Critical Infrastructure Protection, Risk Management, and Resilience

A POLICY PERSPECTIVE

Critical Infrastructure Protection, Risk Management, and Resilience

A POLICY PERSPECTIVE

Kelley A. Pesch-Cronin
Nancy E. Marion

CRC Press
Taylor & Francis Group
Boca Raton London New York

CRC Press is an imprint of the
Taylor & Francis Group, an **informa** business

CRC Press
Taylor & Francis Group
6000 Broken Sound Parkway NW, Suite 300
Boca Raton, FL 33487-2742

First issued in hardback 2019

ISBN-13: 978-1-4987-3490-5 (hbk)

Library of Congress Cataloging-in-Publication Data

Names: Pesch-Cronin, Kelley A., author. | Marion, Nancy E., author.
Title: Critical infrastructure protection, risk management, and resilience :
a policy perspective / Kelley A. Pesch-Cronin and Nancy E. Marion.
Description: Boca Raton, FL : Taylor & Francis Group, [2016] | Includes
bibliographical references and index.
Identifiers: LCCN 2016028977 | ISBN 9781498734905 (hbk)
Subjects: LCSH: Terrorism--United States--Prevention. | Risk
assessment--United States. | Infrastructure (Economics)--United States. |
United States. Department of Homeland Security. | Emergency
management--Law and legislation--United States.
Classification: LCC HV6432 .P473 2016 | DDC 363.6068/1--dc23
LC record available at https://lccn.loc.gov/2016028977

Visit the Taylor & Francis Web site at
http://www.taylorandfrancis.com

and the CRC Press Web site at
http://www.crcpress.com

KP: For Michael, thank you for your amazing
support and encouragement. And for my children,
may you find peace and happiness always.

NM: For Bobby and Moonbeam. Go Bubblepop! It's huge-big!!

CONTENTS

AUTHORS

Dr. Kelley A. Pesch-Cronin is an associate professor at Notre Dame College of Ohio, South Euclid, Ohio. Her research interests include homeland security and emergency management issues, especially as they pertain to policy and politics. Previously, she worked in municipal government and local law enforcement and has coauthored several books in this field.

Dr. Nancy E. Marion is a professor of political science at the University of Akron, Akron, Ohio. Her research areas largely revolve around the intersection of politics and criminal justice. She is the author of numerous articles and books that examine how politics affects criminal justice policy.

1

Critical Infrastructure and Risk Assessment

INTRODUCTION

In August 2005, Hurricane Katrina struck New Orleans, Louisiana. As a Category 3 hurricane, there were sustained winds of 125 miles/hour and massive flooding. Hundreds of residents were displaced from their homes and had no food, water, shelter, or medical assistance. Much of the city was devastated. Businesses were in shambles.

Many residents of the city believed that the federal government did not respond quickly to meet the needs of the communities and businesses from the damaged areas. Many victims sought relief from the government but found none. The federal agency responsible for providing assistance after a national disaster, the Federal Emergency Management Agency (FEMA), was accused of failing to provide help for days after the event. Even then, it seemed that FEMA officials were unprepared to deliver aid and that many government officials, including President George W. Bush, were not aware of the seriousness of the hurricane and the ensuing damages. The lack of attention resulted in an escalation of destruction and multiple deaths.[1]

A few years later, in 2008, another hurricane, Ike, slammed into the Gulf states of Texas, Florida, Louisiana, and Mississippi, again causing widespread damage with multiple injuries and deaths. Afterward, state leaders again accused FEMA of failing to provide needed assistance to residents of those states in a timely manner.[2]

1

The same complaints were heard from residents of New York, New Jersey, and Connecticut after Hurricane Sandy hit the East Coast of the US in 2012, killing more than 100 people. The heavy rains, powerful wind, and storm surges caused massive flooding in major cities. Water surged through the nation's Financial Center and New York's public transportation system. Major power outages affected almost 8 million businesses and homes in 15 states.[3] Major airports, schools, and government offices were closed. Gas shortages only served to complicate the circumstance. Residents were in need of basic necessities of shelter, food, and water and more than 352,000 people registered for assistance from the federal government.[4] While many praised the government's response to Sandy,[5] others made it clear that FEMA's response was delayed and they failed to efficiently provide basic services to those affected by the storm, again escalating the storm's effects.[6]

Catastrophes like these and other devastating events can cause a disruption of vital government services that people rely on each day. Disasters can be caused by either a natural event (a hurricane, earthquake, or flood) or a human act (i.e., a terrorist attack). Either way, residents affected by a calamity often do not have the critical services they need to survive in the days after an event. Government agencies and businesses may be unable to provide basic services needed for a community to maintain itself. Citizens may find themselves without access to water, food, shelter, or power sources. If serious enough, the disruption can pose a serious risk to society: there is a risk that even more citizens will be harmed or killed or additional property will be damaged as looting occurs in the time before services are restored.

Natural events such as Katrina, Ike, and Sandy, and man-made events such as the terrorist attacks of September 11, 2001 or the subsequent anthrax attacks on media outlets and members of Congress demonstrate how vulnerable assets and systems can be. If they are damaged or incapacitated, even for a short time, there can be a debilitating effect on the nation's security, economic system, or public health (see Note 3). People may be prevented from traveling from one place to another easily, and needed goods and products may not be accessible. There may not be effective and reliable communication systems, financial services, power, food, or medical services. Officials across the country may find it difficult to monitor, deter, and if necessary, respond to possible hostile acts. If these disruptions become prolonged, it could have a major impact on the country's health and welfare.

The damages caused by recent events in the US, both natural and man-made, have made it clear that there is a need to reexamine how the country protects its assets and seeks to ensure that critical services are available to citizens in the days and weeks following an event. Both victims and nonvictims have called on government officials to enact policies that will protect the nation's critical infrastructure so they are better able to withstand events, or if damaged, can recover quickly. These disasters made public officials realize that the government needed to put more emphasis on the security of the nation's infrastructure during a disaster or terrorist act, to ensure that basic services are available to citizens. It has become unmistakable that protecting the nation's critical infrastructure is essential to public health and safety of residents, the economic strength, the way of life, and national security.[7] Thus, one of the goals for government officials in the recent years was to ensure the protection of the country's critical infrastructure. This way, the country will be safer, more secure, and even more resilient in the aftermath of an event.

Today, the Department of Homeland Security (DHS) spends billions of dollars annually to prevent (or mitigate), prepare for, respond to, and recover from an incident, whether it be natural or man-made. The government's goal has become national preparedness, which they define as: "The actions taken to plan, organize, equip, train, and exercise to build and sustain the capabilities necessary to prevent, protect against, mitigate the effects of, respond to, and recover from those threats that pose the greatest risk to the security of the Nation."[8] In order to fulfill the *National Preparedness Goal*, the focus of DHS shifted from focusing primarily on terrorism threats to all-hazards threats. This shift has been significant and continues to be debated as to how best to balance the approach to prevention, response, and recovery.

It is critical that government officials and private individuals alike understand government attempts to identify and protect the country's critical infrastructure as they seek to ensure that essential services and goods are available to residents in the aftermath of a disruptive event such as a hurricane, earthquake or flood, or a terrorist attack. The proper identification of structures deemed to be critical infrastructure and the strategies to protect them has become a priority in today's world. Although essential, these steps have also become controversial. It is important to begin our analysis of critical infrastructure protection by defining essential terms that are used frequently by those who seek to protect the nation's critical infrastructure. Over time, the meanings of some terms have changed and become muddled. In some cases, the meanings of some terms vary regionally across the country. For that reason, it is important to define the terminology that will be used throughout the remainder of the book.

3

WHAT IS CRITICAL INFRASTRUCTURE?

The term "critical infrastructure" has changed over time and because of that, the term is sometimes ambiguous or blurred. Prior to the September 11, 2001, terrorist attacks in the US, the term "infrastructure" referred primarily to public works (facilities that were publicly owned and operated) such as roadways, bridges, water and sewer, airports, seaports, and public buildings. The main concern at that time was how functional these services were for the public. This began to change during the early 1990s after the nation witnessed major disasters such as the bombings of the World Trade Center (1993) and the Oklahoma City building (1995). About this time, the threat of terrorism was also emerging in the US and consequently, the definition of what is meant by critical infrastructure has become much broader.

Now the term critical infrastructure is a general term that refers to the framework of man-made networks and systems that provide needed goods and services to the public. In other words, it is the facilities and structures, both physical and organizational, that provide essential services to the residents of a community, which ensure its continued operation. This term includes things such as buildings, roads and transportation systems, telecommunications systems, water systems, energy systems, emergency services, banking and finance institutions, and power supplies. In addition to physical structures and assets, the term incorporates virtual (cyber) systems and people.

In general, critical infrastructure is all of the systems, which are indispensable for the smooth functioning of government at all levels. It is the asset that is vitally important or even essential to a community or to the nation that, if disrupted, harmed, or destroyed, or in some way unable to function, could have a debilitating impact on the security, economics, or national health, safety, or welfare of citizens and businesses.[9] There could also be a significant loss of life if these services are not provided.

Critical infrastructure can be divided into Tier 1 and Tier 2 facilities. Tier 1 facilities and systems are those structures that, if attacked or destroyed by a terrorist attack or natural disaster, would cause significant impacts on either the national or regional level. These would be impacts similar to those that occurred in Louisiana after Hurricane Katrina or resulting from the terrorist attacks of September 11, 2001. Tier 2 facilities and systems are less critical but still needed for a strong community (see Note 7, p. A-6). The distinction between a Tier 1 and a Tier 2 asset is used by officials as they make better decisions about how to allocate resources for critical infrastructure protection. The categories are reviewed annually and are changed as needed. The Tier 1/Tier 2 list is classified and not available to the public (see Note 7, pp. 1–14).

A similar term is key resources. As defined in the Homeland Security Act of 2002 and the 2003 National Strategy, key resources are the assets that are either publicly or privately controlled and are essential to the minimal operations of the economy and government. These documents identified five key resources: (a) national monuments and icons, (b) nuclear power plants, (c) dams, (d) government facilities, and (e) commercial key assets. By 2009, the number of sectors and key resources expanded to 18 and were called critical infrastructure and key resources. Since then, the concept of critical infrastructure and key resources (CIKR) has evolved to encompass the sectors and resources. For the most part, key resources are not separated from critical infrastructure in today's nomenclature, and the terms are used interchangeably.

Local Critical Infrastructure

Each community has assets that provide a service to its residents and need to be protected from both natural and man-made events. What assets are defined or labeled as critical infrastructure can be different in different cities or regions of the country—critical infrastructure assets are different in Cleveland as compared with Los Angeles, or even Tampa or Denver, because they have different weather conditions, different needs, and different assets. In considering a community's critical infrastructure, it is essential to know how valuable an asset is to that community and whether, or to what extent, it needs to be protected. Community leaders must rank assets by placing some kind of a value on them. In some cases, a community's critical infrastructure can be one major structure that is very costly to build, maintain, and operate, like a water purification plant. Clearly, a community relies heavily on this service, but because of the enormous cost, a community can only afford one of them. Protecting this structure would be vital to the community. This asset provides a needed service to residents, and there would be serious impacts on the health of the community should this plant be harmed in some way. Officials need to know if an asset is vulnerable to a natural disaster, or if it would be an attractive target for an attack. It is also important to know if there is a back-up or secondary method for providing the service to residents.

5

Federal Critical Infrastructure

On the federal level, there are thousands of assets that are considered to be critical infrastructure. The Homeland Security Act of 2002 and the Homeland Security Presidential Directive-7 (HSPD-7, 2003) require officials in DHS to identify the nation's critical assets and networks (the national infrastructure). This list is found in a document called the National Asset Database, maintained by the Office of Infrastructure Protection (OIP). There are 77,000 national assets on the list that are located across the country, with about 5% of those assets (only 1,700) labeled as critical.[10] This would include assets such as power plants, dams, or hazardous materials sites.[11] The critical infrastructure assets in the US include a power grid that is essential for daily life that is interconnected with other national systems. There are 4 million miles of paved roadways with 600,000 bridges. There is also a complex rail system in the US that includes 500 freight railroads and 300,000 miles of rail track. There are 500 commercial service airports along with 14,000 general aviation airports. In addition, there are 2 million miles of oil and gas transmission pipelines; 2,800 electric plants; 80,000 dams, 1,000 harbor channels, and 25,000 miles of inland, intracoastal, and coastal waterways servicing more than 300 ports and 3,700 terminals. Clearly, if any of these facilities were to be attacked and damaged, communities and residents may be seriously impacted.[12]

The list of critical assets is sometimes controversial, as officials in the federal, state, and local governments, and the private sector owners, often disagree about what should be included in the directory. For example, the list includes many assets that are considered to be local assets, such as festivals and zoos, which some officials argue should not be included. However, DHS includes all assets in an attempt to create a comprehensive inventory of critical infrastructure around the country. Thus, identifying a comprehensive list of national critical assets continues to be an ongoing debate for the DHS.[13] The number of assets in each sector is found in Table 1.1.

Private Critical Infrastructure

In addition to having local assets and federal assets, there are also privately owned critical infrastructure assets. Most people have the perception that critical infrastructure is owned and operated by the government, but in reality 80% of the critical infrastructure in the US is owned and operated by the private sector.

Table 1.1 Numbers of Critical Assets by Sector

Government facilities	12,019
Emergency services	2,420
Nuclear power plants	178
Chemical/hazardous materials	2,963
Telecommunications	3,020
Water	3,842
Banking and finance	669
Transportation	6,141
Information technology	757
Agriculture and food	7,542
Dams	2,029
Energy	7,889
Postal and shipping	417
Public health	8,402
National monuments and icons	224
Commercial assets	17,327
Defense industrial base	140
Not specified	290

Source: Moteff, J. 2007. *Critical Infrastructure: The Critical Asset Database.* Washington, DC: Congressional Research Service, RL 33648. Retrieved from: http://fas.org/sgp/crs/homesec/RL33648.pdf. Office of the Inspector General. Department of Homeland Security. Progress in Developing the National Asset Database.

Because many assets are owned by private entities, the private sector must be involved in planning for protecting those valuable assets. Many documents, including the National Strategy, the Homeland Security Act, and HSPD-7, address the importance of including all partners in coordinating protection efforts. These documents make it clear that protecting the infrastructure cannot be accomplished effectively simply by the government and the public sectors. Instead, they must work jointly with private sector owners and operators. The government can assist owners and operators of critical infrastructure in many ways, such as providing timely and accurate information on possible threats; including owners in the development of initiatives and policies for protecting assets; helping corporate leaders develop and implement security measures; and/or helping to provide incentives for companies whose officials opt to adopt sound security practices (see Note 7, pp. 1–15).

CRITICAL INFRASTRUCTURE INFORMATION

In addition to critical infrastructure assets, there is also something called critical infrastructure information (CII). This is the data or information that pertains to an asset or critical infrastructure, and is considered to be sensitive but not always classified (secret). An example of CII is knowledge about the daily operations of an asset, or a description of the asset's vulnerabilities and protection plans. CII can also include information generated by the asset such as patient health records or a person's banking and financial records. CII could also be any evidence of future development plans related to the asset, or information that describes pertinent geological or meteorological information about the location of an asset that may point out potential vulnerabilities of that facility (e.g., a dam at an earthquake-prone site). In general, CII refers to any information that could be used by a perpetrator to destroy or otherwise harm the asset or its ability to function.

The importance of protecting CII was first identified in the CII Act of 2002, passed by Congress. It was noted that when a private organization chose to share information with government officials, that information then became a public record and could be accessed by the public through public disclosure laws. Many companies did not want to make that information public, so they were reluctant to work with government agencies and officials. As a way to protect that information and encourage more cooperation, the Congress created a new category of information they called CII. According to the law, any federal official who knowingly discloses any CII to an unauthorized person may face criminal charges. They could be removed from their position, may face a term of imprisonment of up to 1 year as well as fines. The information may be disclosed to other state or local officials, if it is used only for protection of critical infrastructures. The law was passed to ensure that only trained and authorized individuals who need to know the information can access it and use it only for homeland security purposes.

CRITICAL INFRASTRUCTURE PROTECTION

To protect the critical infrastructure and CII, and in order to maintain services if an event occurs, it is essential that officials from the federal, state, and local governments, as well as private owners of the nation's critical infrastructure, develop plans not only to protect their assets from possible harm, but also action plans to respond to an attack or other harm. These plans must be reviewed regularly and updated as potential threats continue to change. The term "critical infrastructure protection" (CIP) refers to those actions that are geared toward protecting critical infrastructures against physical attacks or hazards. These actions may also be directed toward deterring attacks (or mitigating the effects of attacks) that are either man-made or natural. While CIP includes some preventative measures, it usually refers to actions that are more reactive in scope. Today, CIP focuses on an all-hazards approach.

The primary responsibility for protecting critical infrastructure, and for responding if it is harmed, lies with the owners and operators, but the federal government and owners/operators work together to identify critical infrastructure, and then to assess the level of risk associated with that asset. The assets' potential vulnerabilities are determined, and possible methods for reducing the risk are identified. If owners and operators are unwilling or unable to participate in this process, the federal government can intervene and assess the protection level and devise a response.[14] While most critical infrastructure protection is carried out at federal, state, and local level, there is also a global perspective to protecting critical infrastructure as the world becomes more global.

A related term is critical infrastructure assurance (CIA). This revolves around the process by which arrangements are made in the event of an attack or if an asset is disrupted, to shift services either within one network, or among multiple networks, so that demand is met. In other words, it has to do with detecting any disruptions, and then shifting responsibilities so that services can continue to be met. This can often be done without the consumer's knowledge.

RISK

The probability that an asset will be the object of an attack or another adverse outcome is its risk.[15] Risk is the likelihood that an adverse event will occur,[16] and is related to consequences (C), vulnerabilities (V), and threats (T), as described in the following formula. The National Infrastructure Protection Plan (NIPP) expresses this relationship as follows:

$$Risk = (function\ of)\ (CVT)$$

It is essential that CIKR owners and operators assess the potential risk to their assets using these three elements. This way, they can make policies to protect the critical infrastructure and plans to respond if that were to occur. Each element is described in the following.

Consequence

A consequence is the effect or result of an event, incident, or occurrence. This may include the number of deaths, injuries, and other human health impacts; property loss or damage; and/or interruptions to necessary services. The economic impacts of an event are also critical consequences, as many events have both short- and long-term economic consequences to communities or even to the nation.[17] It is important that there is business continuity, which is the ability of an organization to continue to function before, during, and after a disaster (see Note 7, p. A-2).

Vulnerability

A vulnerability is "a physical feature or operational attribute that renders an entity open to exploitation or susceptible to a given hazard" (see Note 17, p. 33). It is easy to think of it as a weakness or flaw in an asset that may cause it to be a target for an attack. An aggressor may seek out a vulnerability and use that to strike the asset. In most cases, the major vulnerability is access control whereby unauthorized people can enter the asset (such as a building or open area) to gather information to plan an attack, or even to carry out an attack. To reduce this possibility, it has become common practice to prohibit unauthorized people from entering these types of areas (see Note 17, p. 33).

Structural vulnerabilities need to be addressed and maintained over an extended time rather than relying on a temporary solution or a "quick fix." This extended approach is referred to as long-term vulnerability reduction. The *National Preparedness Goal* defines the long-term vulnerability reduction core capability as to "build and sustain resilient systems, communities, and CIKR lifelines so as to reduce their vulnerability to natural, technological, and human-caused incidents by lessening the likelihood, severity, and duration of the adverse consequences related to these incidents" (see Note 8, p. 11). According to the DHS, the initial national capability target is to "achieve a measurable decrease in the long-term vulnerability of the Nation against current baselines amid a growing population based and expanding infrastructure base" (see Note 8, p. 11).

Threat

A threat is a "natural or man-made occurrence, individual, entity, or action that has or indicates the potential to harm life, information, operations, the environment, and/or property." This term has also been more simply defined as "an intent to hurt us."[18] Threat has to do with potential harm that can originate from any source, including humans (terrorists or active shooter); natural hazards (different threats for different parts of the country); or technology (a cyberattack). Those charged with protecting critical assets seek to identify possible threats to resources as a way to mitigate harm that could result. It is much easier to identify natural threats such as storms and earthquakes. To a great extent, these threats can be predicted and the possible impact is easier to judge. Plans can be established so that a community is prepared to respond. On the other hand, man-made threats are far less predictable and can occur at any time with unknown consequences, making mitigation and response planning much more difficult.

RISK ASSESSMENT

Risk assessments of critical assets are carried out as a way to identify potential risks that may exist surrounding an asset, which can then lead into developing courses of action to prevent or respond to an attack. Through data collection and analysis, a risk analysis is an attempt to identify not only threats, but also consequences of an attack. In general, a risk assessment asks, "What can go wrong? What is the likelihood that it will go wrong? What are the possible consequences if it does go wrong?"[19] This way, the probability of an incident occurring and the severity (consequence) of that incident will be better understood (see Note 7, pp. 3–7). The analysis can also be used to determine priorities, or what assets are more critical and how should money be spent to protect them. It can also help officials create plans to protect residents and keep their property safe.

Since the September 11, 2001 attack and Hurricane Katrina, public interest in risk analysis has grown dramatically. Risk analysis has become an effective and comprehensive procedure to reduce the possibility of an attack and subsequent damages, and they have become complex.[20] Government officials at the federal, state, and local levels, heads of agencies, and even legislators now incorporate risk analysis into their decision-making processes and address risk more explicitly at all levels.[21]

11

Risk assessments are completed on an asset, a network, or a system. They typically consider three components of risk as noted earlier, and rely on a variety of methods, principles, or rules to analyze the potential for harm. Some risk assessments are heavily quantitative and rely heavily on statistics and probabilities, whereas others are less quantitative.[22] In general, a risk assessment report typically includes five elements. They are as follows:

1. Identification of assets and a ranking of their importance
   The first step in a risk analysis is to determine which infrastructure assets can be considered to be "critical." Since all assets vary as to how important they are, assets can be, and need to be, ranked. Officials must determine what properties are needed in a community to ensure services are required. Examples include buildings, water treatment plants, or power plants. They may also decide that certain people are critical, such as medical professionals, police officials, or government officials. Another possibility is to include information such as financial data or business strategies. Risk assessments are then done on those assets that are identified as the most critical. The time and resources that would be needed to replace the lost asset must also be part of the analysis. If that asset were lost, how quickly could it be replaced? Are there other assets that could substitute for that one? If the asset was lost, how would services be provided? What cascading effects might occur if one asset were lost or damaged? (see Note 22).

2. Identify, characterize, and assess threats
   All potential threats to an asset need to be identified. Details about potential threats that should be considered include the type of threat (e.g., insider, terrorist, or natural threat); the attacker's motivation; potential trigger events; the capability of a person to carry out an attack; possible methods of attack (e.g., suicide bombers, truck bombs, cyberattacks). Analysts can gather information on these topics from the intelligence community, law enforcement officials, specialists and experts in the field, news reports in the media, previous analysis reports, previously received threats, or "red teams" who have been trained to "think" like a terrorist (see Note 22).

3. Assess the vulnerability of critical assets to specific threats
   An asset's vulnerability can be analyzed in many ways. The first is physical. Here, an analyst would determine things like an

outsider's accessibility to an asset. The second is technical, which refers to an asset's likelihood of being the victim of a cyberattack or other type of electronic attack. The third type of vulnerability is operational, or the policies and operating procedures used by the organization. The fourth is organizational, or the effects that may occur if a company's headquarters is attacked (see Note 22).

4. Determine the risk

   Risk is the chance that a disruptive event may occur, as described earlier. Assets are usually rated on their risk, and resources can be allocated to reduce an asset's risk.

5. Identify and characterize ways to reduce those risks

   An important part of a risk assessment is to determine ways to mitigate or eliminate the risk of an attack. This could be something as simple as banning unauthorized people from entering particular areas or reducing traffic around an asset. Of course, other ways to eliminate the risk of an attack may be more complicated such as building physical barriers or relocating assets.

RISK MANAGEMENT

In risk management, officials ask, "What can be done? What options are available and what are the associated tradeoffs in terms of cost, risks, and benefits? What are the impacts of current management decisions on future options?"[23] These are efforts to decide which protective measures to take based on an agreed upon risk-reduction strategy.

CONVERGENCE

Many of the critical infrastructure assets are connected to each other in some way. This integration of infrastructure is called "convergence." This means that if one asset is harmed and unable to serve people, the other assets linked to it may also be unable to perform (see Note 17, p. 31). This is referred to as "cascading" or "escalating" effects. The interconnected nature of critical infrastructure could lead to even more harm to a community than if the assets were independent. In some cases, the interdependencies can be global since many of our assets are linked to those around the world.

An obvious example of convergence can be seen with cyber assets, which is linked to all other assets both in the US and elsewhere. Computers have become an essential part of our society, and every other sector relies, at least in part, on information technology (IT). A cyberattack may affect the power grid, water, financial services, and healthcare, causing great damage in both the short and long term. It would also affect transportation and financial outlets, thus having an impact on the economy. Computer systems control equipment in the chemical, nuclear, and oil industries. Companies rely on IT for an easy communications, personnel management, research, and online commerce. The computer network is so essential that, in the Comprehensive National Initiative, cybersecurity was identified as one of the most serious economic and national security challenges facing the US. Those assets that are interconnected to other assets and networks may be an attractive target for enemies because of the broad harm it may cause.

On the other hand, interconnected assets could be a benefit for communities. In the case that one sector is unable to provide a service, another asset may be able to step in so that there is minimal disruption and the desired level of service can be provided. So clearly, the interconnected nature of critical infrastructure has both positive and negative components.

RECOVERY/RESILIENCY

In the event that an attack or other disaster does occur, a community must take steps to return to "normal," or to the conditions that existed prior to the event and subsequent disruption of services. This process is called Recovery and is part of the emergency management all-hazards response cycle. Recovery has been defined as the ability to adapt and withstand the disruption that occurs after an emergency or event (see Note 8, p. A-2). It is the ability to recover rapidly and bounce back, or regroup, after a disruption, which could be either natural, technological, or human-caused.[24] In most cases, community agencies and facilities are able to return to their full capabilities in a reasonable amount of time after an event. However, in many cases, the costs of rebuilding are too high and it becomes impractical to return to pre-event standards.[25]

A similar concept is resiliency, which refers to the ability of a community to resist, absorb, recover from, or adapt to a change in conditions. As part of the risk management process, resiliency is "the capacity of an organization to recognize threats and hazards and make adjustments that will improve future protection efforts and risk reduction measures." This has to do with a community making changes to reduce the risk of an event or consequences of that event.[26] For example, communities may take steps to ensure that facilities are constructed so that they are able to withstand damage to, or the loss of, a supporting beam or column.[27]

Resiliency is made more difficult because, in many cases, when one infrastructure is impacted, others may be impacted alongside (convergence). Each system is interconnected to many other infrastructures, whether it be cyber, physical, or organizational, making them interdependent. These relationships are constantly changing. A risk to one subset becomes a risk to all (see Note 16, p. 684).

At the same time, however, if one infrastructure is damaged or lost, it can be offset by another infrastructure. If one is damaged, another infrastructure may be able to reallocate their services in a way to fill in the gap and reduce the impact caused by the event. For example, if the water supply is damaged, people in that community are less concerned with whether the water is coming through a central pipe or some peripheral parts of the system. Instead, residents are concerned if the water supply fails to provide water to their homes at all.

Beyond allowing a community to continue to provide services, resiliency also has a deterrent value, or a protective value. If a community is well protected and is prepared to bounce back quickly, an attacker, whose goal it is to disrupt services, may be deterred from attacking. An offender may look at the target's protection when considering a target, and if that target is one that will not fall prey to an attack, the offender may go elsewhere.

A community's resiliency is made up of robustness (strength), resourcefulness (innovation, ability to adapt), and recovery. Robustness (R1) refers to the inherent strength in a structure or system, or its ability to withstand external damage without loss of functionality.[28] Resourcefulness (R2) is the capacity to mobilize needed resources and services in emergencies, and recovery (R3) is the ability to return to a "normal" condition. This can be portrayed in the following:

$$R1 + R2 + R3 = \text{Resilience}$$

Some officials have indicated a fourth factor that should be included in this equation, which is Rapidity, or the speed with which disruption can be overcome and safety, services, and financial stability restored.[29] Certainly, residents want essential services such as power and water restored as quickly as possible in order to return to a "normal" state.

RESOURCEFULNESS

Resourcefulness refers to the ability of a community to gather and coordinate any necessary resources, services, equipment, and personnel in the event of a damaging event. Those communities that are resourceful are able to recover more quickly than others. Some essential parts to this include identifying personnel and equipment that might be critical to a recovery operation; cross training so that first responders can respond quickly to more than one type of event; mutual aid agreements that allow agencies to share resources and ask for help under particular circumstances; purchasing of spare equipment so that there is never a gap in available resources; and maintaining a supply of personnel and equipment that could quickly respond when needed (see Note 25).

HAZARD

A hazard is a source or cause of harm (see Note 19, p. 17). There are different types of hazards. A natural hazard is a potential incident resulting from acts of nature or a weather phenomenon.[30] These would be incidents that are caused by acts of nature such as hurricanes, wildfires, avalanches, earthquakes, winter storms, tornadoes, disease outbreaks, or epidemics (see Note 30, p. 5). Another type of hazard is a technological hazard. These are potential incidents that are the result of accidents or failures of systems or structures (see Note 30, p. B-1). Examples of these include hazardous materials releases, dam or levee failures, an airplane crash, power failure, or radiological release (see Note 30, p. 6). These may be caused by human error or a failure of technology. The final type of hazard is human-caused hazard, which include incidents that are the result of intentional actions of an individual or group of individuals. Examples of this type of hazard include acts of terrorism, an active shooter, biological attacks, chemical attack, cyber incident; a bomb attack, or a radiological attack (see Note 30, pp. B-1, 6).

The "all-hazards" approach is a way to analyze and prepare for a full range of threats and hazards, including domestic terrorist attacks, natural and man-made disasters, accidental disruptions, and other emergencies (see Note 25. pp. 2–5). This is a "grouping classification encompassing all conditions, environmental or man-made, that have the potential to cause injury, illness, or death; damage to or loss of equipment, infrastructure services, or property; or alternatively causing functional degradation to social, economic, or environmental aspects" (see Note 7, p. A-2).

IMPACTS

Impacts describe how an event might affect an asset or the impact it has on the provision of services to residents. An impact could be the damage caused by an event, or the consequences that occur as the result of an event. Impacts are clearly linked to the size and complexity of an event—a more serious event will result in more serious impacts. In a risk analysis, the possible impacts identified should be specific in order to allow officials to have a better understanding of how to manage the risk (see Note 30, p. 11).

PREPAREDNESS

Preparedness has been defined as those activities that are "necessary to build, sustain, and improve readiness capabilities to prevent, protect against, respond to, and recover from natural and man-made incidents." Preparedness is a continuous process whereby vulnerabilities are continually being assessed and response plans continually being updated and revised. Preparedness can be completed by officials at all levels of government and between government and private sector and nongovernmental organizations. As described in the National Incident Management System (NIMS), preparedness has to do with establishing guidelines, protocols, and standards for planning, training and exercises, personnel qualification and certification, equipment certification, and publication management (see Note 7, pp. 1–11).

CYBERSECURITY

The term "cybersecurity" refers to actions that are taken by government or by private owners and operators to prevent damage to, unauthorized use of, or exploitation of, information and communications held electronically. This also includes all actions geared toward restoring these systems after an attack or other harm. The goal of this sector is to ensure the confidentiality, integrity, and availability of online information and data. Activities regarded as cybersecurity include those that are intended to protect and restore information networks and wirelines, wireless satellite, public safety answering points, and 911 communications systems and control systems (see Note 7, p. A-2).

MITIGATION

Mitigation refers to lessening the impact of an event. All communities should develop plans that have the goal of reducing the potential impact of a natural or man-made event. Once a community completes the assessment report that identifies risks and vulnerabilities, officials should devise a mitigation plan. All members of a community should be invited to participate in making the plan, as well as private stakeholders. The plan should define the roles and responsibilities of all interested organizations and individuals. It may also include mutual aid agreements with other jurisdictions or memorandums of understanding that will help ensure that the plan is carried out when needed (see Note 25, pp. 6–16). Some examples of mitigation measures that communities have taken to improve the safety of a facility include increasing physical security measures, hiring additional security guards, and installing barriers around a building. Examples of mitigating cybersecurity measures include enhancing firewalls and updating passwords.

Training is essential to mitigation efforts. Personnel can train on equipment, become familiar with policies, learn to communicate, and work with other agencies. Training exercises that simulate emergencies are important as agencies can assess how well they have planned. Since threats can change, exercises will keep people ready to react (see Note 25, pp. 6–17, 18). This way, when an event occurs, people will be ready and able to assist.

CONCLUSION

This book examines the government's role in identifying and protecting the nation's critical infrastructure as they seek to protect the country from harm and ensure that essential services and goods are available in the aftermath of a disruptive event. It will focus on risk assessment of assets and the development of plans to protect the nation's infrastructure from damage resulting from both natural disasters and attacks. The purpose is to introduce these ideas to the readers in a way that is easy to understand rather than with the use of complicated formulas.

A history of risk assessment and programs for critical infrastructure protection is given in Chapter 2. This helps to give readers a background into early government policies that form the basis of today's asset protection programs. The status of today's protection plans is the focus of Chapter 3. The role of the DHS in critical infrastructure protection is described in Chapter 4, and Chapter 5 provides information on other agencies that help the nation in these efforts. The importance and status of public–private partnerships is presented in Chapter 6. This is of particular importance because a great portion of our country's assets are privately owned. The information in Chapter 7 summarizes the laws pertaining to critical infrastructure protection that have been passed by Congress. Chapter 8 presents the DHS perspective on risk and details three key documents which were created to define the principles, processes, and operational practices of risk management. Chapter 9 provides an overview of earlier risk assessment methods, federal guidelines for risk, and application of the Threat and Hazard Identification and Risk Assessment (THIRA) process. Chapters 10 through 12 summarize the 16 critical infrastructures and their sector-specific agencies. In this section, each chapter provides a sector profile, goals and priorities, and the various methods and approaches each sector takes to assess risk. The text concludes with a discussion of the issues that continue to challenge and shape our responses to critical infrastructure protection, risk management, and resilience efforts in Chapter 13.

REVIEW QUESTIONS

1. Why is it important for the US to protect its CIKR?
2. What is critical infrastructure?
3. Why would a government or agency carry out a risk assessment?
4. What are the elements of a risk assessment?
5. Why would a community be interested in recovery and resiliency?

NOTES

1. Hurricane Katrina 2009. Retrieved from: http://www.history.com/topics /hurricane-katrina.
2. Elliott, J. October 2008. Texas Leaders Blast FEMA for Hurricane Ike Response. *The Chron.* Retrieved from: :http://www.chron.com/news/houston-texas/article/Texas-leaders-blast-FEMA-for-Hurricane-Ike-1789822.php; After Hurricane Ike. November 10, 2008. *The Washington Post.* Retrieved from: http://www.washingtonpost.com/wp-dyn/content/article/2008/11/09 /AR2008110901879.html.

3. US Department of Homeland Security, and US Department of Justice, Global Justice Information Sharing Initiative. December 2008. Critical Infrastructure and Key Resources, Protection Capabilities for Fusion Centers. Retrieved from: https://it.ojp.gov/documents/d/CIKR%20protection%20capabilities%20for%20fusion%20centers%20s.pdf.

4. "Hurricane Sandy Fast Facts" CNN Library. November 5, 2014. Retrieved from: http://www.cnn.com/2013/07/13/world/americas/hurricane-sandy-fast-facts/index.html.

5. Vogel, S. November 1, 2012. Officials and Experts Praising FEMA for its response to Hurricane Sandy. *The Washington Post*. Retrieved from: http://www.washingtonpost.com/politics/decision2012/officials-and-experts-praising-fema-for-its-response-to-hurricane-sandy/2012/11/01/7a6629d8-2447-11e2-ac85-e669876c6a24_story.html.

6. Bucci, S. P., Inserra, D., Lesser, J., Mayer, M. A., Slattery, B., Spencer, J., and Tubb, K. October 24, 2013. After Hurricane Sandy: Time to Learn and Implement the Lessons in Preparedness, Response, and Resilience. The Heritage Foundation. Retrieved from: http://www.heritage.org/research/reports/2013/10/after-hurricane-sandy-time-to-learn-and-implement-the-lessons.

7. DHS, FEMA. September 2010. CIKR Awareness AWR-213, Participant Guide, pp. 1–15, p. A-2, p. A-6.

8. US DHS. 2011. National Preparedness Goal, p. 11, A-2.

9. US DHS. 2011. National Preparedness Goal, p. A-1; US DHS. 2009. National Infrastructure Protection Plan, p. 7; US DHS. 2013. National Infrastructure Protection Plan, p. 29.

10. Liscouski, R. April 21, 2004. Assistant Secretary. Infrastructure Protection, Department of Homeland Security, testimony before the House Select Committee on Homeland Security, Infrastructure and Border Security Subcommittee.

11. Moteff, J. 2007. *Critical Infrastructure: The Critical Asset Database*. Washington, DC: Congressional Research Service, RL 33648. Retrieved from: http://fas.org/sgp/crs/homesec/RL33648.pdf.

12. Collins, P., and Baggett, R. 2009. *Homeland Security and Critical Infrastructure Protection*. Westport, CT: Praeger.

13. Office of the Inspector General. Department of Homeland Security. *Progress in Developing the National Asset Database*.

14. Moteff, J. D. June 10, 2015. *Critical Infrastructures: Background, Policy and Implementation*. Washington, DC: Congressional Research Service, 7-5700. Retrieved from: www.crs.gov.

15. Lowrance, W. 1976. *Of Acceptable Risk*. Los Altos, CA: William Kaufmann.

16. Haimes, Y. Y. 2004. *Risk Modeling, Assessment, and Management*, 2nd ed. New Jersey: John Wiley and Sons: xii; US DHS. 2010. *DHS Risk Lexicon*, p. 27.

17. US DHS. 2013. National Infrastructure Protection Plan, p. 109.

18. US DHS. 2010. *DHS Risk Lexicon*, p. 36; US DHS. 2013. National Infrastructure Protection Plan, p. 33.

19. US DHS. 2010. *DHS Risk Lexicon*, p. 17, pp. 27–28.

20. Barry, C. E., Farr, J. V., and Wiese, I. September 2000. Infrastructure Risk Analysis Model. *Journal of Infrastructure Systems, 6,* 114–117; Ten, C.-W., Manimaran, G., Liu, C.-C. 2010. Cybersecurity for Critical Infrastructures: Attack and Defense Modeling. *IEEE Transactions on Systems, Man and Cybernetics. 40,* 853–865.
21. Haimes, Y. Y. 2004. *Risk Modeling, Assessment, and Management,* 2nd ed. New Jersey: John Wiley and Sons.
22. Motef, J. February 4, 2005. *Risk Management and Critical Infrastructure Protection: Assessing, Integrating, and Managing Threats, Vulnerabilities and Consequences.* CRS Report for Congress. Washington, DC: Congressional Research Service. Retrieved from: https://www.fas.org/sgp/crs/homesec /RL32561.pdf.
23. Ezell, B. C., Farr, J. V., and Wiese, I. September 2000. Infrastructure Risk Analysis Model. *Journal of Infrastructure Systems, 6,* 114–117.
24. DHS, FEMA. April 2013. Advanced Critical Infrastructure Protection, MGT-414, Participant Guide.
25. DHS, FEMA. September 2014. Critical Asset Risk Management, Participant Guide, pp. 2–5, pp. 6–16, pp. 6-16–6-17.
26. US DHS. 2010. *DHS Risk Lexicon,* pp. 26, 46; DHS, FEMA. September 2010. CIKR Awareness AWR-213, Participant Guide, pp. 1–11.
27. Mueller, J., and Stewart, M. G. 2011. *Terror, Security and Money.* New York, NY: Oxford University Press.
28. O'Rourke, T. 2009. Setting Performance Goals for Infrastructure, p. 2.
29. O'Rourke, T.D. 2007. Critical Infrastructure, Interdependencies and Resilience. *The Bridge, 37*(1), 22–29. Retrieved from: http://www.nae.edu /File.aspx?id=7405.
30. US DHS. 2013. Threat and Hazard Identification and Risk Assessment Guide (CPG-201), 2nd ed., p. 5, 6, 11, p. B-1.

2

Early History

INTRODUCTION

Public officials in federal and state governments have been concerned with protecting the country's critical infrastructure for many years, even prior to the terrorist attacks of September 11, 2001. In these early years, the government began to take a closer look at the safety of the nation's infrastructure after early acts of both foreign and domestic terrorism. The assault on the World Trade Center in 1993 in New York City and the bombing of the federal building in Oklahoma City in 1995 increased fears of further attacks. Fears were also increasing as technology improved and the potential for computer hacking surged, highlighting the need for more cybersecurity efforts. In the midst of this, President Clinton signed an Executive Order that identified critical infrastructure sectors, which was the start of a new era in critical infrastructure protection. Since that time, policies for protecting the country's assets have expanded to meet ever-growing threats. This chapter provides a history of critical infrastructure protection policies, providing a background to the current policies that exist in the US today.

EARLY YEARS OF CRITICAL INFRASTRUCTURE PROTECTION

Critical infrastructure protection is not new in the US. During the Cold War, US officials recognized threats of possible attacks and created initiatives to prepare for these possibilities. Officials at that time identified critical infrastructure assets such as power plants and grids, oil and gas pipelines, and other critical facilities that, if harmed, might affect continuity of government and services. These plans were relatively minor and never serious enough to warrant much attention from the federal government. Most threats were seen as insignificant and were left to the state and local law enforcement or individual companies.[1]

More "modern-day" critical infrastructure protection can be traced back to July 15, 1996, when President Clinton signed Executive Order 13010. In this document, the president revealed his plans to establish a new organization he called the President's Commission on Critical Infrastructure Protection (PCCIP). The Commission was one of the first federal attempts to assess legitimate threats against the US (see Note 1). The members of the Commission would, according to Clinton, investigate the scope and nature of potential vulnerabilities and threats to the country's critical infrastructure, with particular attention given to the potential impact of cyberthreats. The Committee members were asked to recommend a comprehensive national plan or strategy for protecting critical infrastructure.[2]

Clinton also identified eight critical infrastructure sectors for the country in Executive Order 13010. These eight sectors were (a) telecommunications, (b) transportation, (c) electric power, (d) banking and finance, (e) gas and oil storage and delivery, (f) water supply, (g) emergency services, and (h) government operations. These sectors could be thought of as "categories" of assets, or simply a way to organize the country's critical infrastructure protection plans.

One other change that Clinton made in this document was to expand the definition of what was considered to be infrastructure. Under this new approach, "infrastructure" was defined as a "framework of interdependent networks and systems comprising identifiable industries, institutions (including people and procedures), and distribution capabilities that provide a reliable flow of products and services essential to the defense and economic security of the United States, the smooth functioning of government at all levels, and society as a whole."[3]

After holding many meetings and completing intensive research, the Commission released their findings in their final report, which was released in 1997. In general, the report indicated that there was no immediate crisis that posed a significant threat to the nation's infrastructure, but there was a need for the government to take some action to protect its assets, especially with regard to cybercrime. Moreover, the report included recommendations geared toward securing the country's infrastructure. One key finding throughout the report was the need for more communication and increased information sharing between the private sector and the government (see Note 2).

After the report was made public, Clinton sought a new plan that would be completed within the upcoming 5 years that would assure that the country's critical infrastructure would be protected from any intentional disruption. The new plan was to include plans for critical infrastructure protection, both physical and cyber. Moreover, according to Clinton, the plan would address the potential for attacks so that any interruption in service delivery would be brief, manageable, and geographically isolated. These plans were described in the Presidential Decision Directive 63 (PDD-63), which was announced in May 1998. PDD-63 was the first unclassified presidential national security directive that presented a new approach to protecting the country's critical infrastructure. It supported partnerships between the government and private ownership that had not been tried before.

In this new document, the term "critical infrastructure" was used to refer to the physical and cyber-based systems that people relied on for operating the economy and the government. PDD-63 defined the critical infrastructure as composed of five essential domains: (a) banking and finance, (b) energy, (c) transportation, (d) telecommunications, and (e) government services. Further, the report identified specific critical infrastructure assets that required protection. These were referred to as "sectors." The sectors included information and communications; banking and finance; water supply; aviation, highways, mass transit, pipelines, rail, and waterborne commerce; emergency and law enforcement services; emergency, fire, and continuity of government services; public health services; electric power, oil and gas production, and storage. These are listed in Table 2.1.

Each sector was assigned a lead agency, which would be responsible for securing and protecting the critical infrastructure in their particular sector. Each lead agency, in turn, was asked to appoint a Sector Liaison Official. This person had the task of communicating with any appropriate private sector organizations and including them in any interactions about protecting assets. Members of the private sector were then asked to choose a person who would agree to serve as the Sector Coordinator. This person would work with the agency's Sector Liaison Official to ensure cooperative efforts. Most agencies appointed their Sector Liaison Official quickly, but it took longer for the agencies to appoint the sector coordinators. PDD-63 also set up a National Plan Coordination Staff to support the plan's development. The staff would be housed in the Critical

Table 2.1 Lead Agencies per Presidential Decision Directive 63

Department/Agency	Sector/Function
Commerce	Information and communications
Treasury	Banking and finance
EPA	Water
Transportation	Transportation
Justice	Emergency law enforcement
Federal Emergency Management Agency	Emergency fire service
Health and human services	Emergency medicine
Energy	Electric power, gas, and oil
Justice	Law enforcement and internal security[a]
Director of Central Intelligence	Intelligence[a]
State	Foreign affairs[a]
Defense	National defense[a]

[a] These are the functions identified by PDD-63 as being primarily under federal control.

Infrastructure Assurance Office (CIAO), which would be located in the Commerce Department. CIAO not only provided support to the sectors as they developed their plans, but also helped the National Coordinators as they integrated the sector plans into a National Plan. Originally, CIAO was to exist for only 3 years to study the vulnerability of the country's critical infrastructures, but the work done by CIAO was so critical that it continued to operate past the 3-year deadline.

In most cases, an individual from a relevant trade organization was chosen to serve as the sector coordinator. For example, the Environmental Protection Agency opted to have the Executive Director of the Association of Metropolitan Water Agencies to serve as the sector coordinator for the water sector. Similarly, in the law enforcement sector (which is no longer a separate sector), the National Infrastructure Protection Center (NIPC) helped to create an Emergency Law Enforcement Services Forum, consisting of senior state, local, and non-Federal Bureau of Investigation (FBI) law enforcement officials. In the case of banking and finance, the sector coordinator was chosen from a major banking/finance institution, who also served as the Chairperson of the Financial Services sector coordinating council. This was an agency that was created by industry officials to coordinate critical infrastructure protection activities with the federal government.

Personnel within the lead agencies were asked to develop plans to help ensure the protection of their assets. The plans were to include an assessment of any possible vulnerabilities that existed for each asset and plans to reduce the sector's vulnerability to an attack. They were also to develop response plans in the case of an attack, remediation plans, and reconstitution plans. The agencies were also asked to include needs for future research and development, possible opportunities for international cooperation, and so forth. The plan was to be completed within 180 days, which were then to be fully implemented within 2 years and updated every 2 years after that (see Note 2).

Another position created in the PDD-63 was the National Coordinator for Security, Infrastructure Protection, and Counter-terrorism. This person was given the task of serving as the chair of the Critical Infrastructure Coordination Group. He or she reported to the President through the Assistant to the President for National Security Affairs. Also created by the PDD-63 was a National Infrastructure Assurance Council, an advisory group that included private owners, representatives from state and local government, and representatives from relevant federal agencies. The Council was to meet and provide the President with reports about the progress (see Note 2).

A new office, the NIPC, was created as part of the PDD-63. This office, which was housed within the Department of Justice (DOJ) and the FBI, was given the job of defending the nation's public and private computer systems from possible cyberattacks and responding to illegal acts carried out by the use of computers and information technologies (see Note 1).

In addition to setting up many new positions and agencies, PDD-63 also recognized the need for a national capability to detect and respond to cyberattacks as they occurred. To do this, Clinton sought a Federal Intrusion Detection Network (FIDNET) that would work with the Federal Computer Intrusion Response Capability (FedCIRC). Additionally, the FBI was asked to expand its computer crime activities and form the NIPC. The NIPC would become the lead agency for federal threat assessment, vulnerability analysis, early warning capability, law enforcement investigations, and coordination of responses. Clinton asked that all agencies provide the NIPC with any information they had about cyberthreats or actual attacks. The NIPC would also work with the private sector through the Information Sharing and Analysis Center (ISAC) that would be operated

27

by the private sector. Because the NIPC was housed in the DOJ, the DOJ became the lead agency for protecting the country's critical infrastructure.

In December 1999, some of the sectors established an organization they called the Partnership for Critical Infrastructure Security. The agency's goal was to share information and strategies for infrastructure protection and to identify any possible interdependencies across sectors. This group was led by members of the private sector, but the Department of Homeland Security (DHS) (and CIAO before that) acted as a liaison and provided administrative support. Sector Liaisons from lead agencies were considered ex officio members. The partnership helped coordinate input from the organization to many of the national strategies and plans for infrastructure protection.

In January 2000, just prior to leaving the presidency, the Clinton Administration released the *National Plan for Information Systems Protection*. In keeping with the focus of PDD-63, the new Plan focused on protecting the cyber-infrastructure.

BUSH ADMINISTRATION

When George W. Bush was elected to the presidency, he chose to make some changes in the policies for critical infrastructure protection. The Bush Administration shifted the focus of infrastructure protection, adding more of a focus on cybersecurity. The concern with asset protection was brought to the forefront after the terrorist attacks of September 11, 2001. At that time, while the administration still had a concentration on maintaining cybersecurity, its focus also included protection of physical threats, especially ones that might cause mass casualties. This was not always a popular approach and there was some debate among officials.

Pre-September 11, 2001

The Bush Administration expanded the policies toward critical infrastructure protection that were first established by President Clinton. President Bush continued to stress that protecting the infrastructure was essential for citizens, the economy, the government, and national security. Bush also talked about the importance of protecting critical infrastructure for the sake of national morale. Administration officials spoke more often about ensuring that any disruption in services be infrequent, of minimal duration, and manageable. The definition of critical infrastructure was expanded during this time to include those targets that, if attacked, would result in a large number of casualties. The emphasis of protection also changed to include more collaboration between private sector owners/operators and the federal government. The Bush administration promised that they would work to help identify critical assets and create a plan for protecting those assets.

Fairly soon after entering office, Bush decided to consolidate the responsibilities of the many groups and agencies within the National Security Council (NSC) into 17 Policy Coordination Committees (PCCs). The responsibility of protecting critical infrastructure was given to the Counter-Terrorism and National Preparedness PCC. There was some debate surrounding a proposal to establish a federal chief information officer (CIO), who would oversee the security of all federal nonnational security-related computer systems. At the same time, this person would also coordinate with the private sector on tasks relating to protecting privately owned computer systems. In the end, Bush chose not to create this position, instead relying on the Deputy Director of the Office of Management and Budget to do that job.

The president also turned to Congress for ideas about the best way to protect the country against acts of terrorism. The Hart-Rudman Commission, otherwise known as the US Commission on National Security/21st Century, suggested the creation of a National Homeland Security Agency. Within this new Agency would be a directorate that would oversee critical infrastructure protection. At first, Bush did not support this plan, but his plans changed after the terrorist attacks on the US on September 11, 2001.

Post-September 11, 2001

After September 11, 2001, President Bush signed the USA PATRIOT Act (PL 107-56) and the Homeland Security Act of 2001 (PL 107-296). In the PATRIOT Act, the definition of critical infrastructure was updated to be "Systems and assets, whether physical or virtual, so vital to the United States that the incapacity or destruction of such systems and assets would have a debilitating impact on security, national economic security, national public health or safety, or any combination of those matters."[4] New terms were also mentioned for the first time, including "key assets" which were described as "individual targets whose destruction would not endanger vital systems, but could create local disaster or profoundly damage our nation's morale or confidence."[5] An example of this would be the

Statue of Liberty, which has both historic and symbolic meaning to people who live in the US.

The Infrastructure Protection Executive Notification Service (ENS), located within DHS, was established as a way for DHS to directly communicate with the chief executive officers of major industrial firms. With the new system, DHS was able to alert companies to any infrastructure incidents, or to make them aware of any threats that may pertain to them. The Department also oversaw the critical infrastructure warning network (CWIN), which is a way to provide secure lines of communication between DHS and other federal, state, and local agencies, the private sector, and international agencies.

Executive Order 13228

President Bush signed Executive Order 13228 on October 8, 2001, less than a month after the terrorist attacks on the US. Through this action, Bush created the Office of Homeland Security. The new Office would be overseen by the Assistant to the President for Homeland Security. The mission of the new agency was to "develop and coordinate the implementation of a comprehensive national strategy to secure the United States from terrorist threats and attacks."[6] The primary task of the new office was to coordinate efforts to protect the US and its critical infrastructure from another attack, and maintain efforts at recovery. When DHS was established, many of the functions of the Office of Homeland Security were transferred there.

Additionally, the Homeland Security Council was added to the administration through the executive order. The council was comprised of the President, Vice-President, Secretaries of Treasury, Defense, Health and Human Services, and Transportation, the Attorney General, the Directors of FEMA, FBI, and Central Intelligence Agency (CIA) and the Assistant to the President for Homeland Security, and later the Secretary of Homeland Security. Other officials from the White House and other officers would be invited to attend the meetings at night. The role of the newly developed Council was to provide advice to the President about all aspects of protecting the country and its critical infrastructure.

Another document signed by President Bush was Executive Order 13231, which he signed on October 16, 2001. In this Executive Order Bush stated that it was US policy "to protect against the disruption of the operation of information systems for critical infrastructure ... and to ensure that any disruptions that occur are infrequent, of minimal duration, and manageable, and cause the least damage possible" (see Note 6). When he signed the document, Bush established the President's Critical Infrastructure Protection Board. The Board was made up of the CIAO and other federal officials and was tasked with recommending policies and coordinating programs "for protecting information systems for critical infrastructure." The Board was also asked to write a National Plan.

The Board was chaired by a Special Advisor to the President for Cyberspace Security. The Special Advisor reported to both the Assistant to the President for National Security and the Assistant to the President for Homeland Security. Besides presiding over Board meetings, the Special Advisor proposed policies and programs as needed if they would help ensure the nation's information infrastructure was protected.

The Executive Order 13231 also established the National Infrastructure Advisory Council. The Council was to advise the President on the security of information systems for critical infrastructure. Moreover, the Council was to work toward increasing partnerships between public and private agencies, monitor the development of ISACs, and encourage the private sector owners to carry out vulnerability assessments of critical information and telecommunication systems.

National Strategy for Homeland Security

In July 2002, the Office of Homeland Security released a report entitled a *National Strategy for Homeland Security*. The Strategy described all government efforts geared toward protecting the nation against terrorist threats of all kinds. It identified actions for protecting the nation's critical infrastructure and key assets as one of six critical mission areas. This strategy added public health, the chemical industry and hazardous materials, postal and shipping, the defense industrial base, and agriculture and food to the list of sectors that have critical infrastructure in them. It also combined emergency fire service, emergency law enforcement, and emergency medicine as emergency services. It also eliminated those functions that belong primarily to the federal governments (e.g., defense, intelligence, law enforcement). Some of the sectors were reassigned to different agencies. Many of the sectors were placed into DHS (postal and shipping services, and the defense industrial base).

The Report also introduced a new type of asset, called key assets, which were identified as potential targets that, if destroyed, may not endanger vital systems across the nation, but would nonetheless create a local disaster or affect the nation's morale. These would be things such as national monuments or historic attractions, dams, large commercial centers, or even sport stadiums.

The Strategy reinforced the need to work closely with the private sector to assess vulnerabilities and develop a plan to deal with those vulnerabilities. In the Strategy, the need to set priorities was stressed, explaining that not all assets are equally critical. The Strategy was updated in October 2007, with few changes to the strategy for protecting critical infrastructure.

The *National Strategy for the Physical Protection of Critical Infrastructures and Key Assets* was published in February 2003, by the Office of Homeland Security. This document also helped to define what was meant by "key assets." This new strategy used a broader perspective in issues related to organizing the nation's efforts to protect its critical assets. It also identified the roles and responsibilities of agencies and people, any actions that needed to be taken, and guiding principles. In this document, the definition of what is critical infrastructure was expanded to include historical attractions, centers of government and commerce, facilities that are associated with our national economy. This would include Wall Street in New York, chemical plants and events where there would be large numbers of people in attendance.

The National Strategy also indicated that protecting critical infrastructure and key assets was a way to reduce the nation's vulnerability to possible terrorist acts. National goals and objectives were set as a way to protect secure specific vital infrastructures. The goals were intended to identify any assets that were deemed to be critical in preserving the health and safety of the nation, the government, economic and national security, and public confidence. In the event of an attack, the primary focus would be on protecting those assets and infrastructure that were identified as critical.

That same month, February 2003, The President's Critical Infrastructure Protection Board released a report, entitled *The National Strategy to Secure Cyberspace*. This document focused on methods to protect information and data stored electronically or available on the Internet.

Homeland Security Presidential Directive-7

On December 17, 2003, the Bush Administration released Homeland Security Presidential Directive 7 (HSPD-7). In this directive, the responsibilities of various agencies in protecting critical infrastructure were outlined. In addition, the role of Sector-Specific Agencies (SSAs) (i.e., Lead Agencies) was more clearly defined. The SSAs were asked to collaborate with officials from their particular sectors and identify, prioritize, and coordinate measures designed to protect the country's infrastructure. The Directive also reiterated the need to create effective relationships between DHS and agencies in other areas.

One change made was to appoint DHS as the lead agency for the sector on chemical and hazardous materials. This person would report to the Secretary of Homeland Security annually regarding their relationships with the private sector. The Directive also reinforced the need for all federal agencies to develop plans for protecting their critical infrastructure.

Through HSPD-7, President Bush asked for a comprehensive National Plan for Critical Infrastructure and Key Resources Protection to be completed by the end of 2004. This document was to include (a) a strategy to identify, prioritize, and coordinate the protection of critical infrastructure and key resources, including how the Department will work with other stakeholders; (b) a summary of activities to be undertaken in order to carry out the strategy; (c) a summary of initiatives for sharing critical infrastructure information and threat warnings with other stakeholders; and (d) coordination with other federal emergency management activities.

In HSPD-7, the Secretary of Homeland Security was to serve as the principal federal official to lead critical infrastructure protection across the country. The responsibility for sectors was assigned to SSAs. The plans developed by the agencies, called the Sector-Specific Plans (SSPs), were supposed to create a more coordinated approach to protect critical infrastructure and key resources.

The National Infrastructure Protection Plan (NIPP) was not completed by the December 2004 deadline. Instead, in February 2005, DHS published an Interim NIPP. Then in November 2005, the Department released a "draft" NIPP. The final version of the NIPP was approved June 30, 2006. The NIPP was then revised in early 2009 to reflect the evolution of the process, including concepts of all-hazards and resiliency. These changes did not represent major shifts in policy or programs.

The Bush Administration devised a new Critical Infrastructure Protection Partnership Model. The new plan expanded the sector liaison and sector coordinator into Government Coordinating Councils and Sector Coordinating Councils for each sector. The goal was to increase representation of both owner/operators and government representation within the sectors. For example, the Water Sector Coordinating Council expanded to include two owner/operator representatives, along with one nonvoting association staff member from each of the following participating organizations: the Association of Metropolitan Water

Agencies, the American Water Works Association, the American Water Works Association Research Foundation, the National Association of Clean Water Agencies, the National Association of Water Companies, the National Rural Water Association, the Water Environment Federation, and the Water Environment Research Foundation. The Water Government Coordinating Council is chaired by the Environmental Protection Agency, the Lead Agency, but also includes DHS, the Food and Drug Administration, the Department of Interior, and the Center for Disease Control. Government Coordinating Councils can also include state, local, and tribal government entities. The Sector Coordinating Councils were asked to establish their own organizational structures and leadership that would act independently from the federal government. Also, under this model, the Partnership for Critical Infrastructure Security was designated the Private Sector Cross-Sector Council. The Sector Coordinating Councils were to provide input into both the NIPP and the individual SSPs.

In March 2006, the DHS used its authority under the Homeland Security Act to form the Critical Infrastructure Partnership Advisory Council (CIPAC). However, the Council was not required to meet standards outlined in the Federal Advisory Committee Act that requires advisory committees to meet in public and to make written materials available to the public. This was done so that the members of the Commission would feel free to share information that they would otherwise be hesitant to do. The DHS serves as the head of the committee, and other members include owner/operators that are members of their respective sector coordinating councils; federal, state, local, and tribal government representatives that belong to their government coordinating councils.

CONCLUSION: A SHIFT IN POLICIES

In the early documents and plans for protecting the nation's critical infrastructure, it was clear that the emphasis of preparedness and protection was primarily on the federal government's response to disasters and emergency events such as earthquakes, floods, or hurricanes. There was only limited preparedness for potential acts of terrorism. However, this approach changed in the months after the terrorist attacks of September 2001. Then, the attention of federal response shifted to preparing for possible terrorist attacks and mitigating potential effects so that service interruption was limited. Plans and documents such as the NIPP sought to make American's critical infrastructure and assets more secure and more resilient.[7] To do that, DHS and SSAs were encouraged to create collaborative partnerships to develop more effective plans. Despite these efforts, plans to protect the country were still in the developmental stage, and more work was continued by President Obama.

REVIEW QUESTIONS

1. What was Executive Order 13010 and why was it important?
2. What was President Clinton's approach to critical infrastructure protection?
3. Explain the significance of PDD-63.
4. How did President Bush's approach to protecting the nation's assets differ from President Clinton's?
5. How did the concept of critical infrastructure change over time?
6. What did President Bush seek to do when he signed Executive Order 13228?
7. Explain the importance of the National Strategy for Homeland Security.

NOTES

1. Cordesman, A. H., and Cordesman, J. G. 2002. *Cyber-Threats, Information Warfare, and Critical Infrastructure Protection: Defending the U.S. Homeland.* Westport, CT: Praeger.
2. Moteff, J. D. June 10, 2015. *Critical Infrastructures: Background, Policy and Implementation.* Washington, DC: Congressional Research Service, 7-5700. Retrieved from: www.crs.gov.
3. Clinton, B. July 17, 1996. *Executive Order 13010—Critical Infrastructure Protection.*
4. 107th U.S. Congress. 2001. *Uniting and Strengthening America by Providing Appropriate Tools Required to Intercept and Obstruct Terrorism Act of 2001* (Public Law 107-56), Section 1016(e).
5. Office of Homeland Security. 2002. *National Strategy for Homeland Security*, p. 31.
6. Bush, G. W. October 8, 2001. *Executive Order 13228—Establishing the Office of Homeland Security and the Homeland Security Council.* Online by Gerhard Peters and John T. Woolley, *The American Presidency Project.* Retrieved from: http://www.presidency.ucsb.edu/ws/?pid=61509; *Executive Order 13231—Critical Infrastructure Protection in the Information Age.* October 16, 2001. http://www.presidency.ucsb.edu/ws/?pid=61512.
7. DHS, FEMA. September 2010. *CIKR Awareness AWR-213, Participant Guide*, pp. 1–8.

3

Current Critical
Infrastructure Protection

INTRODUCTION

Today, critical infrastructure (CI) protection is a top priority for officials in all levels of governments, including federal, state, local, and tribal structures. It is also a priority for both public owners and private owners and operators of CI. No matter who is involved, the goal is to protect our infrastructure from damage resulting from a man-made incident such as a terrorist attack, but also from a natural event such as a hurricane or earthquake. In either case, the object is to return a community to a normal (or close to normal) state of affairs as quickly as possible. Chapter 2 provided an early history of asset protection, and this chapter provides a description of the current policies for protecting the nation's infrastructure. These policies are in a continual state of flux as the government continues to improve CI protection in response to ever-changing threats.

OBAMA ADMINISTRATION

President Barack Obama, since taking office in 2009, has not made many changes to the infrastructure protection policies that were originally generated by Presidents Clinton and Bush. Instead, he has continued to build on existing structures. Early in his Presidency, in February 2009, President Obama asked for a review of the homeland security and counterterrorism structures that were located within the White House. He also asked for an evaluation of the federal government's policies regarding cybercrime and cybersecurity. The results of the analysis were released in May 2009. Based on these reviews, the President merged the Homeland Security Council and the National Security Council into one agency, which he called the National Security Staff. The report also included a recommendation to appoint one person from the White House who would be responsible for overseeing federal policies regarding cybersecurity.

Strategic National Risk Assessment

In 2010, the Secretary of Homeland Security wrote the Strategic National Risk Assessment (SNRA). This was a classified assessment that formed the basis of Presidential Policy Directive 8 (PPD-8), which was announced by President Obama in 2011 (described in the section "Presidential Policy Directive-8"). The goal of the SNRA was to help identify the types of incidents that posed the greatest threat to the security of the nation. The committee that assisted the investigation included officials from the Director of National Intelligence and the Attorney General. An unclassified version of the report was released to the public in December 2011. Among other things, the report analyzed weaknesses in the nation's security and gave suggestions for how those could be addressed.

The committee drew from multiple sources, including historical records and experts from different disciplines. The Committee assessed the frequency and consequence of risks, to answer the question, *with what frequency is it estimated that an event will occur, and what are the consequences of the incident(s) if it does occur?* The Committee examined the threats and consequences associated with six categories of harm: (a) loss of life, (b) injuries and illnesses, (c) direct economic costs, (d) social displacement, (e) psychological distress, and (f) environmental impact.

The risks from possible threats and hazards that had the potential to have a significant impact on the nation's assets were discussed. The members identified risk factors, and then identified core capabilities and capability targets that would be described in the *National Preparedness Goal*. The committee members relied on a new approach to asset protection that relied on collaborative thinking about strategic needs for prevention, protection, mitigation, response, and recovery requirements. It also promoted the necessity for all levels of government to share a common understanding and awareness of threats and hazards so that they could prepare for, and respond to, events both independently and collaboratively. This was critical because, as noted by the committee, preparation and response are often more effective when multiple responders from local, state, and federal agencies are involved. It was also recognized that the whole community should be involved.

Possible events that could affect the nation's security were grouped into three categories: (a) natural hazards; (b) technological/accidental hazards; and (c) adversarial, human-caused threats/hazards. The report also created six possible harms: (a) loss of life, (b) injuries and illnesses, (c) direct economic costs, (d) social displacement, (e) psychological distress, and (f) the environment. The SNRA Committee found that there were a wide range of threats and hazards that posed a significant risk to the nation, affirming the need for an all-hazards, capability-based approach to preparedness planning. Some of the key findings reported included the following:

1. Natural hazards, including hurricanes, earthquakes, tornados, wildfires, and floods, present a significant and varied risk across the country.
2. A virulent strain of pandemic influenza has the possibility of killing hundreds of thousands of Americans and affecting millions more, resulting in economic loss.
3. Technological and accidental hazards, such as dam failures or chemical substance spills or releases, could result in devastating fatalities and severe economic impacts. The likelihood of this happening may increase because of aging infrastructure.
4. Terrorist organizations or their affiliates may attempt to acquire, build, and use weapons of mass destruction (WMD). Conventional terrorist attacks, including those by "lone actors" employing explosives and armed attacks, present a continued risk.
5. Cyberattacks can have their own catastrophic consequences and can also cause other hazards, including power grid failures or financial system failures, which magnify the potential impact of cyber incidents.[1]

The SNRA Committee identified events that had the potential to pose the greatest risk to the security of the nation.[2] These are listed in Table 3.1. The Committee recognized that it was possible that many of the events they listed could potentially occur more than once every 10 years, meaning that the nation's preparedness would probably be tested at some point in the next 10 years. They also stressed that risks to CI are always changing, and the nation must always be prepared for new hazards.

Table 3.1 SNRA National Level Events

Threat/Hazard Group	Threat/Hazard Type	National Level Event Description
Natural	Animal disease outbreak	An unintentional introduction of the foot-and-mouth disease virus into the domestic livestock population in a US state
Earthquake		An earthquake occurs within the US resulting in direct economic losses greater than $100 million
Flood		A flood occurs within the US resulting in direct economic losses greater than $100 million
Human pandemic outbreak		A severe outbreak of pandemic influenza with a 25% gross clinical attack rate spreads across the US populace
Hurricane		A tropical storm or hurricane impacts the US resulting in direct economic losses of greater than $100 million
Space weather		The sun emits bursts of electromagnetic radiation and energetic particles causing utility outages and damage to infrastructure
Tsunami		A tsunami with a wave of approximately 50 ft. impacts the Pacific Coast of the US
Volcanic eruption		A volcano in the Pacific northwest erupts impacting the surrounding areas with lava flows and ash and areas east with smoke and ash
Wildfire		A wildfire occurs within the US resulting in direct economic losses greater than $100 million
Technological/ Accidental	Biological food contamination	Accidental conditions where introduction of a biological agent (e.g., *Salmonella*, *E. coli*, botulinum toxin) into the food supply results in 100 hospitalizations or greater and a multistate response
Chemical substance spill or release		Accidental conditions where a release of a large volume of a chemical acutely toxic to human beings (a toxic inhalation hazard, or TIH) from a chemical plant, storage facility, or transportation mode results in either one or more offsite fatalities, or one or more fatalities (either on- or offsite) with offsite evacuations/ shelter-in-place
Dam failure		Accidental conditions where dam failure and inundation results in one fatality or more

(Continued)

Table 3.1 SNRA National Level Events (*Continued*)

Threat/Hazard Group	Threat/Hazard Type	National Level Event Description
Radiological substance release		Accidental conditions where reactor core damage causes release of radiation
Adversarial/ Human-caused	Aircraft as a weapon	A hostile nonstate actor(s) crashes a commercial or general aviation aircraft into a physical target within the US
Armed assault		A hostile nonstate actor(s) uses assault tactics to conduct strikes on vulnerable target(s) within the US resulting in at least one fatality or injury
Biological terrorism attack (nonfood)		A hostile nonstate actor(s) acquires, weaponizes, and releases a biological agent against an outdoor, indoor, or water target, directed at a concentration of people within the US
Chemical/ biological food contamination terrorism attack		A hostile nonstate actor(s) acquires, weaponizes, and disperses a biological or chemical agent into food supplies within the US supply chain
Chemical terrorism attack (nonfood)		A hostile nonstate actor(s) acquires, weaponizes, and releases a chemical agent against an outdoor, indoor, or water target, directed at a concentration of people using an aerosol, ingestion, or dermal route of exposure
Cyberattack against data		A cyberattack which seriously compromises the integrity or availability of data (the information contained in a computer system) or data processes resulting in economic losses of $1 billion or greater
Cyberattack against physical infrastructure		An incident in which a cyberattack is used as a vector to achieve effects which are beyond the computer (i.e., kinetic or other effects), resulting in one fatality or greater or economic losses of $100 million or greater
Explosives terrorism attack		A hostile nonstate actor(s) deploys a man-portable improvised explosive device (IED), vehicle-borne IED, or vessel IED in the US against a concentration of people, and/or structures such as critical commercial or government facilities, transportation targets, or critical infrastructure (CI) sites, etc., resulting in at least one fatality or injury

Source: Department of Homeland Security. December 2011. *Strategic National Risk Assessment* (dhs.gov).

Executive Order 13563

On January 18, 2011, President Obama issued Executive Order 13563, which was entitled "Improving Regulation and Regulatory Review." In this document, Obama reaffirmed the mandates set forth in Executive Order 12866, known as "Regulatory Planning and Review." In the new Executive Order, Obama directed all federal agencies to develop a preliminary plan to review their regulations to determine whether any of the existing rules should be updated or altered in any way to make the agency's regulatory program more effective.

One example of this was the DHS Preliminary Plan, which became public on May 26, 2011. A primary focus of their plan was to include members of the public as part of the review process. They also sought to include members of the public in the development of the plan and then the implementation of it.[3]

Presidential Policy Directive-8

On March 30, 2011, President Obama signed the Presidential Policy Directive-8 (PPD-8), entitled *National Preparedness*. This document replaced Homeland Security Presidential Directive-8 (HSPD-8) that was signed by President George W. Bush in 2003. In the new document, Obama developed a way to further strengthen the nation's security and resilience by making the nation better prepared for events. He concentrated on an all-hazards approach to security that included planning for possible terrorist acts, including cyberattacks, technological events, and also natural disasters. Additionally, the president recognized that national preparedness and security must involve all people who have a personal stake in CI or security, including those in government, the private sector, and individual citizens. The document requires that everyone be involved in the process for protecting assets instead of just government officials, which was primarily what was done in the past.

Five mission areas were identified in PPD-8. They are Prevent, Protect, Mitigate, Respond, and Recovery, described as follows:

1. Prevent: This was recognized as the most important of the mission areas. While people cannot prevent natural weather-related events, it is possible to prevent man-made events. This includes taking any actions necessary to avoid, prevent, or stop a threatened or actual act of terrorism, or preventing imminent threats of any kind. Prevention-related activities may include: increased

inspections; more surveillance and security operations; efforts geared toward increased public health (e.g., immunizations); surveillance and testing of agricultural products; law enforcement operations aimed at deterring or disrupting illegal activity.

2. Protect: This involves taking actions necessary to secure the homeland against acts of terrorism and man-made or natural disasters. Keywords in this area are "defense," "protection," "protect," "security," and any kind to include "cybersecurity." This refers to efforts for protecting all citizens, residents, visitors, as well as physical assets against threats, and hazards in a way that allows people to continue their way of life.

3. Mitigate: This refers to actions geared toward reducing the loss of life and property that could occur after an event by lessening the impact of disasters. Keywords are "risk reduction," "improve resilience," and "reduce future risk."

4. Respond: In this category, the focus is on ensuring that people have the services needed after an event to save lives, protect property and the environment, and meet basic human needs. This includes responding quickly and ensuring that people have services they need to survive. To do that, it is essential that policies are created that coordinate federal, state, and local activities.

5. Recovery: This stage focuses on the providing services needed to assist affected communities to return to a "normal" state as quickly as possible. Keywords are "rebuilding," "restoring," "promoting," "interim," and "long term."[4] Efforts here focus on the timely restoration of services, strengthening and rebuilding of infrastructure, housing, and health facilities, as well as social, cultural, and historic elements of a community.[5]

In addition, there are also six elements noted in PPD-8: *National Preparedness Goal*; *National Preparedness System*; *National Preparedness Report*; *National Planning Frameworks*; *Federal Interagency Operational Plans*; and *Build and Sustain Preparedness*.

National Preparedness Goal

PPD-8 required the Secretary of Homeland security to create a new *National Preparedness Goal*.[6] According to Obama, "The National Preparedness Goal shall be informed by the risk of specific threats and vulnerabilities— taking into account regional variations—and include concrete, measurable, and prioritized objects to mitigate that risk."[7]

The goal identifies and defines core capabilities that, according to the president, the country needs in order to achieve preparedness and, in the end, better national security. When met, the core capabilities will help the country to be prepared for all types of incidents that could pose a risk to the nation's security. These core capabilities are essential for officials to implement the five mission areas as described earlier. The goal defines success as "A secure and resilient Nation with the capabilities required across the whole community to prevent, protect against, mitigate, respond to, and recover from the threats and hazards that pose the greatest risk."[8]

A fundamental concept throughout the document is the emphasis on the whole community approach. This means that all interested groups and organizations need to work together in a variety of ways and make the best use of resources to be fully prepared for an event (see Note 4, pp. 1–13). In December 2011, Federal Emergency Management Agency (FEMA) relea sed a report entitled *A Whole Community Approach to Emergency Management: Principles, Themes and Pathways for Action.*[9] In this document, officials describe the idea of whole community approach. It means that all members of a community, including emergency management practitioners, community leaders, organizations, government officials, private business owners and operators, and citizens can each help to assess the needs of their own community and decide the best method to organize and strengthen their assets, capacities, and interests. They will decide the best ways to prepare to potential threats and hazards. This concept is described in Table 3.2.

Table 3.2 Key Principles of the Whole Community Approach

1. Understand and meet the actual needs of the whole community: community engagement can lead to a deeper understanding of the unique and diverse needs of a population, including its demographics, values, norms, community structures, networks, and relationships. The more we know about our communities, the better we can understand their real-life safety, sustaining needs, and their motivations to participate in emergency management-related activities prior to an event.

2. Engage and empower all parts of the community: engaging the whole community and empowering local action will better position stakeholders to plan for and meet the actual needs of a community and strengthen the local capacity to deal with the consequences of all threats and hazards. This requires all members of the community to be part of the emergency management team, which should include diverse community members, social and community service groups and institutions, faith-based and disability groups, academia, professional associations, and the private and

(Continued)

Table 3.2 (*Continued*) Key Principles of the Whole Community Approach

nonprofit sectors, while including government agencies who may not traditionally have been directly involved in emergency management. When the community is engaged in an authentic dialogue, it becomes empowered to identify its needs and the existing resources that may be used to address them.

3. Strengthen what works well in communities on a daily basis: a *Whole Community approach* to building community resilience requires finding ways to support and strengthen the institutions, assets, and networks that already work well in communities to address issues that are important to community members on a daily basis. This includes structures and relationships that are present in the daily lives of individuals, families, businesses, and organizations before an incident occurs.

Source: Federal Emergency Management Agency. December 2011. A Whole Community Approach to Emergency Management. FDOC 104-008-1, http://www.fema.gov/media-library-data.

National Preparedness System

The National Preparedness System refers to a document published in November 2011 that outlines an approach, resources, and tools needed to assist communities and the nation in meeting the National Preparedness Goal. It includes national planning frameworks that cover the five areas of prevention, protection, mitigation, response, and recovery, as mentioned earlier. The frameworks each use a common terminology and approach, and are each built around the all-hazards approach to preparedness. In addition, the system is also built on an "All-of-Nation" approach to preparedness. The system has six parts: (a) identifying and assessing risk; (b) estimating capability requirements; (c) building and sustaining capabilities; (d) planning to deliver capabilities; (e) validating capabilities; (f) reviewing and updating (see Note 4, pp. 1–13).

National Preparedness Report

Under the PPD-8, the Secretary of Homeland Security must submit a National Preparedness Report to the President each year. This report is to include a summary of the progress that has been made toward achieving the National Preparedness Goal. The Secretary is also required to identify any gaps in activities. The report could be used by the president when establishing the annual budget so that funds could be allocated to support existing activities or create new activities to fill the gaps (see Note 4, pp. 1–13).

National Planning Frameworks

There are five frameworks that focus on the mission areas of PPD-8 (Prevention, Protection, Mitigation, Response and Recovery). The frameworks demonstrate how different groups and agencies will cooperate to meet the needs of individuals, families, communities, and states in their efforts to prevent, protect, mitigate, respond to, and recover from any disaster or event (see Note 4, pp. 1–13).

The frameworks were created in a way that they are scalable and could be adapted to each individual community or event. The frameworks only establish the overall theme or strategy (coordinating structure) for communities, which must then build and deliver the core capabilities identified in the National Preparedness Goal. It was stressed that there is a need for a common terminology that will be used across all of the frameworks as a way to ensure interoperability across all mission areas. The frameworks address the roles of individuals, nonprofit entities, government agencies, nongovernmental organizations (NGOs), the private sector, and communities in planning for response to events. Most importantly, the frameworks contain detailed information on the 31 core capabilities, which help to define desired outcomes, set capability targets, and specify appropriate resources.

Federal Interagency Operational Plans

These plans describe the federal government's strategies to deliver the core capabilities outlined in the five frameworks described earlier. These plans help to define how federal policies and officials can provide support to state and local officials as they establish plans for responding to an event. The federal plans will also describe essential tasks and responsibilities and specific provisions for integrating resources and personnel with other governments (see Note 4, pp. 1–14).

Build and Sustain Preparedness

This element stresses that the effort to build and maintain the country's preparedness is ongoing and will constantly build on existing activities (see Note 4, pp. 1–14).

This element has four key sections, which are as follows:

1. A comprehensive campaign, including public outreach and community-based and private sector programs
2. Federal preparedness efforts
3. Grants, technical assistance, and other federal preparedness support
4. Research and development

Executive Order 13636

On February 12, 2013, President Obama issued Executive Order 13636, *Improving Critical Infrastructure: Cybersecurity*. In this document, the president stressed that the nation's security depends on a reliable and functioning CI and a secure cyber environment. He also stressed that the best way to achieve a safe environment is with better communication and cooperation with the owners and operators of CI. Clearly, increased communication could lead to more efforts to collaborate on, develop, and implement risk-based approaches to cybersecurity. For these reasons, Obama asked the federal government to coordinate their activities with the owners and operators of CI and improve information sharing between the groups. As another way to improve information sharing, Obama asked the Attorney General, the Secretary of Homeland Security, and the Director of National Intelligence to develop unclassified reports on any cyberthreats that are reported, and to share those reports with the targeted group.

In another part of the executive order, Obama sought to develop a cybersecurity framework for CI to improve the nation's cybersecurity. This framework would establish standards, methodologies, procedures, and processes that the owners of CI could use to reduce their cybersecurity risks. The new plan, when done, would be a cost-efficient approach to helping owners and operators identify, assess, and manage cyber risks. The plan will help owners and operators identify potential vulnerabilities, then provide innovative suggestions for addressing those risks. The process of creating the framework would be overseen by the Director of the National Institute of Standards and Technology (NIST), but other interested people would be allowed to participate. This would include sector coordinating councils, owners and operators of critical assets, Sector-Specific Agencies (SSAs), regulatory agencies, universities, and other relevant groups. The framework would be the basis for the Voluntary CI Cybersecurity Program.

The framework was released in February 2014. Upon its release, all owners or operators of CI were encouraged to use the framework to improve the security of their networks. Any agencies that had the responsibility of regulating the security of CI were asked to review their policies to determine if they were sufficient, and if not, they were asked to consider adopting the recommended ones, or at least modifying what they had to align more with the standards found in the framework. The Secretary of Homeland Security was also asked to create incentives for participating in the voluntary program.

The Enhanced Cybersecurity Services program was expanded through Obama's executive order. This program allows classified information on cybersecurity threats and other technical information to be shared with infrastructure network service providers. Obama asked government agencies to expand the program to all CI sectors so that more information about threats and other technical information would be shared with a bigger audience more quickly. In order for this to work, Obama asked to change the way security clearances to those employed by infrastructure owners and operators were granted, making the process quicker.

At the same time, the president wanted to ensure that privacy and civil liberties of all individuals were protected. He asked that the Chief Privacy Officer and the Officer for Civil Rights and Civil Liberties of the DHS oversee the programs and recommend ways to ensure that citizens' rights were protected.

Executive Order 13691

In February 2015, Obama issued Executive Order 13691, called *Promoting Private Sector Cybersecurity Information Sharing*. In this document, he addressed the importance of sharing information pertaining to cybersecurity. Obama gave the Secretary of DHS the responsibility of establishing Information Sharing and Analysis Organizations (ISAOs), which are very much like the Information Sharing and Analysis Centers (ISACs) in PDD-63. There would also be an ISAO Standards Organization that would work with all of the CI stakeholders to develop voluntary standards and guidelines for establishing and operating ISAOs. In the Executive Order, Obama also designated the National Cybersecurity and Communications Integration Center (NCCIC) as a CI protection program, allowing it to receive and transmit cybersecurity information between the federal government and the ISAOs as protected CI information.

Presidential Policy Directive-21

In February 2013, President Obama announced Presidential Policy Directive-21 (PPD-21), which had the title *Critical Infrastructure Security and Resilience*. This new plan superseded Homeland Security Presidential Directive (HSPD-7) from the Bush administration. PPD-21 reflected the increased interest in resilience and the all-hazard approach that has evolved in CI protection policy over the last few years. The purpose of the directive was to establish a national policy to strengthen and maintain a secure CI that is also resilient to attacks. This is important for the continuity of national essential functions. Both physical and cyber infrastructure was included.

In PPD-21, cooperation was stressed. Companies were asked to cooperate not only with the government but sometimes with competing industries in efforts to increase security. As noted by Obama, CI protection must be a shared responsibility between federal, state, local, tribal, and territorial entities, along with public and private owners and operators of the assets. He also noted the importance of working with international partners to strengthen infrastructure that was physically located outside the US.

The number of sectors and how they are organized were changed in PPD-21 (see Table 3.3). In the 2006 National Infrastructure Protection Plan (NIPP), there were 17 CI sectors established, as outlined in HSPD-7. But since PPD-21 revoked HSPD-7, the 18 sectors were reorganized into 16 CI sectors.

PPD-21 identifies the energy and communications sectors as uniquely critical and deserving of extra attention (see Note 4, pp. 1–7). National Monuments and Icons was designated as a subsector of Government

Table 3.3 16 Critical Infrastructure and Key Resources Sectors

1. Chemical Sector: Department of Homeland Security (DHS) is the Sector-Specific Agency (SSA)
2. Commercial Facilities Sector: DHS is the SSA
3. Communications Sector
4. Critical Manufacturing: DHS
5. Dams: DHS
6. Defense Industrial Base Sector
7. Emergency Services Sector
8. Energy Sector
9. Financial Services Sector
10. Food and Agriculture Sector Department of Agriculture and Department of Health and Human Services are co-SSAs
11. Government Facilities Sector: DHS and General Services Administration (GSA)
12. Healthcare and Public Health Sector
13. Information Technology Sector
14. Nuclear Reactors, Materials and Waste Sector; DHS
15. Transportation Systems Sector: DHS and Department of Transportation
16. Water and Wastewater Systems Sector: Environmental Protection Agency (EPA)

Facilities; Postal and Shipping was designated as a subsector of Transportation; Banking and Finance was renamed Financial Services; and Drinking Water and Water Treatment was renamed Water and Waste Water Systems. In March 2008, DHS announced the creation of an additional sector, Critical Manufacturing. The sector encompasses groups from the primary metal, machinery, electrical equipment, and transportation equipment manufacturing industries. PPD-21 also gave the energy and communications sectors a higher profile, because of the Administration's assessment of their importance to the operations of the other infrastructures.

PPD-21 also called for other federal departments and agencies to play a key role in CI security and resilience activities through their appointment as SSA. An SSA is a federal department or agency that is responsible for, among other things, security, and resilience programs and related activities of designated sectors. Each sector was assigned a SSA (see Table 3.3). For example, DHS is the SSA for the commercial facilities and dams sectors, and the Department of Energy (DOE) and the Environmental Protection Agency (EPA) are the SSAs for the energy and water sectors, respectively. DHS also shares SSA responsibilities with the Department of Transportation (DOT) for the transportation sector, and the General Services Administration (GSA) for the government facilities sector.[10] The lead agency assignments are noted in Table 3.4.

1. While energy shows as one sector, it is actually represented by two separate sectors: electric power (except for nuclear power facilities); and the production, refining, and some distribution of oil and gas. The DOE is the lead agency for both. However, the Department of Homeland Security (DHS) (through the Transportation Security Administration) is the lead agency for the distribution of oil and gas via pipelines. Nuclear power is considered to be its own sector.
2. Transportation includes all modes of transportation: rail, mass transit (rail and bus), air, maritime, highways, pipelines, and so forth. The Transportation Security Administration (part of the DHS), in collaboration with the DOT, is the lead agency for all but the maritime subsector, which has the Coast Guard (also within the DHS), as its lead agency.

President Obama asked for an evaluation of the existing public–private partnership model to determine if it could be improved. To do this, he sought to collect baseline data and existing system requirements that would be the starting point for a more efficient exchange of information.

Table 3.4 Current Lead Agency Assignments

Department/Agency	Sector/Subsector
Agriculture	Agriculture, food
Agriculture	Meat/poultry
Health and Human Services	All other
Treasury	Financial services (Formerly Banking and Finance)
EPA	Water and wastewater systems (formerly drinking water and water treatment systems)
Health and Human Services	Public Health and Healthcare
Defense	Defense Industrial Base
Energy	Energy
Homeland Security	Transportation systems (now includes postal and shipping)
Homeland Security	Information technology
Homeland Security	Commercial nuclear reactors, materials, and waste
Homeland Security	Chemical
Homeland Security	Emergency services
Homeland Security	Dams
Homeland Security	Commercial facilities
Homeland Security	Government facilities (now includes national monuments and icons)
Homeland Security	Critical manufacturing

After this was established, a new plan would be developed, called the Research and Development Plan for CI, which would be a working document that would be updated every 4 years.

Throughout PPD-21, the president outlined the roles and responsibilities of different groups as the following:

1. The Secretary of Homeland Security "shall provide strategic guidance, promote a national unity of effort, and coordinate the overall Federal effort to promote the security and resilience of the Nation's critical infrastructure." This person should evaluate national capabilities and challenges to protecting assets, analyze threats and vulnerabilities, and develop a national plan. The DHS was also asked to identify and prioritize infrastructure, maintain

centers that provide situational awareness (i.e., emerging trends, imminent threats, or status of incidents), provide information and analysis on information, assess vulnerabilities, and coordinate federal government responses to significant incidents.

2. SSAs were asked to provide sector specific information and expertise about their specific sector, and then coordinate their activities and plans with DHS and other agencies. They can also provide technical assistance if needed either to mitigate incidents or respond to incidents.

3. The Department of State was asked to work with representatives from other countries to strengthen the security and resilience of any CI located outside of the US.

4. The Department of Justice (the FBI) was identified as the organization that would lead counterterrorism and counterintelligence investigations to disrupt and reduce foreign intelligence and actual or attempted attacks on the nation's infrastructure.

5. Department of Interior should identify and coordinate security and resilience efforts for all monuments and icons.

6. The Department of Commerce was given the responsibility to engage the private sector, research, and academic organizations as a way to improve security of cyber-based systems, and help to develop new ways to protect CI.

7. The Intelligence Community should provide intelligence assessments regarding possible threats.

8. The GSA was given the task of providing contracts for CI systems that include audit rights for the security and resilience of assets.

9. The Nuclear Regulatory Commission should oversee the protection of commercial nuclear power reactors, as well as the transportation of nuclear waste.

10. The Federal Communications Commission was asked to identify vulnerabilities in the Communications Sector and work to address those.

In addition to all of this, there were three strategic imperatives outlined by President Obama in the Directive. These were as follows[11]:

1. To refine and clarify functional relationships across the federal government as a way to advance CI security and resilience. If needed, relationships among stakeholders should be defined or even redefined. The functions of federal agencies need to be clarified to reflect an increase in knowledge and changes in threats. To

do this, President Obama asked for two national centers operated by DHS that would work to enhance CI protection. One would focus on physical infrastructure and the other on cyber protection.

2. Enable efficient exchange of information between all levels of government as well as with all owners and operators of CI. There is a need for more information sharing within the government and with the private sector.

3. Implement an analysis of incidents or threats to inform planning and operational decisions regarding CI protection. This should include operational and strategic analysis.

NIPP 2006

In PPD-21, President Obama required that the NIPP be updated and revised. The NIPP had originally been published in 2006, but the administration believed it was time to update that plan. The updated plan was to include a focus on the how the sectors rely on the energy and communications infrastructure and ways to mitigate the associated risks. Clearly, there had been significant changes in the risk, policy, and operating environments surrounding the country's CI since the NIPP was first published.

The 2006 version of the NIPP outlined an integrated national plan for managing risk for the country's CI. The process included identifying assets and threats, then conducting threat assessments in which vulnerabilities were analyzed in light of consequences and risk mitigation activities. Those activities would be prioritized based on cost-effectiveness. The 2006 NIPP also called for implementation plans for these risk reduction activities.

Each lead agency was asked to work in collaboration with other agencies in its sector to write a Sector-Specific plan. When the plans were completed, DHS was to integrate the individual Sector-Specific Plans into a national plan. This could then be used to identify the assets that, if damaged, could pose a significant risk to the entire nation. Any risk reduction plans that required federal assistance would also be identified. The sector officials were asked to review the plans every 3 years and reissue revised plans if needed. This would help ensure that the plans would remain current and relevant to all security partners.

Only seven plans were made public, and the others were given the designation "For Official Use Only." The Government Accountability

Office (GAO) reviewed nine of the plans and found that all complied with the NIPP process. However, some of the plans were more complete than others and provided more analysis than others. There were significant differences in the amount of detail provided and the general thoroughness of the reports. Moreover, while all of the plans provided detail about the threat analyses conducted by the sector, eight of the plans described no incentives that the sector could use to encourage owners and operators to carry out voluntary risk assessments, as required by the NIPP. These incentives were needed since many of the companies in the sectors were privately owned, they were not regulated by the government. Instead, the government was forced to rely on voluntary compliance with the NIPP.

The GAO finished their report by making two key recommendations to DHS. First, they recommended that the DHS provide better definitions of CI information needs; and second, that there be a better explanation of how this information could be used to attract more users.

NIPP 2013

After a brief revision in 2009, the NIPP was again revised in 2013 after President Obama, in PPD-21, called for officials to update the document. He requested the update based on a belief that there had been significant changes in the CI risk, policy, and operating environments, as well as our general knowledge about CI protection. In essence, government officials and others were to complete a "gap analysis" to fix any gaps that may exist in asset protection. The 2013 National Plan builds upon previous NIPPs and emphasizes goals of CI security and resilience. The ultimate goals were to: (a) identify, deter, detect, disrupt, and prepare for threats and hazards to the nation's CI; (b) reduce vulnerabilities of critical assets, systems, and networks; and (c) mitigate the potential consequences of incidents or adverse events that do occur to infrastructure (see Note 4, p. 1–9).

The revised NIPP was developed through a collaborative process that included stakeholders from the 16 CI sectors, all 50 states, and from all levels of government and industry. The Committee members worked to identify priorities and articulate goals that would help to mitigate risk to infrastructure and help be resilient in the case of an attack. As published, the following are the vision, mission, and goals:

Vision: A nation in which physical and cyber infrastructure remain secure and resilient, with vulnerabilities reduced, consequences minimized, threats identified and disrupted, and response and recovery hastened.

Mission: Strengthen the security and resilience of the nation's CI by managing physical and cyber risks through the collaborative and integrated efforts of the CI community.

Goals:

1. Assess and analyze threats to, vulnerabilities of, and consequences to CI to inform risk management activities.
2. Secure CI against human, physical, and cyberthreats through sustainable efforts to reduce risk, while accounting for the costs and benefits of security investments.
3. Enhance CI resilience by minimizing the adverse consequences of incidents through advance planning and mitigation efforts, and employing effective responses to save lives and ensure the rapid recovery of essential services.
4. Share actionable and relevant info across the infrastructure community to build awareness and enable risk-informed decision making.
5. Promote learning and adaptation during and after exercises and incidents.[12]

The 2013 NIPP, entitled *Partnering for Critical Infrastructure and Resilience*, is largely the same as the two earlier versions, but with more integration of resiliency and the all-hazard approach. However, the basic partnership model and the risk management framework were maintained. The revised NIPP stresses the importance of developing partnerships between national, regional, state, and local government and owners and operators. It was made clear that coordination with infrastructure stakeholders is necessary to protect the public's safety and ensure national security.

The revised NIPP made it clear that managing the risks from threats and hazards requires an integrated approach as a way to identify, deter, detect, disrupt, and prepare for threats and hazards to the nation's CI; reduce vulnerabilities of critical assets, systems, and networks; and then mitigate the potential consequences to CI of incidents or adverse events that do occur.[13]

The new report recognized that the country's well-being relies on security and resiliency of CI, so the primary goal of any program must be the efforts to protect CI. To do that, the NIPP establishes a procedure to define what assets are considered to be national CI and how to protect them. International collaboration is also part of asset protection efforts. The new report also gives attention to cybersecurity (see Note 13).

Cooperation with the all partners was stressed, particularly with private sector owners and operators of CI, alongside of federal, state, local, tribal and territorial governments, regional entities, NGOs, and academia (see Note 4, pp. 1–8). The document stressed that these groups should work together to manage risks and achieve better security. Because everyone is involved in the process, many perspectives will be included, resulting in better information sharing (see Note 13, pp. 1–8). To increase cooperation, many groups were included in the process. These include sector coordinating councils, government coordinating councils, and cross-sector councils.

Better communication was also needed by federal agencies to help to prevent the "silo effect" whereby an agency carries out a program but does not communicate that with other agencies. This can lead to wasted resources, but also inefficiencies and gaps in services.

The 2013 NIPP highlights seven core tenets and twelve action items to guide the national effort over the next 4 years. These are described in Table 3.5.

The NIPP uses a five-step risk management framework that is applicable to the general threat environment as well as to specific threats or incidents. The five steps can be applied to physical (tangible property), cyber (electronic communications and information), and human security (knowledge of people susceptible to attack). The five steps are as follows[14]:

1. Set goals and objectives: Define specific outcomes, conditions, end points, or performance targets that collectively constitute an effective risk management posture.
2. Identify infrastructure and assets: Build, manage, refine, and improve a comprehensive inventory of the assets, systems, and networks that make up the nation's CI.
3. Assess and analyze risks: Evaluate the risk, taking into consideration the potential direct and indirect consequences of all-hazards threats and known vulnerabilities. These risks can be compared in order to develop a more complete view of asset, system, and/or network risks and associated mission continuity, where applicable. It is also possible to establish priorities based on risk attached to an asset.
4. Implement protective programs and resilience strategies (implement risk management activities): Select appropriate actions or programs to reduce or manage the risk identified, and identify and provide the resources needed to address priorities.

Table 3.5 2013 NIPP: Guiding Tenets and Call to Action

Tenets	Call to Action
Risk should be identified and managed in a coordinated and comprehensive way across the critical infrastructure (CI) community	Build upon partnership efforts
Understanding and addressing cross-sector (inter)dependencies is essential	Set national focus through jointly developed priorities
Gaining knowledge of risks and interdependences requires information sharing	Determine collective actions through joint planning efforts
The partnership approach recognizes the unique perspectives and comparative advantages of the diverse CI community	Empower local and regional partnerships to build capacity
Regional and state, local, tribal and territorial (SLTT) partnerships are crucial to improve security and resilience.	Leverage incentives to advance security and resiliency
Infrastructure critical to US transcends national boundaries, requiring cross-border cooperation	Innovate in managing risk
Security and resilience should be considered during the design of assets, systems, and networks	Enable risk-informed decision making through enhanced situational awareness
	Analyze infrastructure (inter) dependencies and cascading effects
	Promote recovery following incidents
	Strengthen development and delivery of technical assistance, training and education
	Improve security and resilience by research and Development
	Focus on outcomes
	Evaluate progress toward achieving goals
	Learn and adapt

5. Measure effectiveness: Use metrics and other evaluation procedures at the appropriate national, state, local, regional, and sector levels to measure progress and to assess the effectiveness of the CI Protection programs. In this case, those involved are able to track their progress and use the data as a baseline for comparison and continuous improvement through program implementation.

CONCLUSION

Since becoming president, Barack Obama has, for the most part, slowly expanded the policies, organizations, and programs that govern the protection of the nation's CI and assets. He has focused on expanding the involvement of all interested parties in the planning process and improving communication among all involved. President Obama has also focused on the all-hazards approach to protecting CI, and has expanded protection efforts into cybersecurity policies.

REVIEW QUESTIONS

1. How has President Obama addressed CI protection?
2. What was the intent of PPD-8?
3. Describe the impact of PPD-21.
4. What are the key principles of the whole community approach?
5. What are the changes made in Executive Order 13691?
6. What are some differences between the 2006 NIPP and the 2013 version?

NOTES

1. DHS, FEMA. September 2010. *CIKR Awareness AWR-213, Participant Guide.* Washington, DC: US DHS, pp. 1–19.
2. Department of Homeland Security. December 2011. *Strategic National Risk Assessment* (dhs.gov).
3. US DHS. July 27, 2015. *DHS Implementation of Executive Order 13563.* Retrieved from: http://www.dhs.gov/dhs-implementation-executive-order-13563.
4. DHS, FEMA. September 2014. *Critical Asset Risk Management, Participant Guide,* pp. 1–17.
5. US DHS. 2005. *National Response Plan Brochure.* Washington, DC: US DHS.

6. US DHS, FEMA. 2012. *Learn About Presidential Policy Directive 8*; also DHS, FEMA. September 2014. *Critical Asset Risk Management, Participant Guide*, pp. 1–12.
7. Obama, B. 2011. Presidential Policy Directive 8.
8. US DHS. 2011. *National Preparedness Goal*, p. 1.
9. Federal Emergency Management Agency. December 2011. A Whole Community Approach to Emergency Management. FDOC 104-008-1. Retrieved from: http://www.fema.gov/media-library-data.
10. US Department of Homeland Security, and US Department of Justice, Global Justice Information Sharing Initiative. December 2008. *Critical Infrastructure and Key Resources, Protection Capabilities for Fusion Centers*. Retrieved from: https://it.ojp.gov/documents/d/CIKR%20protection%20capabilities%20 for%20fusion%20centers%20s.pdf.
11. The White House: Office of the Press Secretary. 2013. *Presidential Policy Directive—Critical Infrastructure Security and Resilience*.
12. US DHS. 2013. *National Infrastructure Protection Plan*, p. 5; DHS, FEMA. September 2014. *Critical Asset Risk Management, Participant Guide*, pp. 1–11.
13. US DHS. 2013. *National Infrastructure Protection Plan*.
14. DHS, FEMA. September 2010. *CIKR Awareness AWR-213, Participant Guide*, pp. 3–8.

4

Department of
Homeland Security

INTRODUCTION

There are many agencies, which play a key role in homeland security and critical infrastructure protection. These agencies seek to identify potential weaknesses that exist in the nation's critical infrastructure and identify ways to mitigate those threats to protect lives and property, and to ensure that services will continue to be provided. Sometimes these agencies provide assistance in planning and implementing protection strategies, sometimes providing financial assistance. Organizations involved in critical infrastructure protection exist on the federal, state, and local levels. This chapter will examine the various agencies responsible for risk assessment and risk management in the homeland security enterprise.

HISTORY

Just 11 days after the terrorist attacks of September 11, 2001, President Bush formed the Office of Homeland Security that would be located within the White House. The first director appointed to oversee the Office was Pennsylvania Governor, Tom Ridge. The new office was given the task of creating a comprehensive plan to keep the country safe from future terrorist attacks and respond to any future attacks.

In November 2002, the Congress passed the Homeland Security Act (PL 107-296) that created a cabinet-level department called the Department of Homeland Security (DHS). Parts or all of 22 different existing federal agencies were combined to form the new department, which began operating on March 1, 2003 (see Table 4.1).[1] Under the Act, the department was responsible for preventing terrorist attacks, reducing the vulnerability of the nation to such attacks, and responding rapidly in the case of an attack. When it came to critical infrastructure protection, DHS was given the responsibility to develop a comprehensive national plan for securing the country's assets and for recommending "measures necessary to protect the Nation's critical infrastructure and key resources (CIKR) in coordination with other agencies of the federal government and in cooperation with State and local government agencies and authorities, the private sector, and other entities."[2]

Other offices and agencies were transferred to the newly created DHS. One of those was the National Infrastructure Protection Center (NIPC),

Table 4.1   Agencies Relocated to DHS

US Customs Service (Treasury)
Immigration and Naturalization Service (INS) (Justice)
The Federal Protective Service
Transportation Security Administration (TSA) (Transportation)
Federal Law Enforcement Training Center (Treasury)
Animal and Plant Health Inspection Service (Agriculture)
Office for Domestic Preparedness (Justice)
Federal Emergency Management Agency (FEMA)
Strategic National Stockpile and the National Disaster Medical System (HHS)
Nuclear Incident Response Team (Energy)
Domestic Emergency Support Teams (Justice)
National Domestic Preparedness Office (FBI)
CBRN Countermeasures Program (Energy)
Environmental Measurements Laboratory (Energy)
National BW Defense Analysis Center (Defense)
Plum Island Animal Disease Center (Agriculture)
Federal Computer Incident Response Center (GSA)
National Communications System (Defense)
National Infrastructure Protection Center (FBI)
Energy Security and Assurance Program (Energy)
US Coast Guard; US Secret Service

Source: US DHS. June 24, 2015. *Who Joined DHS*. Retrieved from: http://www
.dhs.gov/who-joined-dhs.

which is an agency that works to protect the security of the nation's computer systems. Another agency, the Critical Infrastructure Assurance Office (CIAO) was also moved to DHS. As part of the Department of Commerce, this agency oversees security measures pertaining to energy, financial services, transportation, telecommunications, and other critical assets. The Federal Computer Incident Response Center (FedCRIC), also helps respond to computer-related incidents. Two other agencies, the National Infrastructure Simulation and Analysis Center (NISAC), and the National Communication System (NCS) were also transferred into the new department.

Over the years, DHS has continued to evolve as it seeks to protect the country from terrorist acts and at the same time, protect the country's critical infrastructure from harm. When it comes to asset protection, DHS is responsible for reducing the vulnerability of CIKR to terrorist attacks and other hazards.[3] They are also involved with maintaining and protecting a secure computer system. This entails cooperation with industry as well as officials from state, local, tribal, and territorial governments. This way, consistent policies can be created to keep the critical infrastructure and information systems safe. DHS continues to analyze and reduce cyberthreats and potential vulnerabilities in computer systems. They also work to distribute threat warnings to owners and operators of critical infrastructure, and coordinate the government's response to cyber incidents when they occur.[4]

Another primary goal of DHS is to ensure that services will be provided to citizens in the event of a disaster. If an event occurs, DHS helps to ensure that there will be a coordinated and comprehensive response and provide assistance to those who are in need. They have made cooperative agreements with other federal, state, local, and private sector agencies to ensure that recovery efforts will be quick and effective. The response can be increased sharing of critical information, providing financial assistance, providing training for personnel and law enforcement partners, and by assisting with any rebuilding and recovery efforts that are needed.[5]

LEADERSHIP

Former Governor Ridge, served as the first Secretary of Homeland Security, serving from January 24, 2003, to February 1, 2005. He was succeeded by Michael Chertoff, who became the Secretary on

February 15, 2005, and stayed until January 21, 2009. On July 13, 2005, after completing a review of the agency, Chertoff announced a six-point agenda, based on the review. He also significantly reorganized the department.[6]

One of the changes Chertoff made was to rearrange some of the offices or directorates. He wanted to restructure the Information Analysis and Infrastructure Protection Directorate (IAIPD) and rename it the Directorate of Preparedness. The new directorate would include portions of the Office of State and Local Government Coordination and Preparedness, including the grant functions and some of the preparedness functions. Moreover, Chertoff's reorganization involved the creation of a new position, the Assistant Secretary for Infrastructure Protection. The mission of the new directorate became managing grants and overseeing other national preparedness efforts, such as training for first responders, increasing citizen awareness, protecting public health, and ensuring the safety of infrastructure and cybersecurity.

Chertoff was followed as the DHS Secretary by Janet Napolitano, who held the post from January 20, 2009 until she left on September 6, 2013. In 2010, Napolitano oversaw the completion of a Quadrennial Homeland Security Review (QHSR) in which agency personnel worked closely with the White House staff and members of other federal, state, local, and tribal agencies. The members created goals for homeland security, along with a unified, strategic framework to help agencies meet those goals. In doing so, the agency performed a "Bottom-Up Review (BUR)" that would match the agency's activities with the organizational structure. This way, it would ensure the goals would be met (see Note 6).

The current Secretary of DHS is Jeh Johnson, who became the fourth Secretary of Homeland Security on December 23, 2013. Before becoming the head of DHS, Johnson held the position of General Counsel for the Department of Defense where he oversaw over 10,000 attorneys. He also served as the General Counsel of the Department of the Air Force, and as the Assistant US Attorney for the Southern District of New York. While at the Defense Department, Johnson helped to develop counterterrorism policies for the US and assisted in reforms to military commissions system at Guantanamo Bay. Johnson received his legal training in Columbia Law School, graduating in 1982.

DHS continues to evolve under Johnson. For example, in 2010, the Federal Protective Service (FPS) moved from Immigration and Custom Enforcement (ICE) to the National Protection and Programs Directorate (NPPD). One reason for the move was, according to Obama, that the role of the FPS, which is to protect federal buildings, was more closely related to DHS' goal of protecting the nation's critical infrastructure. In 2013, the tasks performed by the Office of Risk Management and Analysis were transferred to the Office of Policy. In 2013, the United States Visitor and Immigrant Status Indicator Technology (US-VISIT) program was incorporated into the Office of Biometric Identify Management. And then in 2014, some responsibilities of the Office of Infrastructure Protection (OIP) were handed over to the Office of Cyber and Infrastructure Analysis.

DHS continues to determine what infrastructure assets can be considered to be critical infrastructure. This is done through the National Critical Infrastructure Prioritization Program and the Critical Foreign Dependencies Initiative, along with the NISAC and the Office of Infrastructure Analysis. These agencies attempt to identify those assets, found both in the US and overseas, that are critical to the nation's ability to thrive. To do this, the agencies collect data on any threats to which the asset is exposed, any potential vulnerabilities, and any possible consequences that might result if that asset is harmed. DHS makes this information available to owners and operators of critical infrastructure so they are informed. When possible, the agencies offer recommendations on how to reduce risks to assets.

Moreover, analysts in DHS carry out assessments on a regional level to assess the resiliency of assets through their Regional Resiliency Assessment Program (RRAP). These reports provide vulnerability assessments of critical infrastructures within a particular geographic region. Participation of private sector owners/operators and officials from state and local governments in the assessment process of regional assets is voluntary.

BUDGET

It is difficult to trace funding and spending patterns for critical infrastructure protection because so many different agencies play a role in this task, such as the NPPD, the Transportation Security Administration (TSA), Federal Emergency Management Agency (FEMA), the Coast Guard, Secret Service, and the Science and Technology Directorate. However, the budget of the Infrastructure Protection and Information Security Program (IPIS) allows for a preliminary analysis of the budgets.

As shown in Table 4.2, the Obama administration requested in the Fiscal Year (FY) 2017 that IPIS would be given $1,312 million to carry out their functions. This would be an increase of $123 million over the amount they received in FY2015.[7]

Table 4.2 Funding for the Infrastructure Protection and Information Security Program (in millions of dollars)

Program/Project Activity	FY 2014 Actual	FY2015 Enacted	FY 2016 Presidential Request
Infrastructure Protection	$263	$271	$295
Identification, Analysis, and Planning	63	64	76
Sector Management and Governance	63	65	71
Regional Field Operations	57	57	53
Infrastructure Security Compliance	81	85	95
Cybersecurity	790	753	818
Cybersecurity Coordination	4	4	4
US-CERT Operations	101	99	99
Federal Network Security	199	171	131
Network Security Deployment	381	377	480
Global Cybersecurity Management	26	26	20
Critical Infrastructure Cyber Protection and Awareness	73	71	77
Business Operations	5	6	7
Communications	131	164	198
Office of Emergency Communications	37	37	33
Priority Telecommunications Services	53	53	64
Next Generation Networks	21	53	80
Programs to Study and Enhance	10	10	10
Critical Infrastructure Protection	9	10	11
Total, Infrastructure Protection and Information Security	**$1,185**	**$1,189**	**$1,312**

Source: Department of Homeland Security. National Protection and Programs Directorate. Infrastructure Protection and Information Security. Fiscal Year 2016 Congressional Justification. FY2015 enacted data taken from Explanatory Statement Submitted by Mr. Rogers of Kentucky, Chairman of the House Committee on Appropriations, Regarding H.R. 240. *Congressional Record, 161,* 6. *January 13, 2015. H.R. 284.*

Note: Columns may not add due to rounding.

ORGANIZATION

There are many agencies within DHS that help to protect the country's critical infrastructure. Each one plays a specific role in identifying assets, recognizing threats, and planning for recovery in the case of an event. Since its creation, DHS has established three directorates that are vital to critical infrastructure protection. They include the Management Directorate, the Science and Technology Directorate, and the NPPD.

Management Directorate

This organization is responsible for budget issues and dispersing funds for protecting critical infrastructure. Clearly, this is important to protecting critical infrastructure because of the high cost of protecting assets. Many grant programs, which help fund protection plans originate or are managed by this office.

Science and Technology Directorate

The Science and Technology Directorate provides support for research and development regarding critical infrastructure protection. The agency performs research in topics such as explosive detection, blast protection, and safe cargo containers. They monitor threats and develop ways to prevent those threats. The directorate also works with the OIP to develop and maintain a National Critical Infrastructure Protection R&D Plan.

Within the Science and Technology Directorate, three directors (or offices) have been established. These include the Director of Support to the Homeland Security Enterprise and First Responders, the Director of Homeland Security Advance Research Projects Agency, and the Director of Research and Development Partnership. Together, these directors work to create products for first-responders so they can respond to events safely and effectively. They seek to ensure that officials at all levels use the same terminology so there is ease of communication among those in the field. The researchers stay abreast of cutting-edge technology and work with other labs to advance our knowledge of both threats and response techniques.[8]

National Protection and Programs Directorate

Under Presidential Policy Directive-21 (PPD-21), the NPPD is given the task of developing ways to identify the nation's critical infrastructure and prioritize them so that funds can be distributed accordingly. Officials in the agency also seek to reduce possible risks to critical infrastructure, including both physical and virtual threats. One way this directorate achieves their goal is by training others (owners and operators) on identifying risks and mitigating them.[9]

Currently, the following offices are included in the NPPD are the FPS; the OIP, the Office of Cybersecurity and Communications (CS&C), the Office of Biometric Identify Management, and the Office of Cyber and Infrastructure Analysis.

Federal Protective Service
The FPS is a federal law enforcement agency that is responsible for protecting federal facilities and anyone in them (employees and visitors). On accession, the agency will provide protection for special events where large numbers of people may gather. In addition to this, the agency personnel conducts security assessments of buildings to ensure they are safety for those inside, and also provide K-9 explosive detection if needed.[10]

Office of Infrastructure Protection
The precursor to the OIP was the IAIPD, which was formed under the Homeland Security Act of 2002. This office was responsible for developing a national plan to protect critical infrastructure and to increase information sharing within DHS and other federal government offices. The agency was made up of the CIAO (from the Department of Commerce), the FedCRIC (from GSA), the NCS (from the Department of Defense), and the NIPC (from the FBI). The agency collected information on threats and incidents from the government and private sector, analyzed it, and disseminated it to others.

This office was reorganized and replaced with the OIP. The OIP was given the task of coordinating the efforts for national critical infrastructure protection. All infrastructures recognized as significant were categorized and placed into one of the 17 sectors. These included Chemical, Commercial Facilities, Dams, Emergency Services, Energy, Banking and Finance, Agriculture and Food, Government Facilities, Nuclear, Public Health and Healthcare, National Monuments and Icons, Information Technology, Materials and Waste, Postal and Shipping, Telecommunications, Defense Industrial Base, Drinking Water and Water Treatment Facilities, and Transportation (including Aviation, Maritime, Railroad, Mass Transit, Highway). Each sector was assigned a federal agency that would oversee it. These were also known as Sector-Specific Agencies (SSAs) (see Chapter 2).

Today, the OIP is the agency responsible for coordinating national programs designed to reduce the risks to key buildings and other critical infrastructure. One of their tasks is to identify the nation's important assets and then assesses their vulnerability to a possible attack.[11] Analysts in the OIP conduct vulnerability and consequence assessments for the owners and operators of critical assets, as well as for members of state, local, tribal, and territorial agencies, so that they have more knowledge about potential risks and vulnerabilities to critical infrastructure. OIP collects data, analyzes that data, and provides results to shareholders. They also provide information on emerging threats and hazards so that appropriate actions can be taken. The office also offers training to partners to help them manage the risks to their assets, systems, and networks.[12]

A second responsibility of OIP is to carry out plans that will protect the asset, whether it is a physical or cyber asset. As the OIP carries out programs to prepare for an event, they are concerned with ensuring a timely response from the government and private agencies to help those affected, which will then lead to a rapid recovery. To do this, OIP has established partnerships with officials in all levels of government and with owners and operators from the private sector and coordinates a response to an attack, both nationally and locally.

Divisions
The OIP is comprised of multiple divisions, which are (see Note 2, pp. 2–8) as follows:.

Chemical Security Compliance Division
Chemical Security Compliance Division (CSCD) oversees the Chemical Facility Anti-Terrorist Standards (CFATS). This agency assesses high-risk chemical plants, oversees security planning for these plants, and ensures that the plants meet risk-based performance standards.

Infrastructure Information Collection Division
Infrastructure Information Collection Division (IICD) is responsible for collecting information and data on vital infrastructure and provide it to public and private sector partners that work with DHS.

Infrastructure Analysis and Strategy Division
Infrastructure Analysis and Strategy Division (IASD) includes special analytical teams that perform modeling, simulation and analysis of critical infrastructure to assist DHS in revising the National Infrastructure Protection

Plan (NIPP). IASD oversees the Homeland Security Infrastructure Threat and Risk Analysis Center (HITRAC) and the NISAC.

Protective Security Coordination Division
Protective Security Coordination Division (PSCD) assesses possible vulnerabilities of critical infrastructure and consequences to that asset if an event occurs. They then use this information to develop protective programs. It also coordinates protection plans and recovery operations in an "all-hazards environment."

Contingency Planning and Incident Management Division
Contingency Planning and Incident Management Division (CPIMD) coordinates and implements preparedness activities of OIP, including training exercises, contingency planning and incident management. This division also manages the National Infrastructure Coordinating Center (NICC).

Partnership and Outreach Division
Partnership and Outreach Division (POD) develops relationships with owners and operators of critical infrastructure so that strategic information can easily be exchanged. This agency also provides outreach to stakeholders to increase their capacity to protect assets.

Infrastructure Security Compliance Division
Infrastructure Security Compliance Division (ISCD) oversees the implementation of the CFATS. ISCD's program oversees high-risk chemical facilities to ensure that these buildings meet required safety standards.

OIP oversees five of the critical infrastructure sectors. As the site-specific agency, OIP provides guidance and coordinates the implementation of the NIPP framework. They help to ensure that protection activities are fully integrated across the sectors. Because of this role, OIP maintains contact with officials in many critical industries in the US such as DuPont, Dow Chemical, Eastman Kodak, and Shell Oil (see Note 2, pp. 2–9).

Sectors
The five sectors that OIP watches over are as follows:

Chemical Branch
OIP is responsible for preparedness and infrastructure protection for all commercial chemical facilities. Because there are several hundred

thousand facilities in the US that use, manufacture, store, transport, or deliver chemicals in some way, this is a critical role.

Commercial Facilities Branch

OIP oversees protection for commercial sites such as hotels, office buildings, convention centers, stadiums, theme parks, apartment buildings, and shopping centers, among others. These are places where thousands of people may gather and are areas likely to be attacked.

Dams Branch

OIP is responsible for protection of assets, systems, networks, and functions related to dam projects, navigation locks, levees, hurricane barriers, mine tailings impoundments, or other similar facilities. In this position, OIP oversees the safety of the Hoover Dam, the Grand Coulee, and the Glen Canyon dam.

Emergency Services Branch

OIP works with other government agencies that prepare for and provide emergency services after an event.

Nuclear Branch

OIP prepares and protects nuclear infrastructure assets such as nuclear power plants, research and test reactors, nuclear fuel cycle facilities, radioactive waste management facilities, nuclear material transport systems, deactivated nuclear facilities, radioactive material users, and radioactive source production and distribution facilities. Damage to these facilities could result in great harm to property and many lives lost.

Office of Cybersecurity and Communications

The CS&C works to increase the security of the cyber network in the nation. The agency works to identify and prevent and threats to information stored on the internet. They also house the National Cybersecurity and Communications Integration Center (NCCIC) to monitor threats to the internet. CS&C is the SSA for two sectors: Communications and Information Technology.

There are five divisions within CS&C. These include the Office of Emergency Communications, the NCCIC, the Stakeholder Engagement and Cyber Infrastructure Resilience, the Federal Network Resilience, and the Network Security Deployment.

71

Office of Emergency Communications
The Office of Emergency Communications was created in an effort to increase communication between different agencies on all levels of government. They support interoperability of communications so that all first-responders and officials use similar terminology. To do this, they provide training opportunities and planning sessions to increase communications.

National Cybersecurity and Communications Integration Center
The NCCIC officials seek to improve communications regarding cyber-related incidents. They also seek to increase awareness of cyber vulnerabilities and incidents, and methods for mitigating those.

Stakeholder Engagement and Cyber Infrastructure Resilience
This agency works to communicate more effectively with private and industry partners with an interest in cyber initiatives. They work with industry to improve the security of the internet and cyber-infrastructure. They also seek to collaborate with private operators to identify possible threats and mitigate damages from an attack.

Federal Network Resilience
The Federal Network Resilience group seeks to improve cybersecurity by working with other federal agencies such as the Office of Management and Budget, the General Services Administration, and the Department of Defense, among others.

Network Security Deployment
The Network Security Deployment office seeks to increase cybersecurity to federal agencies. Through the National Cybersecurity Protection System, they seek to detect any possible intrusions, analysis of that intrusion, and prevention.

Office of Biometric Identity Management
The Office of Biometric Identity Management provides services for biometric identification to federal, state, and local government officials so that they can identify individuals and determine if they are a risk. These services include collecting biometric data, analysis, and storage.[13]

Office of Cyber and Infrastructure Analysis
It is the responsibility of the Office of Cyber and Infrastructure Analysis to evaluate possible consequences of disruption to the nation's cyber

infrastructure in the case of an attack or other events, including the effects on public health and safety, the economy, and national security. They seek to identify critical infrastructure that could be impacted by a cyber event.

OTHER OFFICES INSIDE DHS

In addition to the directorates, there are many other offices within DHS that impact critical infrastructure protection. These are described in the following:

Homeland Security Information Network-Critical Sectors

Homeland Security Information Network-Critical Sectors (HSIN-CS) is an Internet-based source of information and communication that allows agencies (including DHS and others) to distribute information about threats and events in a secure, encrypted manner. DHS funds and maintains the system for the members who are members of CIKR sectors. Each CIKR sector has a separate site, which is designed by the sector's Government Coordinating Council and Sector Coordinating Council and provides information relevant to that sector. DHS uses this network to build relationships with other federal agencies as well as those in the private sector.

Federal Emergency Management Agency

FEMA, is the nation's lead agency that oversees the federal response to disasters, both natural and man-made.[14] The agency provides support for citizens so they can protect against, respond to, recover from, and mitigate all hazards. Unlike most agencies that focus on disaster response, FEMA has existed since 1979 after President Carter reorganized five different agencies that had a role in disaster response into a new agency.[15]

In the beginning, the public's response to FEMA was positive. FEMA helped residents of New York's "Love Canal" in Niagara Falls in the late 1970s[16] and then they provided assistance to those living near Three Mile Island, a nuclear power station near Harrisburg, Pennsylvania, after a meltdown and release of nuclear waste.[17] However, FEMA's reputation was damaged after its slow response to Hurricane Hugo in 1989, the Loma Prieta earthquake in 1989, and Hurricane Andrew in 1992. Victims complained that FEMA's response was disorganized.[18] In 1993, President Clinton elevated it to a Cabinet-level agency and hired a new director, James Lee Witt. Witt changed the agency's response to an "all-hazards, all phases" approach so that FEMA would be prepared to respond to all types of hazards, and in all phases of a crisis.[19]

With the new changes, FEMA once again became a responsive organization. In 1993, they helped the victims of floods in the Midwestern US with emergency teams and coordinating officers who came to the disaster areas immediately.[20] In 1994, FEMA oversaw relief efforts after a major earthquake in Los Angeles. In 1995, FEMA responded with assistance to the victims of the Oklahoma City bombings. Because of their quick response to this event, FEMA's role expanded to responding to possible terrorist attacks.[21]

After the terrorist attacks of September 11, 2001, FEMA concentrated on its response to future terrorist acts. President Bush made the agency more narrowly focused on security, terrorism preparedness, and mitigation so that they would be prepared to respond quickly to a terrorist, nuclear weapon, chemical attack, or a natural disaster. Then, when the Homeland Security Act of 2002 was passed, FEMA became part of the DHS.[22]

When Hurricane Katrina hit Louisiana and the Southern US, residents were not provided with food and water supplies, nor was there adequate medical assistance. FEMA's response was again criticized for being slow and confused. Many people died because of thirst and other such conditions. There was also widespread looting throughout the city as people sought ways to survive.[23] It seemed that FEMA was too focused on protecting against possible terrorist attacks and thus not prepared to respond to a natural disaster.[24]

In 2006, Congress proposed bill to overhaul FEMA as part of the Homeland Security Appropriations bill for the Fiscal Year 2007 (PL 109-295).[25] The changes were part of Title VI, which was officially named the "Post-Katrina Emergency Management Reform Act (PKEMRA) of 2006," more commonly referred to as the Post-Katrina Act.[26] FEMA would remain part of DHS but would have an elevated status and more autonomy. Table 4.3 provides more information about the post-Katrina Act.

In 2012, the new FEMA was tested after Hurricane Sandy (also known as "Superstorm Sandy") hit the Northeast US in October 2012[27]

Table 4.3 Provisions of the Post-Katrina Act (PKEMRA)

The development of a system to locate missing family members after a disaster. The new system was called the National Emergency Family Registry and Locator System and the Child Locator Center.

The creation of recovery offices in five states to allow for provisions of needed assistance in a timely and effective manner after a future disaster.

The creation of a "Housing Strategy" that would provide a list of housing resources that would be available for disaster victims for all incomes and specifically for those populations with special needs.

The establishment of training programs to ensure that first responders are effective, grants are supervised, the National Response Plan was administered and implemented.

The creation of a new National Integration Center (NIC) within FEMA to manage both the National Incident Management System (NIMS) and the National Response Plan (NRP). In addition, NIC is responsible for coordinating volunteer activity and first responders.

The creation of ten regional offices within FEMA, each to be headed by a Regional Administrator. Each Administrator is to work alongside nonfederal partners to develop resources related to the national catastrophic response system. They are also tasked with establishing emergency communications systems, overseeing regional strike teams that coordinate initial response efforts, developing regional plans that support the National Response Plan, developing mutual aid agreements in the region, identifying special response modes for those with special needs, and maintaining a Regional Response Coordination Center. Every Regional Administrator must also create a Regional Advisory Council to provide advice on emergency management issues and identify gaps in response plans.

and killing between 117 and 159 people.* There was agreement that the federal response to Hurricane Sandy was far improved as compared with the response after Hurricane Katrina. It was obvious that officials from DHS and FEMA established stronger partnerships with state and local governments and were more prepared prior to the disaster.[28]

Today, FEMA's mission "is to support our citizens and first responders to ensure that as a nation we work together to build, sustain and improve our capacity to prepare for, protect against, respond to, recover from, and mitigate hazards."[29] They effectively prepare for, and respond to, disasters,

---

* The exact number of people who died as the result of Hurricane Sandy is unknown. While data from the Centers for Disease Control and Prevention, which used data from the American Red Cross, estimates that 117 died, the National Oceanographic and Atmospheric Administration indicates that 159 people died directly or indirectly by the storm.

and terrorist attacks. They cooperate with local officials to prepare for events so that when they do occur, communities will be more resilient.[30] Personnel within the agency help to "identify actions that should be taken before, during, and after an event that are unique to each hazard."[31]

The agency has many offices that specialize in different areas related to responding to future events. They include an Office of Policy and Program Analysis; Office of Disability Integration and Coordination; Office of National Capital Region Coordination; Office of External Affairs; Regional Operations; Protection and National Preparedness; Office of Response and Recovery; Office of Senior Law Enforcement Advisor; and the Office of Equal Rights.

FEMA is involved in two vital areas. One is planning, preparing, and mitigating the effects of a disaster. Here, FEMA works with local communities to help them prepare for disasters, and then mitigate the effects. The Mitigation Directorate is the office within FEMA that oversees planning and preparations for a possible national disaster. They help identify potential risks found in a community, and make plans to reduce injuries, deaths, or loss of property that could result.

The second role of FEMA is to assist all victims of natural disasters or acts of terrorism. FEMA provides victims with immediate needs such as, food, water, and housing. In many situations, FEMA operates disaster recovery centers in those areas that have been affected by an event. The centers are operated by trained workers and FEMA officials who provide information, legal advice, and financial assistance to those who need help.[32] FEMA's emergency response services[33] are described in Table 4.4.

As a way to help protect the nation's critical infrastructure, FEMA oversees numerous grant programs for state and local governments. Some of the grants are intended to help fund programs that are geared to protecting critical hassets or mitigating the harm that could occur if an attack were to happen. These grants include the State Homeland Security Grant Program, the Urban Area Security Initiative, the Public Transportation Security Assistance and Railroad Security Assistance, and the Port Security Grant Program. Table 4.5 shows the amount of funding provided by the federal government in these programs in the FY2015.[34]

FEMA National Advisory Council
An organization within FEMA is the National Advisory Council (NAC). This agency was established in June 2007 by the Post-Katrina Emergency

Table 4.4   FEMA's Response Services

National Disaster Medical System (NDMS): comprised medical professionals who provide medical assistance to victims of a disaster.

Urban Search and Rescue (USAR): involves locating, rescuing, and stabilizing any victims trapped in confined spaces.

Disaster Mortuary Operations Response Team (DMORT): the eleven teams are comprised of individuals who have specialized training in recovery, identification, and processing of deaths at a disaster scene, and provide mortuary and forensic services after a crisis.

Disaster Medical Assistance Team (DMAT): the 55 teams are composed of doctors and paramedics who provide assistance to burn victims, children, or victims who have been crushed.

National Medical Response Teams (NMRT): these four teams address the medical needs of victims in the aftermath of accidents involving chemical, biological or nuclear weapons or materials.

Mobile Emergency Response Support (MERS): this division provides multi-media communications, information processing, logistics, and operational support to agencies during emergencies to support recovery efforts.[a]

Veterinary Medical Assistance Teams (VMAT): four teams that are made up of veterinarians, pathologists, animal health technicians, microbiologists and others who assist animal disaster victims and provide care to search dogs.

International Medical Surgical Response Teams (IMSuRTs): three teams that are able to quickly establish a surgical facility anywhere in the world to assist victims.

Others: National Nursing Response Teams (NNRT), and the National Pharmacy Response Teams (NPRT).[b]

Source: FEMA. August 17, 2012. Mobile Emergency Response Support. Retrieved from: *https://www.fema.gov/mobile-emergency-response-support*; FEMA, July 16, 2012. National Disaster Medical System. Retrieved from: *http://www.fema.gov/news-release/2004/04/21/national-disaster-medical-system*; FEMA, October 28, 2012, Urban Search and Rescue. Retrieved from: *http://www.fema.gov/urban-search-rescue*.

[a] Federal Emergency Management Administration. August 17, 2012. Mobile Emergency Response Support. Retrieved from: https://www.fema.gov/mobile-emergency-response-support.

[b] Federal Emergency Management Administration. July 16, 2012. National Disaster Medical System. Retrieved from: http://www.fema.gov/news-release/2004/04/21/national-disaster-medical-system; Federal Emergency Management Administration. October 28, 2012. Urban Search and Rescue. Retrieved from: http://www.fema.gov/urban-search-rescue.

Table 4.5 FY 2015 Funding for FEMA Grants

Grant Program	FY 2015 Allocation (in Millions)
State Homeland Security Program	$467
Urban Area Security Initiative	600
Public Transportation Security Assistanceand Railroad Security Assistance	100
Port Security Grant Program	100

Source: DHS. January 13, 2015. National Protection and Programs Directorate. Infrastructure Protection and Information Security. Fiscal Year 2016 congressional justification. FY2015 enacted data taken from Explanatory Statement Submitted by Mr. Rogers of Kentucky, Chairman of the House Committee on Appropriations, Regarding H.R. 240. *Congressional Record. 161*, 6. H.R. 286.

Management Reform Act as a way to develop better coordination of federal policies for preparedness, protection, response, recovery, and mitigation for all events. The Council was tasked with assisting the development and revision of the National Preparedness Goal, the National Preparedness System, the National Incident Management System (NIMS), the National Response Framework (NRF), and other national plans.

The NAC consists of 35 members who have been appointed by and serving at the pleasure of the administrator and include state, local, and tribal governments; nonprofit, and private sector. The members are geographically diverse and are a cross-section of officials, emergency managers, and emergency response providers from state, local, and tribal governments, the private sector, and nongovernmental organizations.[35] These members advise the FEMA administrator on all aspects of emergency management.

Advisory Councils

In general, advisory councils provide advice and recommendations to the government or to private agencies about the best methods to protect critical assets. They can also increase information sharing between and among the public and private agencies (see Note 2, pp. 2–15). Two significant councils are the National Infrastructure Advisory Council (NIAC) and the Critical Infrastructure Partnership Advisory Council (CIPAC) (see Note 2, pp. 2–15).

The NIAC provides advice to the President, through the Secretary of Homeland Security, on issues pertaining to the security of critical infrastructure and assets, both physical and cyber. It can also provide advice to the directors of other agencies that are responsible for critical infrastructure protection, such as the Departments of Transportation and Energy. The mission of NIAC is to improve the cooperation between the public and private sectors in protecting assets (see Note 2, pp. 2–16).

The CIPAC also helps to foster effective coordination between federal, state, local, tribal, territorial, and regional infrastructure protection programs. It provides a forum for these groups to discuss activities to support and coordinate resource protection (see Note 2, pp. 2–16). CIPAC membership plan, coordinate, and implement security programs related to critical infrastructure protection.

Homeland Infrastructure Threat and Risk Analysis Center

HITRAC is found within the DHS and is the Department's Intelligence–Infrastructure Protection Fusion Center. The membership of the Center includes analysts from both the OIP and the Office of Intelligence and Analysis (I&A). These personnel have the expertise to carry out infrastructure risk assessment responsibilities that were established in the Homeland Security Act of 2002. HITRAC performs Sector-Specific Threat Assessments, Sector-Specific Risk Assessments, Individual State Threat Assessments, and other assessments as needed. To assist in this process, they have a Critical Infrastructure Red Team that examines threats, vulnerabilities and plans for mitigating risk to critical infrastructure.

Office of Intelligence and Analysis

The I&A helps to improve information sources that will assist in protecting critical infrastructure.[36] The Information Analysis and Infrastructure Protection Directorate (IAIPD) performs many tasks. One is to gather information from other sources that will assist them in identifying and assessing the risk of a possible terrorist threat. The second is to assess the vulnerabilities of critical infrastructure to determine the possible risks posed by attacks. The IAIPD has developed a comprehensive list of infrastructure assets (specific sites and facilities). From this list, the directorate has identified those assets that are considered to be critical assets. Those on the list are then prioritized.[37]

I&A is the executive agent for the State and Local Fusion Center Program within the US DHS. Its goal is to create partnerships with fusion centers and major cities to improve information flow between DHS and the centers, and improve the effectiveness of the centers as a network.

This office has multiple resources to assist a fusion center in their attempt to protect critical infrastructure. One is providing the fusion centers with information on national threats. They can also help to provide information to fusion centers as well as the technology needed to assess or analyze that data. They can provide security clearances for members in state and local governments so that information can be shared with them. Training is also a helpful service they provide to fusion centers.

Transportation Security Administration

The TSA was placed under the DHS when it was formed in 2002. The TSA oversees the security of the nation's transportation sectors. Officials screen airline passengers and their baggage to ensure that no dangerous material is brought onboard an aircraft. TSA also regulates the installation and maintenance of equipment to detect for explosives. TSA agents provide security for airport perimeters. They also oversee the Air Marshals.[38]

State, Local, Tribal, and Territorial Government Coordinating Council

The State, Local, Tribal, and Territorial Government Coordinating Council (SLTTGCC), under the NIPP, serves as a forum to ensure that state, local, tribal, and territorial homeland security officials or their designated representatives are integrated fully as active participants in national CIKR protection efforts. The SLTTGCC provides the organizational structure to coordinate across jurisdictions on state and local-level CIKR protection guidance, strategies, and programs.[39]

National Infrastructure Coordinating Center

The NICC is an agency that coordinates information for critical infrastructure sectors and DHS. The agency provides situational and operational awareness across the sectors as a way to increase awareness. It also provides a central point where the sector officials can request information or ask for assistance.

Technical Resource for Incident Prevention

Technical Resource for Incident Prevention (TRIPwire) is an online information sharing network for groups including bomb squads, law enforcement personnel, and other emergency services personnel that informs them about current terrorist tactics, techniques, and procedures. The agency was developed by the DHS Office for Bombing Prevention (OBP), which continues to maintain it. The group relies on expert analyses and reports alongside relevant documents, images, and videos that were gathered directly from terrorist sources to assist law enforcement to anticipate, identify, and prevent incidents.

National Infrastructure Simulation and Analysis Center

The NISAC is the DHS's modeling, simulation, and analysis program that was mandated by Congress. The center prepares and shares analyses of CIKR, along with their interdependencies, consequences, and other complexities. NISAC provides three types of products: preplanned long-term analyses, preplanned short-term analyses, and unplanned priority analytical projects. The reports produced provide information for mitigation design and policy planning and address the cascading consequences of infrastructure disruptions that could occur across all 18 CIKR sectors at national, regional, and local levels.

CONCLUSION

The DHS is an agency that is involved in critical infrastructure protection. Its goal is to make the US able to prepare for, or respond to an event of national significance. There are many other organizations that share this goal. There is no doubt that these groups will continue to adapt as they respond to new threats or adapt to changes in the security realm and respond to the security needs of the nation.

REVIEW QUESTIONS

1. Provide a description of the history and development of the DHS.
2. What are the three directorates found within the DHS and what do they do?

3. What is the role of FEMA in infrastructure protection?
4. What are some of the other offices found within DHS that play a role in infrastructure protection?

NOTES

1. US DHS. June 24, 2015. Who Joined DHS. Retrieved from: http://www.dhs.gov /who-joined-dhs
2. DHS, FEMA. September 2010. *CIKR Awareness AWR-213, Participant Guide.* Washington, DC: US DHS, pp. 2–16.
3. US DHS. July 20, 2015. *Prevent Terrorism and Enhance Security.* Retrieved from: http://www.dhs.gov/prevent-terrorism-and-enhance-security.
4. US DHS. October 2, 2012. *Safeguard and Secure Cyberspace.* Retrieved from: http://www.dhs.gov/safeguard-and-secure-cyberspace.
5. US DHS. July 17, 2015. *Building a Resilient Nation.* Retrieved from: http:// www.dhs.gov/building-resilient-nation.
6. US DHS. July 13, 2015. *Creation of the Department of Homeland Security.* Retrieved from: http://www.dhs.gov/creation-department-homeland-security.
7. Department of Homeland Security. National Protection and Programs Directorate. Infrastructure Protection and Information Security. Fiscal Year 2016 Congressional Justification. FY2015 enacted data taken from Explanatory Statement Submitted by Mr. Rogers of Kentucky, Chairman of the House Committee on *Appropriations, Regarding H.R. 240. Congressional Record, 161, 6. January 13, 2015. H.R. 284.*
8. US DHS. 2011. *DHS Science and technology Directorate Strategic Plan.* Retrieved from: https://www.dhs.gov/xlibrary/assets/st/st-strategic-plan.pdf.
9. US DHS. August 2015. *National Strategy for the Physical Protection of Critical Infrastructures and Key Assets.*
10. US DHS. *The Federal Protective Service.* Retrieved from: https://www.dhs .gov/topic/federal-protective-service.
11. *Office of Infrastructure. Protection Strategic Plan: 2012–2016.*
12. US DHS. July 16, 2015. *Office of Infrastructure Protection.* Retrieved from: http://www.dhs.gov/office-infrastructure-protection.
13. US DHS. *Office of Biometric Identity Management.* Retrieved from: https://www .dhs.gov/obim.
14. FEMA Website. *FEMA: 35 Years of Commitment.* Retrieved from: http://www .fema.gov/fema-35-years-commitment.
15. Carter, J. March 31, 1979. Executive Order 12127—Federal Emergency Management Agency. Online by Gerhard Peters and John T. Woolley, *The American Presidency Project.* Retrieved from: http://www.presidency.ucsb. edu/ws/?pid=32127; Taylor, A. September 12, 1992. Andrew Is Brutal Blow for Agency. *CQ Weekly,* p. 2703. Retrieved from: http://library.cqpress.com /cqweekly/WR102408159.

16. Carter, J. August 2, 1979. Environmental Priorities and Programs Message to the Congress. Online by Gerhard Peters and John T. Woolley, *The American Presidency Project*. Retrieved from: http://www.presidency.ucsb .edu/ws/?pid=32684.
17. Walker, S. J. 2005. *Three Mile Island: A Nuclear Crisis in Historical Perspective*. Berkeley, CA: University of California Press.
18. Prah, P. M. November 18, 2005. Disaster preparedness. *CQ Researcher, 15*, pp. 981–1004. Retrieved from: http://library.cqpress.com/cqresesarcher /document. php?id=cqresrre2005111800&type=hitli; Taylor, A. September 12, 1992. Andrew Is Brutal Blow for Agency. *CQ Weekly*, p. 2703. Retrieved from: http://library.cqpress.com/cqweekly/WR102408159; Roberts, P. S. June/July 2006. FEMA after Katrina. *Policy Review*, pp. 15–33.
19. Roberts, P. S. June/July 2006. FEMA after Katrina. *Policy Review, 137*, pp. 15–33.
20. Veron, I. J. July 17, 1993. High Marks for FEMA—for Now. *CQ Weekly*, p. 1862. Retrieved from: http://library.cqpress.com/cqweekly/WR103401932.
21. Prah, P. M. November 18, 2005. Disaster preparedness *CQ Researcher, 15*, pp. 981–1004. Retrieved from: http://library.cqpress.com/cqresesarcher /document.php?id=cqresrre2005111800&type=hitli.
22. Adams, R. September 12, 2005. FEMA Failure a Perfect Storm of Bureaucracy. *CQ Weekly*, pp. 2378–2379. Retrieved from: http://library .cqpress.com/cqweekly/weeklyreport109-000001853459; Roberts, P. S. June /July 2006. FEMA after Katrina. *Policy Review*, pp. 15–33.
23. *The Federal Response to Hurricane Katrina: Lessons Learned*. February 2006. Washington, DC: Government Printing Office. Retrieved from: http:// georgewbush-whitehouse.archives.gov/reports/katrina-lessons-learned/.
24. Prah, P. M. November 18, 2005. Disaster preparedness. *CQ Researcher, 15*, pp. 981–1004. Retrieved from: http://library.cqpress.com/cqresesarcher/document. php?id=cqresrre2005111800&type=hitli; Hsu, S. S., and Susan, B. G. September 6, 2005. FEMA Director Singled Out by Response Critics. *Washington Post*. Retrieved from: http://www. washingtonpost.com/wp-dyn/content/article /2005/09/05/AR2005090501590.html; Crittenden, M. R. September 10, 2007. Emergency Plan Deemed a Disaster-in-Waiting. *CQ Weekly*, p. 2551. Retrieved from: http://library.cqpress.com/cqweekly/weeklyreport110-000002580266.
25. Yoest, P. December 18, 2006. 2006 Legislative Summary: FEMA Restructuring. *CQ Weekly*, p. 3355. Retrieved from: http://library.cqpress.com/cqweekly /weeklyreport109-000002418336.
26. Library of Congress, Congressional Research Service. March 6, 2007. Federal Emergency Management Policy Changes after Hurricane Katrina: A summary of Statutory Provisions. Retrieved from: http://www.fas.org/sgp/crs/homesec /RL33729.pdf.
27. National Oceanic and Atmospheric Administration. 2013. *Billion-Dollar Weather/Climate Disasters*. National Climatic Data Center.

28. Naylor, B. November 3, 2012. Lessons From Katrina Boost FEMA's Sandy Response. NPR. Retrieved from: http://www.npr.org/2012/11/03/164224394/lessons-from-katrina-boost-femas-sandy-response.
29. FEMA. *About the Agency*. Retrieved from: http://www.fema.gov/about-agency.
30. Naylor, B. August 27, 2010. Has FEMA Recovered from Hurricane Katrina? *NPR*, Morning Edition. Retrieved from: http://www.npr.org/templates/story/story.php?storyId=129466751.
31. FEMA. *Plan, Prepare and Mitigate*. Retrieved from: http://www.fema.gov/plan-prepare-mitigate.
32. Blair, K. May 9, 2014. FEMA Disaster Recovery Centers Opening This Weekend. *Pensacola News Journal*. Retrieved from: http://www.pnj.com/story/news/2014/05/09/femas-disaster-recovery-center-opens-saturday/8911747/.
33. FEMA. August 17, 2012. Mobile Emergency Response Support. Retrieved from: https://www.fema.gov/mobile-emergency-response-support; FEMA, July 16, 2012. National Disaster Medical System. Retrieved from: http://www.fema.gov/news-release/2004/04/21/national-disaster-medical-system; FEMA, October 28, 2012, Urban Search and Rescue. Retrieved from: http://www.fema.gov/urban-search-rescue.
34. DHS. January 13, 2015. National Protection and Programs Directorate. Infrastructure Protection and Information Security. Fiscal Year 2016 congressional justification. FY2015 enacted data taken from Explanatory Statement Submitted by Mr. Rogers of Kentucky, Chairman of the House Committee on Appropriations, Regarding H.R. 240. Congressional Record. 161, 6. H.R. 286.
35. DHS, FEMA. March 20, 2015. *National Security Council*. Retrieved from: https://www.fema.gov/national-advisory-council.
36. US DHS. *Operational and Support Components*. Retrieved from: http://www.dhs.bov/components-directorates-and-offices.
37. Motef, J. February 4, 2005. *Risk Management and Critical Infrastructure Protection: Assessing, Integrating, and Managing Threats, Vulnerabilities and Consequences*. CRS Report for Congress. Washington, DC: Congressional Research Service. Retrieved from: https://www.fas.org/sgp/crs/homesec/RL32561.pdf.
38. Elias, B., Peterman D. R., and Frittelli J. *Transportation Security: Issues for the 114th Congress,* CRS Report for congress, RL33512. Washington, DC: Congressional Research Service.
39. US Department of Homeland Security, and US Department of Justice, Global Justice Information Sharing Initiative. December 2008. *Critical Infrastructure and Key Resources, Protection Capabilities for Fusion Centers*. Retrieved from: https://it.ojp.gov/documents/d/CIKR%20protection%20capabilities%20for%20fusion%20centers%20s.pdf.

5

Other Federal Risk Management Agencies

INTRODUCTION

There are many other federal agencies in addition to the Department of Homeland Security (DHS) that play a role in critical infrastructure protection. This chapter will explore the federal responsibilities for critical infrastructure protection and risk assessment outside of the DHS.

DEPARTMENT OF STATE

Created in 1789, the US Department of State oversees international relations with other countries. The mission statement for the Department of State indicates that the Department "is to shape and sustain a peaceful, prosperous, just, and democratic world and foster conditions for stability and progress for the benefit of the American people and people everywhere."[1] Personnel at the Department of State seek to advance US national security, promote the country's economic interests, provide services, and reaffirm the US' role throughout the world.[2]

When it comes to protecting the nation's critical infrastructure, the State Department provides funding for programs that protect life, property, and information of the Department as part of the Worldwide Security Protection Program. They fund many programs that are geared toward protecting the worldwide security infrastructure. For example, they have an ongoing program to protect the security of computer systems, by collecting cyber incident information, monitoring the system, and continuing to perform threat analysis. Their budget in 2012 was $1,355,000,000, and they had 1,711 employees.[3]

In addition, the State Department has agreements with other countries for protection of critical infrastructure. For example, the US has an agreement with the Kingdom of Saudi Arabia (2008) in which the US has agreed to sell them technical assistance for, among other things, critical infrastructure protection. This may include providing advice, training, and equipment.[4] An agreement was also made with Panama in 2007 to protect critical assets. In this agreement, it was noted that critical infrastructure can be destroyed or damaged by terrorist acts, and that it is important to "find effective ways to prevent, deter, mitigate consequences of, and be prepared to respond to, potential threats to critical infrastructure." The agreement contains a promise to work to "prevent, mitigate, and deter potential terrorist threats to critical infrastructure, through the development and implementation of national measures and the strengthening of regional and international cooperation." It is important that critical infrastructure be identified, along with the risks and threats posed to it. The most famous example of a critical infrastructure in Panama is the Panama Canal.[5]

In the 2007 joint performance summary between the State Department and the Agency for International Development, it was noted that one of the goals of fiscal year (FY) 2006 was to "reduce opportunities for terrorist exploitation of container traffic" at ports. This was done through the Container Security Initiative. As a result, most ports across the world agreed to implement the program. As a result, the potential vulnerabilities of ports were addressed, reducing the opportunities for terrorists to use containers as weapons, and protect the maritime transportation sector and, in the event of an event, allows quicker resumption of the seaways and ports.[6]

DEPARTMENT OF JUSTICE

The Department of Justice (DOJ) plays an essential role in protecting the nation's critical infrastructure. Presidential Decision Directives-63 (PDD-63) assigned the DOJ to be the lead sector liaison for emergency law enforcement services. In addition, Executive Order 13231 assigned the Attorney General to serve on the President's Critical Infrastructure

Protection Board and to be cochair of the Incident Response Coordination and Physical Security committees. According to the officials within the Department and other federal documents, the organizations within the DOJ, playing a role in critical infrastructure protection responsibilities are: the Computer Crime and Intellectual Property Section (CCIPS); the National Infrastructure protection Center (NIPC); the National Counter Intelligence Executive (NCIX); and the Cyber Crime Division.

CCIPS: within the Criminal Division, the CCIPS investigates and prosecutes cyberattacks on our nation's critical assets. This section also addresses policy and legislation issues such as information sharing among the military, the intelligence community, law enforcement, civilian agencies, and the private sector, as well as government network intrusion detection and strategic planning. CCIPS coordinates with the Department of Defense, the Critical Infrastructure Assurance Office (CIAO), the NIPC, the National Security Council (NSC), and interagency groups that work on issues related to critical infrastructure protection, including work on the national plan to defend cyberspace and the cyber portion of the 5-year counterterrorism plan.

NIPC: NIPC is a multiagency organization that is located within the FBI. It helps to detect, analyze, and warn residents and businesses of potential cyberthreats. They also provide information on actual attacks to computer systems, should they occur. The center is also responsible for the tasks associated with the FBI's role as lead agency and sector liaison for the Emergency Law Enforcement Services Sector. As sector liaison, NIPC provides information on cyberthreats and crimes involving or affecting critical infrastructure to law enforcement. NIPC also coordinates the federal government's response to cyber incidents, mitigating attacks, and investigating threats. NIPC regularly coordinates with federal, state, local and law enforcement and intelligence agencies that are represented in other federal agencies (i.e., the Department of Defense, CIA, NSA and Secret Service, and others) and on the president's Critical Infrastructure Protection Board. They also communicate regularly with officials in Canada and Great Britain.

An additional role of the NIPC is to operate the National InfraGard program. This is a cooperative, outreach effort between officials in the federal government and private sector businesses, academic institutions, state and local law enforcement agencies, and other participants who communicate and work together to increase the security of the nation's assets. The goal of InfraGard is simply to increase the flow of communication and information between these groups so that the owners and operators of infrastructure assets can better protect their resources. InfraGard also helps to educate its members and provide training on infrastructure and protection measures, and provides them with threat advisories when needed.

The exchange of information is possible because each InfraGard member has been vetted and identified as a person who might need to know the information for security reasons. This process also allows the FBI to work with the members when they are investigating incidents or gathering intelligence about a threat or an event. InfraGard holds meetings within each chapter, and maintains a public website alongside a secure private website, which has critical infrastructure-related information for the members of InfraGard.

InfraGard currently has over 26,000 members in 86 chapters around the US. All 56 FBI field offices support at least one InfraGard chapter. InfraGard maintains partnerships with the FBI's Directorate of Intelligence, Counterterrorism Division, Counterintelligence Division, Criminal Investigative Division, and Weapons of Mass Destruction Directorate. They also share information and have created partnerships with DHS and other federal agencies.

NIPC is comprised of three divisions, the first of which is the Computer Investigations and Operations section. This is the operations and response arm of the agency. It is responsible for collection, analysis, and distribution of pertinent information to its members. Through the FBI's field offices around the country, the agency also conducts computer investigations as needed. The second section of the NIPC is the Analysis and Warning Section, which distributes warnings about threats and attacks to its members. They also provide support to companies during investigations about possible computer intrusions. The third section of NIPC is the Training, Outreach, and Strategy Section, which provides outreach to members, including the private sector and local law enforcement. They also carry out training programs for investigators and law enforcement personnel on cyber and infrastructure protection. NIPC's funding to support these activities for FYs 2000 to 2002 has been $21 million, $26 million, and $72 million, respectively.

The NCIX was established under Executive Order 14231 and Presidential policy directive 75 (PPD-75). NCIX works in conjunction with the President's Critical Infrastructure Protection Board to address all potential threats from hostile foreign intelligence services. The members of NCIX are appointed by the Director of the FBI. This agency is the leader of national-level counterintelligence, so it helps to identify critical assets throughout the nation, implement strategic counterintelligence analyses, develop a national threat assessment, formulate a national counterintelligence strategy, create an integrated counterintelligence budget, and develop an agenda of program reviews and evaluations.

The DOJ's cybersecurity unit was announced in December 2014. The personnel in this unit will provide expert legal advice on criminal electronic surveillance statutes for law enforcement agencies that conduct cyber-investigations. They will also work with private sector officials and members of Congress as needed. The agency will be housed within the CCIPS, but will help law enforcement obtain the resources they need to solve cybercrimes and prosecute them. Another key aspect of the cybersecurity unit is prevention of cybercrimes and increasing the public's understanding of the issue.

Federal Bureau of Investigation

The Federal Bureau of Investigation (FBI), located within the DOJ, is the nation's law enforcement agency that investigates possible cyber-based crimes, including computer intrusions and instances of major cyber fraud. The FBI has developed ways to share cyber-related information with state and local governments that could be sensitive or classified, but could also prevent cybercrimes from occurring. One of those methods is InfraGard, discussed earlier. In addition, the FBI's National White Collar Crime Center in partnership with the Internet Crime Complaint Center is to process complaints regarding Internet-related criminal acts. Upon receiving a complaint, agents will investigate it, and, if needed, refer the complaint to federal, state, local, and international law enforcement agencies. They will also issue an alert to affected entities, if pertinent.[7]

The FBI also works internationally to protect critical infrastructure around the country. In July 2014, the FBI (specifically the Weapons of Mass Destruction Directorate) and Interpol sponsored a Symposium for International law enforcement groups on Critical Infrastructure. During the event, the Director of the FBI, James Comey, spoke to those attending about the need to explore and share best practices for managing threats made against critical infrastructure. He stressed that it is essential that law enforcement from all parts of the world identify common approaches to protecting critical infrastructure and key resources. He also discussed the need for increased open communication and information sharing with partners in the US and abroad.[8]

DEPARTMENT OF COMMERCE

The US Commerce Department plays a role in protecting the nation's critical infrastructure, and the communications networks in particular. In Presidential Policy Directive-63 (PPD-63), the Department of Commerce was given three major tasks: (a) to be the CIAO, (b) to be the lead agency responsible for the information and communications sector, and (c) to research into critical infrastructure protection.[9]

Another source of the Department's infrastructure protection responsibilities was the Telecommunications Authorization Act of 1992, which created Commerce's National Telecommunications and Information Administration (NTIA). This agency serves as the main adviser to the president on telecommunications and information policies. NTIA oversees grant programs that increase the use of broadband and other technologies. The NTIA leads outreach and provides assistance to the agencies in the communications sector. It was hoped that the NTIA would raise industry awareness about the true nature of threats and vulnerabilities to those in the sector, and then increase efforts for better information sharing (see Note 9).

The act also established FirstNet as an independent agency within the NTIA, which attempts to reinforce the nation's cybersecurity. FirstNet's responsibilities include increasing cooperation with private companies and federal, state, regional, and local agencies in order to ensure the security and resiliency of the FirstNet network and protecting it from cyberattacks (see Note 7).

Another principal agency within the Department of Commerce is the National Institute of Standards and Technology (NIST). This agency is a nonregulatory agency within the Department that supports innovation and industrial competitiveness. This agency took center stage after President Obama issued Executive Order 13636, on February 12, 2013. In this statement Obama stated, "cyber threat to critical infrastructure continues to grow and represents one of the most serious national security challenges we must confront." He then asked the agency to develop a Cybersecurity Framework to reduce potential cyber risks to the nation's critical infrastructure, thus allowing the economy to thrive. To do this, NIST was assigned to work cooperatively with the private industry to develop a framework of standards, using existing international standards and procedures as a model. They recognize that the private sector and the government must cooperate in order to address issues effectively. Moreover, they recognize that businesses must not only be aware of cybercrime threats but also be willing to adopt the standards as a way to protect both their businesses and the national economy.[10] The idea was that business owners may be more willing to adopt the standards if they had a role in creating them. Other agencies, including DHS and the Department of Treasury, would then provide guidance to businesses on how to implement the Framework in their sectors, as well as provide incentives to companies for adopting their cybersecurity practices to line up with the Framework.[11]

After studying the problem with the input of stakeholders, representatives from the Department of Commerce wrote a report that included recommended incentives for businesses to participate in the program.[12] They made multiple suggestions or recommendations to the President regarding actions the Government could take that would result in a successful program. These suggestions included:

- NIST should engage cybersecurity stakeholders who are concerned with critical infrastructure protection when developing policies related to the standards, particularly those members of the insurance industry who understand the cybersecurity policies. The potential partnership between NIST and insurance company representatives could result in more effective plans to reducing cyber events.
- Representatives from NIST and other federal agencies should be aware of the potential legal and financial risks that owners and operators of critical assets face from possible tort liabilities occurring as a consequence of cyberattacks and the long-term effects that attacks have on a company's willingness to participate in the program. They noted that many companies could face legal action from customers if their personal information is stolen as the result of a cybercrime. This could make companies less willing to provide information about their company's cyber policies or attacks that they may have had. The Committee requested that an analysis be completed on legal cases that have been brought against the owners and operators of critical infrastructure as a way to assess new policies to limit the legal liability of companies who become victims of cyberattacks.
- Consider requiring that companies participate in the Program as a requirement for receiving grants for critical infrastructure protection from the Department of Commerce. Moreover, other federal agencies should also be asked to use participation in the program as a factor when awarding federal grants.

91

- Ensure that the program addresses the issues and problems that occur each day in the "real-world." This can be addressed by including Program participants and vendors in the development of the Standards.
- Implement a Fast-Track Patent Pilot Program for any company that faces the threat of losing their trade secrets through theft. As an incentive for these companies to participate in the Program, it was suggested that the government develop a system with the US Patent and Trademark Office (USPTO) for a "Fast-Track Patent Pilot."
- Develop an optional public recognition program for those companies who agree to be part of the Program. Some companies may want their customers to know that they have participated in a program to increase their security and protect the private information of its customers. However, since other companies would not want this to be made public this would have to be a voluntary option.
- Provide technical assistance to those companies who choose to participate in the program. This would be assistance in implementing the standards that are set in the program (see Note 12).

The Framework for Improving Critical Infrastructure Cybersecurity was released by the Department of Commerce. The document outlines standards that will help organizations to improve the both the security and resilience of critical infrastructure. With the report, organizations will be able to analyze their current level of cybersecurity, set their own goals for improving cybersecurity, and create a plan to improving and maintaining their cybersecurity.

There are three main sections in the framework: the core, tiers, and profiles. The first section, the core describes five functions—identify, protect, detect, respond, and recover—that can help an organization understand the status of their own cybersecurity program. The second section, tiers, helps a company analyze the extent to which their cybersecurity risk management policies are in line with the goals described in the framework. The third section, profiles, help companies advance their cybersecurity policies so they meet the standards set forth in the document.[13]

DEPARTMENT OF TRANSPORTATION

According to PDD-63, the Department of Transportation serves as the lead sector liaison for aviation, highways, mass transit, pipelines, rail, and waterborne commerce. More recently, when President Obama issued

Executive Order 13231, he assigned the Secretary of Transportation to serve on the President's Critical Infrastructure Protection Board and also to serve as the cochair of the Infrastructure Independencies Committee.

Within the Transportation Department is the Office of Intelligence and Security (OIS). These personnel analyze, develop, and coordinate national policies concerning, among other things, issues related to the protection of the transportation infrastructure. To do this, the office cooperates with members of the public and private sectors, international organizations, academia, and interest groups. OIS also serves as the transportation sector liaison, as described in PDD-63. They work with numerous other groups including the Association of American Railroads who serve as sector coordinators. They are the primary liaison with DHS, the Office of Cyberspace Security, and the Intelligence and law enforcement communities. OIS is the transportation sector's primary point of contact for all security issues.

FEDERAL COMMUNICATIONS COMMISSION

The Federal Communications Commission (FCC) has the responsibility to regulate interstate and international communications in the US through radio, television, wire, satellite, and cable. They also maintain these networks during emergencies or natural disasters. Officials have the ability to adopt, administer, and enforce rules related to cybersecurity of the communications critical infrastructure. According to FCC regulations, communications providers are required to report on the security of com munications infrastructures, including any service disruptions or outages that may impact the safety of the public or the ability for emergency response.

In addition, the FCC has developed partnerships with the private sector owners and operators. They have instituted advisory committees such as the Communications, Security, Reliability, and Interoperability Council which seeks to advise the FCC on actions that can be taken to improve the security of both commercial and public safety communications systems. They also make recommendations concerning technical standards and gaps pertaining to the emergency communications system (i.e., the 911 system).

FCC is also required, under presidential directive, to work with DHS and other federal departments and agencies to identify and prioritize communications critical infrastructure and any vulnerabilities they face. The FCC is to work with stakeholders to address those vulnerabilities.

They are also asked to cooperate with foreign governments and international organizations to increase the security and resilience of critical infrastructure within the communications sector (see Note 7).

ENVIRONMENTAL PROTECTION AGENCY

PDD-63 designates the environmental protection agency (EPA) to serve as the lead agency and sector liaison for protecting the nation's water supply (i.e., drinking water and water treatment systems). Moreover, Presidential Decisions Directives 39, 62, and 63 mandate that EPA officials take part in a federal response program aimed at preparing for and responding to terrorist incidents so that clean water is available as quickly as possible after an event.

The Office of Water is the lead EPA office in fulfilling EPA's national critical infrastructure protection responsibilities. After the terrorist attacks of 2001, the Office of Water expanded its responsibilities to focus on providing technical and financial assistance to those who are carrying out vulnerability assessments. They also provide assistance for emergency response planning for drinking water and wastewater utilities. Another role of the Office of Water is to develop new technologies that will help water utilities to protect their assets and public health. To do this, they carry out research programs in cooperation with other federal agencies and nongovernmental organizations. The Office of Water also works to increase the communication processes between privately owned or locally owned utilities and government officials regarding preparedness and response activities in the water sector. The office is also developing plans regarding the interdependencies between the water sector and others including energy and transportation.

DEPARTMENT OF INTERIOR

The Department of Interior is the Sector-Specific Agency for national monuments and icons, such as the Statue of Liberty (which actually ranks among the top ten of the Department's critical infrastructure assets). The National Monuments and Icons Sector-Specific Plan (SSP) promotes collaborative efforts at all levels of government to increase cooperation and improve the protection of assets. The goal of the Department is to "protect and provide access to our Nation's natural and cultural heritage and honor our trust responsibilities to Indian Tribes and our commitments to island communities." Recently, the department has recognized that information security is essential as a way to protect systems from unauthorized access. One example of this requirement is that records are maintained regarding visitors to these assets. All visitors must record the purpose of their visit, and who accompanies them. If a person attempts to get into the asset, or is able to access a site without authorization, that must be reported.[14]

The Department's safety plans are implemented by the US Park Police and the National Park Service. The National Monuments Sector oversees a variety of assets located throughout the US and includes monuments, physical structures, or objects that are recognized both nationally and internationally as a symbol that represents the Nation's history, traditions, and values. These structures often have national, cultural, religious, historic, or political significance. They may also be memorials to people or events.[15] A ranking system helps to determine if a monument or icon is one of National Critical, National Significant, Regional Critical, or Local Significant asset. National assets include Flaming Gorge, Folsom, Shasta, Grand Coulee, Hoover, and Glen Canyon dams.[16] Further, assets found in the Nation's capital as well as the Statue of Liberty, Independence Hall, the Liberty Bell, and Mount Rushmore National Monument.

An agency within the Department of the Interior is the Bureau of Reclamation. Their mission is "to manage, develop, and protect water and related resources in an environmentally and economically sound manner in the interest of the American public." The Bureau seeks to identify critical assets among their facilities. This includes items such as switchyards, transmission lines, and equipment that comprise the Bulk Electricity System that are owned and operated by the Bureau of Reclamation. This would include hydro-generation control centers, power plants, and transmission centers. They also perform a risk assessment on these facilities as a way to address vulnerabilities and improve security.[17]

Officials inside the Bureau have identified Critical Cyber Assets (CCAs) within its critical assets to identify all cyber-based assets. This will help them identify which ones are "essential."

The Bureau of Reclamation, in cooperation with Oak Ridge Associated Universities (ORAU), conducts emergency exercises at sites that have been identified as being critical infrastructures. ORAU is an organization made up of PhD granting academic institutions that works with agencies to further research and education. This will help officials know, first, if the dams could withstand an event, and how to improve security at these sites. The exercises involve planning, tabletop exercises, and workshops.[18]

DEPARTMENT OF AGRICULTURE/DEPARTMENT OF HEALTH AND HUMAN SERVICES

The Department of Agriculture, along with the Department of Health and Human Services, has been assigned to be the Sector-Specific Agency for Food and Agriculture (meat, poultry, and egg products). This sector is important because most of the assets are privately owned (i.e., restaurants, farms, food factories, and stores).

DEPARTMENT OF ENERGY

The Department of Energy is the lead agency for sector liaison for energy, including the production refining, storage, and distribution of oil and gas, and electric power except for commercial nuclear power facilities. Many energy assets are privately owned, so it is important for officials in this department to work closely with those owners in developing strategies to protect those assets.

DEPARTMENT OF TREASURY

The Department of the Treasury is the lead agency for sector liaison for banking and finance. Because banking and finance plays such a critical role in the economy, financial institutions are subject to significant regulation and examination standards. Many financial firms have chosen to collaborate with government officials through public–private partnerships. One of them is the Financial Services Sector Coordinating Council for Critical Infrastructure Protection and Homeland Security (FSSCC), LLC, and another is the Financial Services-Information Sharing and Analysis Center (FS-ISAC). These agencies seek to inform financial firms on different methods to strengthen their cybersecurity and reduce the possibility of attack.

CONCLUSION

Many federal agencies have a role in protecting critical infrastructure across the nation. The goal is not only to protect the infrastructure from an attack, but also to recover quickly if that infrastructure is damaged.

These departments and agencies must work with each other, and also in cooperation with private owners and operators to increase security of their assets and reduce the risk of an attack.

REVIEW QUESTIONS

1. How is the Department of State involved with critical infrastructure protection?
2. Why is it important for federal agencies to work in conjunction with private owners of critical infrastructure?
3. What is the role of the DOJ in critical infrastructure protection?
4. What is InfraGard?
5. How does the Department of Commerce help to protect critical assets?

NOTES

1. U.S. Department of State. November 2014. *FY 2014 Agency Financial Report.* Retrieved from: http://www.state.gov/s/d/rm/index.htm#mission.
2. US Department of State. *Diplomacy in Action.* Retrieved from: http://www.state.gov/r/pa/map/index.htm.
3. US Department of State. *Congressional Budget Justification, Fiscal Year 2014.* Retrieved from: http://www.state.gov/documents/organization/207266.pdf.
4. U.S. Department of State. May 2008. *Technical Cooperation Agreement Between the United States of America and the Kingdom of Saudi Arabia.* Retrieved from: http://www.state.gov/documents/organization/109344.pdf.
5. US Department of State. March 1, 2007. *Declaration of Panama.* Retrieved from: http://www.state.gov/p/wha/rls/81491.htm.
6. US Department of State and US Agency for International Development. *Joint Performance Summary, FY 2007.* Retrieved from: http://www.state.gov/documents/organization/59173.pdf.
7. US Government Accountability Office. January 2014. Critical Infrastructure Protection: More Comprehensive Planning Would Enhance the Cybersecurity of Public Safety Entities' Emerging Technology, GAO-14-125. Retrieved from: http://www.gao.gov/assets/670/660404.pdf.
8. U.S. FBI. July 8, 2014. *FBI, Interpol Host Critical Infrastructure Symposium.* Retrieved from: https://www.fbi.gov/news/stories/2014/july/fbi-interpol -host-critical-infrastructure-symposium/fbi-interpol-host-critical -infrastructure-symposium.
9. Cordesman, A. H., and Cordesman, J G. 2002. *Cyber-Threats, Information Warfare, and Critical Infrastructure Protection: Defending the U.S. Homeland.* Westport, CT: Praeger.

10. US Department of Commerce. February 18, 2013. *The Department of Commerce's Role in Improving Critical Infrastructure Cybersecurity.* Retrieved from: http://2010-2014.commerce.gov/blog/2013/02/18/department-commerces-role-improving-critical-infrastructure-cybersecurity.

11. US Department of Treasury. *Treasury Department Report to the President on Cybersecurity Incentives Pursuant to Executive Order 13636.* Retrieved from: http://www.treasury.gov/press-center/Documents/Supporting%20Analysis%20Treasury%20Report%20to%20the%20President%20on%20Cybersecurity%20Incentives_FINAL.pdf.

12. US Department of Commerce. *Recommendations to the President on Incentives for Critical Infrastructure Owners and Operators to Join a Voluntary Cybersecurity Program.* Retrieved from: http://www.ntia.doc.gov/files/ntia/Commerce_Incentives_Discussion_Final.pdf.

13. U.S. Department of State, National Institute of Standards and Technology. February 12, 2014. *NIST Releases Cybersecurity Framework Version 1.0.* Retrieved from: http://www.nist.gov/itl/csd/launch-cybersecurity-framework-021214.cfm.

14. US Department of the Interior, Bureau of Reclamation. March 15, 2012. *Physical Security Plan XXXX Dam and Powerplant.* Retrieved from: www.usbr.gov.

15. US DHS, Department of the Interior. 2010. *National Monuments and Icons Sector-Specific Plan.* Retrieved from: https://www.hsdl.org/?view&did=691263.

16. U.S. Department of the Interior, Bureau of Reclamation. June 29, 2015. *Advances in Security Technology and Procedures to Safeguard Reclamation SCADA Systems.* Retrieved from: http://www.usbr.gov/resaerch/projects/detail.cfm?id=2331.

17. U.S. Department of the Interior, Bureau of Reclamation. September 27, 2010. *Critical Asset Identification Methodology.* Retrieved from: http://www.usbr.gov/recman/temporary_releases/irmtrmr-35-AppA.pdf.

18. US Department of the Interior, Bureau of Reclamation. 2015. *ORAU Helps Department of Interior Conduct Full-Scale Emergency Exercises at Major US Dams.* Retrieved from: https://www.orau.org/national-security-emergency-management/success-stories/exercises-planning/bureau of reclamation.aspx.

6

Public–Private Partnerships

INTRODUCTION

Immediately after the terrorist attacks of 2001, most critical infrastructure protection efforts focused on action by the federal government. However, people quickly realized that it was essential to include the private sector in the planning process because a large portion of the critical infrastructure are owned and operated by the private sector. A planning process that did not include a major portion of the stakeholders would not be worthwhile. Moreover, the asset is often located in the communities. Over the years, partnerships have developed between government agencies and the owners and operators of the nation's infrastructure, with Department of Homeland Security (DHS) taking the lead in coordinating critical infrastructure protection activities. These have increased the sharing of information relating to possible threats, vulnerabilities, and even interdependencies. This chapter describes the relationships that have developed between the public and private sectors for risk assessment and homeland security issues.

PRIVATE VERSUS PUBLIC SECTORS

The term "public sector" refers to agencies that are owned or operated by the government. Examples of these offices are federal, state, or local departments and agencies, water treatment plants, and power plants. These groups often get financial support from the government, through taxes. They are responsible for protecting people and property in their jurisdiction. Unfortunately, state and local governments are often not able to keep up with changes in critical infrastructure. They do not have the funding and expertise to keep on par with the private sector.[1]

The term "private sector" refers to any unit that is not operated by the state or federal government. This can include private firms and companies, corporations, private banks, television or radio stations, or nongovernmental organizations. Their goal is to make a profit or generate wealth. Therefore, the actions they take are geared toward minimizing any financial risk and maximizing profit. These organizations may attempt to influence government policy through the legislative process, but they do not have the formal authority to set policy. Those who work in the private must respond to authorities that are outside of the government such as parent companies, business partners, or even outside financial institutions.[2]

The private sector owns a large portion of the nation's critical infrastructure, up to 85%.[3] These owners and operators are the people who have the most information and understand the threats and vulnerabilities of that sector better than any other person or group. They will know the best or most appropriate action that should be taken if something should occur.

The concept of a public–private partnership refers to an agreement that is worked out between a public agency and a private sector agency. The goal of the agreement is to draw on the skills and resources of each separate group so that a task can be accomplished efficiently. Developing a working partnership can result in an efficient and effective delivery of services.

INFORMATION SHARING

Each group has different knowledge or expertise and skills that can be shared with others. Private owners have unique concerns and information that they need to discuss with the public sector so that those concerns are addressed and vice versa. To be effective, critical infrastructure protection must be a cooperative effort between the public and the private sector. It is essential that those in both the private and public sector readily communicate with each other on a regular basis.

When information is shared, both the public and private sectors are benefitted. The public sector (i.e., government agencies) receives critical information about possible threats and vulnerabilities to assets. With that information they will then be able to develop and implement effective plans to respond to and recover effectively from any potential incidents.[4]

The private sector also benefits from increased information sharing. First, the agency may receive expert assistance in performing a risk analysis of their asset, resulting in an improved response plan that will better protect that asset. It can be assumed that the government has access to classified information that the private company does not have, thereby increasing the accuracy of the threat analysis and response plan. In addition, there may be a greater access to financial resources to increase the security of the asset. There may also be a better coordination between many agencies for assets in similar areas. Other possible benefits are better research and development into that area, as well as research concerning cross-sector interdependency (see Note 4, pp. 1–17).

When information is not shared, it may lead to an inaccurate assessment of an asset's vulnerability to risk, or to being attacked, leaving an asset at a higher risk. If an asset is undervalued and the risk not clearly identified, that asset may be harmed to a greater extent if attacked. This can cause harm not only to the asset but to citizens as well. It will not be protected enough, making it more vulnerable to attack. On the other hand, if the identified risk associated with an asset makes it appear more significant than it is, the organization may waste resources in protecting it.

The private and public sector are both hesitant to share information with each other for many reasons. Many private owners and operators are concerned that the information they are being asked to share might, if made available to the public or other competitors, result in damage to their company or its image, which may in turn affect their competitive position within the industry. The private sector may be concerned with confidentiality, or keeping the company's secrets, as they fear that their corporate secrets may be given to the public or to competing owners. They may also be concerned with the integrity of that information and seek assurances that the information will not be changed. In addition, the private sector may not want to share information about their asset because of the fear that the information may be used against them by government officials as part of a regulatory enforcement action. In other words, they may be afraid that, by sharing information, they are exposing themselves to increased or unwanted government oversight. In some cases, the company in question may be afraid that the information is made public, exposing losses to the public and possibly affecting their reputation or brand. Another fear is that the information released may expose them to investigations and increased liability, or the information released may be used to potential terrorists and others who are intent on disrupting their infrastructure.

101

On the other hand, the government may be unlikely to share information because it is sometimes critical to keep method and procedures for protecting critical infrastructure protection plans confidential as a way to prevent an attack. There still may be a need to hide information or policies geared toward protecting an asset or how that is done. A release of information may compromise intelligence activities or investigations. For many, there is a lack of trust that any information shared will remain restricted.

EXECUTIVE ORDER 13010

Many documents regarding critical infrastructure protection, including Presidential Policy Directive-63 (PPD-63) and Homeland Security Presidential Directive-21 (HSPD-21), note the importance of including the private sector in the planning process. In July 1996, President Clinton established the President's Commission on Critical Infrastructure Protection (PCCIP). He asked the members of the Commission to assess the vulnerabilities of the country's critical infrastructures, and then create a new plan to protect them. The committee's report was made public in 1997. In the report, the Commission members noted that increased information exchange was needed between all participants in critical infrastructure protection so that the government could analyze that information to determine vulnerabilities, and also to predict or prevent an attack. The Commission indicated that it was necessary to develop methods for two-way sharing of information within each infrastructure, but also across different sectors, and between sectors.

The PCIP proposed Information Sharing and Analysis Centers (ISACs) that would be comprised of representatives from both government and the private sector. The ISAC would provide a forum in which information from all sources could easily be shared and then analyzed to identify vulnerabilities related to that asset. Information could also be shared after an incident to determine why that event happened and how to make changes to prevent a similar event in the future. However, the PCIP soon realized that this information, while ideal in theory, would be hampered by fears held by business owners that corporate secrets would be made public. Thus, it was necessary that those in the private sector have assurances that any confidential information they shared with others would be protected.

Soon after this report was published, President Clinton released Presidential Decision Directive-No. 63 (PDD-63). In this document, Clinton requested that government officials, in particular the National Coordinator for Security, Infrastructure Protection and Counter-Terrorism, begin to cooperate more with private owners and operators of critical infrastructures and begin to share information pertaining to critical infrastructure. He asked the National Coordinator to look into possible liability issues that could emerge as a result of private companies sharing more information. Once those were identified, Clinton sought proposals for removing those obstacles. Clinton also wanted to have recommendations for ways to ensure that any confidential information shared by businesses would remain confidential.

As PDD-63 was implemented, many owners and operators of critical infrastructures formed ISACs, with the intent of sharing more information with federal officials. A report by the General Accounting Office in 2001 found that there was very little information exchanged between the private agencies and the federal government. According to the Director of the National Infrastructure Protection Center, the reason for this was the concern on the part of the private companies that the information they shared would remain confidential. Moreover, officials in the Partnership for Critical Infrastructure Security stated that it was not clear that any of the Freedom of Information Act (FOIA) exemptions would ensure that information would be protected.

INFORMATION SHARING AND ANALYSIS CENTER

ISACs are sector-specific entities that facilitate interaction and communication both between and among members. In short, they enable information sharing between the government and the private sector. Examples of ISACS include a Supply Chain ISAC, a Public Transportation ISAC, a Water ISAC, an Electricity Sector ISAC, Emergency Management and Response ISAC, Information Technology ISAC, Energy ISAC, Chemical Sector ISAC, Healthcare Services ISAC, Highway ISAC, Food and Agriculture ISAC, Multistate ISAC, a Real Estate ISAC, a Research and Educational Networking ISAC, a Biotechnology and Pharmaceutical ISAC, and a Maritime ISAC. A more detailed analysis of the Transportation ISAC is presented in Table 6.1.

The goal of these groups is to advance physical and cyber protection of critical infrastructure throughout the country. According to PDD-63, an ISAC would be responsible for collecting, analyzing, and sharing incident and response information among its members. They were intended

Table 6.1   Example of an ISAC

The Surface Transportation ISAC (ST-ISAC) was created upon the request of the Department of Transportation. This group provides a secure physical and information technology (IT)-related security capability for owners, operators, and users of the transportation infrastructure. Security and threat information is gathered from sources around the world. They are then analyzed and the results are distributed to members. The goal is to help protect vital systems from being attacked and harmed. The ST-ISAC is owned by the EWA Information and Infrastructure Technologies, Inc. and co-owned by the association of American Railroads and the American Public Transportation Association.

to increase the exchange of information among government agencies and the private sector. The original idea was to have one ISAC, but that was later changed so that each sector would have its own center. It was thought that ISACs would be a place where facts from an attack or other incident would be reported, analyzed, and shared with others. They became a clearinghouse of information about any possible threats, mitigation efforts, or recovery efforts.

In addition to sharing information, ISACs are involved in critical infrastructure protection in other ways. ISACs are constantly monitoring events and oversee an early threat and detection warning system. They work closely with Sector Coordinating Councils (SCCs) to provide detailed analysis of events or threats to its membership. If an event occurs, the ISAC will help coordinate the response, and share relevant information with others in that sector and in other sectors, and among public and private agencies. They also help to plan, coordinate, and carry out training exercises.[5]

The membership and scope of every ISAC is different, but they share some similar characteristics. For example, each of the groups promotes sector-specific information and intelligence sharing regarding all-hazard threats, vulnerabilities, and any incidents that may occur. They work with other agencies concerning mitigation efforts to reduce the risk of an attack. They also create dialogue between related organizations and government agencies to identify best practices. In doing so, they seek to educate others and make them more aware of the environment in a safe and secure way.[6] While they do all of this, the ISAC team ensures that any proprietary or sensitive information is protected.

Some of the material that is made available through an ISAC includes information from US and foreign government sources that is not publicly available; National and International Computer Emergency Response Team (CERT) information that is not publicly available; information from law enforcement and public safety agencies; manufacturing information from hardware and software vendors; research by independent researchers and sector experts; and geospatial analysis of threats.

The ISACs are overseen by the ISAC Council, which operates to advance the physical and cybersecurity of the critical infrastructures across the US. They seek to advance interactions between and among the ISACs and with the government.

CYBERSPACE POLICY REVIEW

In May 2009, President Obama established a committee to review the nation's cyberspace security policy. The committee, called the Cyberspace Policy Review Committee, made recommendations to the president about ways to improve cybersecurity. One of the recommendations the committee made was for the president to appoint an Executive Branch Cybersecurity Coordinator, which he did. The Committee also recommended that the Executive Branch work more closely with all key players who are involved in the US cybersecurity policy, including state and local government officials and those in private sector. This would help to ensure a more organized and unified response to future cyber incidents and strengthen existing public–private partnerships to find solutions to ensure cybersecurity (see Note 6).

FUSION CENTERS

Fusion Centers are one important way for federal, state, local, tribal, and territorial agencies to facilitate sharing of information and intelligence. Many states and large cities have established fusion centers as a way to communicate with each other and share information and intelligence within their own jurisdictions as well as with the federal government. The fusion centers ensure that both classified and unclassified information can be shared among the group, with expertise at all levels sharing information (see Note 6). The information is shared from stakeholders and experts in the particular subject matter.[7]

Fusion Centers have access to data resources that are necessary in order to carry out analysis. They also support protection-related exercises that are planned by federal, state, and regional officials. The analysis in the fusion centers work alongside of other analysts, law enforcement officials, public safety officials, and private sector representatives as a way to analyze information. Some of the information that can be exchanged within a fusion centers include site-specific security risks, interdependencies with other sectors, any suspicious activity reports, adversary techniques, best practices in asset protection and resiliency, standard operating procedures for incident response, and emergency communications capabilities.

INFRAGARD

InfraGard is an organization within the FBI between them and members of the private sector who seek to increase information sharing and analysis between the organizations regarding both cyber and physical critical infrastructure protection. The private sector members include businesses, academic institutions, state, and local law enforcement agencies, and others. Each of the members shares key information and intelligence that is somehow related to the protection of the US critical infrastructure from both physical and cyberthreats. InfraGard chapters are formed throughout the country. This is described in more detail in Chapter 5.

REGIONAL AND STATE PARTNERSHIPS

In 2010, the National Infrastructure Advisory Committee issued the results of a study entitled *Optimization of Resources for Mitigating Infrastructure Disruption Study*. Some of the central topics of the study were current practices for aligning infrastructure resilience with community resilience; defining programs that could be defined as "successful" so that they could be replicated in other communities; and ways that communities and sectors can achieve synergies.

When examining a community's resources, the Committee members sought to know if synergies could be established across the public–private enterprise and if there were opportunities to enhance collaborative planning. In the final report, the group recommended that more partnerships between public and private agencies be created so that there would be better communication between groups. They also recommended that the State, Local, Tribal, and Territorial Government Coordinating Council (SLTTGCC), and other similar organizations, could serve a pivotal role in providing expert advice to the federal government on issues pertaining to critical infrastructure protection.

The report noted that it was essential that the resources that if a community's infrastructure is protected and resilient, the community as a whole will be more resilient. They focus on supporting and strengthening a community's resilience, and the need to identify significant weaknesses in infrastructure that may limit the ability of a community to be resilient (see Note 6).

HOMELAND SECURITY INFORMATION NETWORK

The Homeland Security Information Network (HSIN) is a secure web-based system that was established by DHS to increase information sharing and collaboration efforts between government agencies and the private sector that have a concern with protecting critical infrastructure. HSIN is composed of Communities of Interest (COI) that allows users in all 50 states to share information with others in their communities through a safe environment in real-time. It also allows members to discuss problems or seek information from other communities. Through HSIN, groups are able to convene meetings in a virtual meeting space, or through instant messaging and document sharing (see Note 6).

US-CERT

As another way to share more information, DHS created the US Computer Emergency Readiness Team (US-CERT). This agency makes information related to computer-related vulnerabilities and threats available to others. They also provide information about responses to an incident. US-CERT collects incident reports from others around the country and analyzes that information to looks for patterns and trends in computer-based crime. Officials here manage the National Cyber Alert System, that provides general information to any organization or individual who subscribes.

PROTECTIVE SECURITY ADVISORS PROGRAM

Originally developed in 2004, the Protective Security Advisors (PSAs) program is part of DHS' National Protection and Programs Directorate (NPPD), which is found within the Office of Infrastructure Protection (OIP). The PSAs are experts who have been trained in critical infrastructure protection and in mitigation procedures for infrastructure protection. The Program is comprised of regional directors who oversee analysts who are all OIP infrastructure protection and resilience programs and other services provided to state, local, territorial, and tribal government officials. In addition, the analysts ensure that the owners and operators of critical infrastructure in the private sector are also given the information. As of December 2010, there were 93 regional directors and PSAs working in 74 districts throughout the 50 states and Puerto Rico.

The PSA program focuses on three areas: enhancing infrastructure protection; assisting with incident management; and facilitating information sharing. In the first area, enhancing infrastructure, regional directors, and PSAs help owners and operators of critical infrastructure by providing training, grants, and vulnerability assessments when they are requested. They help in the process of identifying possible risks to critical infrastructure and then mitigating those risks. They also provide assistance to law enforcement agencies as they plan and carry out exercises and other planning scenarios or if there is a special event that needs security such as a political or sporting event.

The second area is assisting with incident management. Regional directors and PSAs may be the first people who respond after an emergency or other disaster. During an event, they will cooperate with state and local emergency operations centers (EOC) and at the Federal Emergency Management Agency (FEMA) Joint Field Office to keep DHS and other government offices up to date on any interdependencies, cascading effects, or damaging assessments to critical infrastructure. They can also help to provide advice on recovery activities.

The third area is facilitating information sharing. Here, regional directors and PSAs help the flow of information among all levels of government and the private sector. During times when there are no emergencies, the directors and PSAs may hold briefings and meetings with critical infrastructure protection partners to disseminate information. In the case of an event, Regional directors and PSAs will communicate with others about critical infrastructure response and recovery. They will provide information on conditions and events to the National Infrastructure

Coordinating Center, DHS, and state, local, and private sector representatives. Regional directors and PSA officers will communicate with the
owners and operators of critical infrastructure damage.

PRIVATE SECTOR PREPAREDNESS PROGRAM

After Congress passed an amendment to the Homeland Security Act in
2007, the Secretary of Homeland Security assigned FEMA, in conjunction
with the DHS OIP, the DHS Private Sector Office, and the DHS Science
and Technology Directorate, to develop a private sector preparedness program (PS-Prep Program). In accordance with the new initiative, FEMA
initiated the PS-Prep Program in 2009. This is a voluntary program for
those in the private sector to improve the preparedness of private sector
and nonprofit organizations for an event.

The PS-Prep program involves establishing guidelines, best practices,
regulations, and codes of practice. With this program in place, the owners
and operators of privately owned critical infrastructure assets can use the
standards to improve their protection plans.[8]

PRIVATE SECTOR RESOURCES CATALOG

The DHS has launched the Private Sector Resources Catalog, aimed specifically towards the needs of private sector owners. The catalog provides
a list of DHS publications available for the owners, including resources on
training, guidance, alerts, newsletters, programs, and other services available to those in the private sector.[9]

They have also created the *Critical Infrastructure Protection and
Resilience Toolkit*.[10] This was created as a tool to assist the owners and
operators of critical infrastructure assets at both the local and regional
levels to help them prepare for, protect against, respond to, mitigate
against, and recover from any possible threats or hazards. The toolkit
includes information that describes the role of local and regional communities and of private organization in protection efforts. The toolkit
also includes resources for planning and training exercises that can help
identify vulnerabilities and resiliency issues in their communities. DHS
has also provided sample responses to a variety of frequently asked
questions concerning the role of private owners in critical infrastructure protection. Links to other useful reference materials and training

resources are provided, as well as information on possible partnerships and other ways to share critical information.

CRITICAL INFRASTRUCTURE PARTNERSHIP ADVISORY COUNCIL

The DHS established the Critical Infrastructure Partnership Advisory Council (CIPAC) in 2006 as a way to increase communication between federal programs and state, local, territorial, and tribal agencies that provide for infrastructure protection. CIPAC is comprised of critical infrastructure owners and operators and the trade organizations that are members of the SCCs. The Council also includes representatives from federal, state, local, and tribal governmental groups who are members of the Government Coordinating Councils for each sector.

The CIPAC helps to coordinate federal infrastructure protection programs with private sector owners and operators. It provides a forum in which they can discuss issues or participate in activities that will increase coordination of critical infrastructure protection. The members often meet to discuss planning, security concerns, operational activities, incident response, or recovery. They may also discuss information about possible threats, vulnerabilities, or protective measures (see Note 5).

FEMA GRANTS

The DHS/FEMA sponsor an annual grant program to provide financial assistance for programs that seek to increase the nation's infrastructure protection and security of its assets. The program is overseen by the Grant Programs Directorate (GPD). The focus of GPD is to establish and promote communication with state, local, and tribal stakeholders and increase the nation's level of preparedness as well as its ability to protect against, and respond to an attack or event. In all, the grant programs helps to fund many activities related to homeland security and emergency preparedness. Some of the programs are about planning, organization, equipment purchase, training, exercises, and management and administration costs.[11] The grants programs for FY 2012 are listed in Table 6.2.[12]

Table 6.2   Active Grants

- Homeland Security Grant Program (HSGP): provides more than $830 million for states and urban areas to prevent, protect against, mitigate, respond to, and recover from acts of terrorism and other threats.
- State Homeland Security Program (SHSP): provides $294 million to support the implementation of state homeland security strategies to build and strengthen preparedness capabilities at all levels. The 9/11 Act requires States to dedicate 25% of SHSP funds to law enforcement terrorism prevention activities.
- Urban Areas Security Initiative (UASI): provides more than $490 million to enhance regional preparedness and capabilities in 31 high-threat, high-density areas. The 9/11 Act requires states to dedicate 25% of UASI funds to law enforcement terrorism prevention activities.
- Operation Stonegarden (OPSG): provides more than $46 million to enhance cooperation and coordination among federal, state, local, tribal, and territorial law enforcement agencies to jointly enhance security along the US land and water borders.
- Emergency Management Performance Grants (EMPG) Program: provides more than $339 million to assist, state, and local governments in enhancing and sustaining all-hazards emergency management capabilities.
- Tribal Homeland Security Grant Program (THSGP): provides $6 million to eligible tribal applicants to implement preparedness initiatives to help strengthen the US against risk associated with potential terrorist attacks and other hazards.
- Nonprofit Security Grant Program (NSGP): provides $10 million to support target hardening and other physical security enhancements for nonprofit orgs determined to be at high risk of a terrorist attack and located within one of the FY 2012 UASI-eligible urban areas.
- Intercity Passenger Rail (Amtrak) Program: provides $10 million to protect critical surface transportation infrastructure and the traveling public from terrorism, and increase the resilience of the Amtrak rail system.
- Port Security Grant Program (PSGP): provides more than $97 million to help protect critical port infrastructure from terrorism, enhance maritime domain awareness, and strengthen risk management capabilities in order to protect against improvised explosive devices and other nonconventional weapons.
- Transit Security Grant Program (TSGP): provides more than $87 million to owners and operators of transit systems to protect critical surface transportation and the traveling public from acts of terrorism and to increase the resilience of transit infrastructure.

Source: Federal Emergency Management Agency. Homeland Security Grant Program. Retrieved from: http://www.fema.gov/homeland-security -grant-program.

TRAINING AND EXERCISE SUPPORT

The DHS, through the National Preparedness Directorate, has established many programs to help local communities train their first responders and others for an event, either natural or man-made. Through the National Domestic Preparedness Consortium (NDPC) Training Program, DHS and FEMA officials provide training to emergency responders in the US and its territories. Three levels of training are provided: (a) awareness level training, (b) performance level training, and (c) management level training.

Awareness level training programs are designed for many a wide array of groups and introduce basic concepts to participants. They are intended to teach classes about key principles and policies related to infrastructure protection and security. These courses usually focus on basic topics related to prevention of incidents and preparation for them (including mitigation techniques).

The second type of training courses is performance level training courses. In these, DHS officials help to train participants so they can carry out specific tasks or have specific skills that are needed when responding to, or recovering from, an event. For example, some of the courses focus on how to deal with chemical spills or radioactive materials.

The third type of training course made available by DHS is management level training classes. These are meant to improve the leadership skills for those who are in management or in other supervisory positions.

If needed, DHS will also assist communities and first-responders with exercises so that any potential deficiencies in either personnel needs or response plans can be identified. The Homeland Security Exercise and Evaluation Program (HSEEP) provides assistance in designing exercises, conducting them, and then evaluating them. Exercises may include seminars, workshops, drills, games, tabletop exercises, functional exercises, or full-scale exercises.

CONCLUSION

In 2013, the Government Accountability Office reviewed the extent of cooperation among the federal, state, and local governments regarding cybersecurity. They discovered that the federal government had increased communication and had shared more information about cyberthreats and attacks. They also found that federal agencies had established grants to improve information technology. However, the GAO made it clear that more cooperation with stakeholders in the emergency services sector was needed.[13]

It is clear that the newly developed partnerships between the federal government and the private sector, which emerged after the terrorist attacks in 2001, have improved the communication between these two groups. In the end, this helps for better planning for protecting the nation's critical infrastructure. In the future, improved relationships and more exchange of information will help protect the nation from harm even further.

REVIEW QUESTIONS

1. What are the advantages to sharing information about critical infrastructure protection? Why would some companies be hesitant to do so?
2. Describe an ISAC and why it is important in protecting assets.
3. Explain what is meant by a Fusion Center and its role in critical infrastructure protection.
4. What does the HSIN do?
5. What are the three areas of concentration for the PSAP?
6. Why is the CIPAC important?

NOTES

1. Cordesman, A. H., and Cordesman, J. G. 2002. *Cyber-Threats, Information Warfare, and Critical Infrastructure Protection: Defending the U.S. Homeland.* Westport, CT: Praeger.
2. Radvanovsky, R., and McDougall, A. 2013. *Critical Infrastructure.* Boca Raton, FL: CRC Press.
3. Stevens, G. M., and Tatelman, T. B. September 27, 2006. *Protection of Security-Related Information.* Congressional Research Service. Retrieved from: http://fas.org/sgp/crs/secrecy/RL33670.pdf.
4. DHS, FEMA. September 2010. *CIKR Awareness AWR-213, Participant Guide.* Washington, DC: US DHS, pp. 1–17.
5. US DHS. 2013. *National Infrastructure Protection Plan.*
6. DHS, FEMA. April 2013. *Advanced Critical Infrastructure Protection MGT-414 Participant Guide.*

7. US Department of Homeland Security, and US Department of Justice, Global Justice Information Sharing Initiative. December 2008. *Critical Infrastructure and Key Resources, Protection Capabilities for Fusion Centers.* Retrieved from: https://it.ojp.gov/documents/d/CIKR%20protection%20capabilities%20 for%20fusion%20centers%20s.pdf.
8. DHS, FEMA. September 2014. *Critical Asset Risk Management, Participant Guide,* pp. 6–12.
9. http://www.dhs.gov/xabout/gc_1273165166442.shtm.
10. http://emilms.fema.gov/IS921/921_Toolkit/index.htm.
11. http://www.fema.gov/grants.
12. Federal Emergency Management Agency. Homeland Security Grant Program. Retrieved from: http://www.fema.gov/homeland-security-grant-program.
13. US Government Accountability Office. January 2014. *Critical Infrastructure Protection: More Comprehensive Planning Would Enhance the Cybersecurity of Public Safety Entities' Emerging Technology, GAO-14-125.* Retrieved from: http://www.gao.gov/assets/670/660404.pdf.

7

Laws and Regulations

INTRODUCTION

The Congress has proposed and passed many laws that authorize new policies or methods to protect the country's critical infrastructure (CI). While many proposals were not passed, the debate that ensued during the process helped to educate the public and raise awareness about CI protection and cybersecurity. This chapter includes information on the proposals considered by Congress for protecting critical assets, whether or not they became law.

106TH CONGRESS (1999–2000)

Even before the terrorist attacks of 2001, the Congress and other officials were concerned about protecting the nation's CI. In the 106th Congress, the members passed HR 4205 (PL 106-398). In Section 1033 of this bill, the Defense Secretary was authorized to guarantee up to $10 million of the payment of a loan that was made to a commercial firm for the purpose of improving the protection of CI assets, and even to refinance any improvements that were previously made for such protection. To do this, the Congress gave the Secretary authorization to use up to $500,000 each year from the Department of Defense budgets. In another part of the bill, Section 1053, the Congress asked the President to provide them with a report on the specific steps that the federal government was taking to develop CI protection strategies.

107TH CONGRESS (2001–2002)

The terrorist attacks of September 11, 2001, occurred in the middle of the 107th Congressional session. As a result, there was more attention focused on protecting CI and the nation's ability to respond to a similar future event. The Congress passed many new laws as a direct response to these events—particularly within the transportation sector and border security. A major change resulting from the new legislation this year was the creation of the Department of Homeland Security (DHS) through the Uniting and Strengthening America by Providing Appropriate Tools Required to Intercept and Obstruct Terrorism (USA PATRIOT) Act of 2001 (HR 3162; PL 107-107).

PATRIOT Act

This was a complex bill that had many parts. In general, the PATRIOT Act allows for more information sharing by law enforcement and intelligence agencies so that CI can help officials to disrupt potential terrorist plots and other criminal activity. This bill provided a new definition of CI.

When it came to CI, this bill required the Director of the US Secret Service to develop a national network of electronic crime task forces that would be located throughout the US. These task forces would work to prevent, detect, and investigate various forms of electronic crimes, including potential terrorist attacks against CI and financial payment systems.

The most attention to CI in the PATRIOT Act was the Critical Infrastructures Protection Act of 2001. A portion of the bill defines CI as "systems and assets, whether physical or virtual, so vital to the United States that their incapacity or destruction would have a debilitating impact on security, national economic security, national public health or safety, or any combination of those matters." The law mandated that it was US policy that any physical or virtual disruption of the operation of CI in the country will be rare, brief, geographically limited in effect, manageable, and minimally detrimental to the economy, human, and government services, and US national security. Further, in order to achieve this, a public–private partnership involving corporate and nongovernmental organizations should be established. It also required that a comprehensive and effective program that will ensure the continuity of CI be created. To do these things, the new law mandated that a National Infrastructure Simulation and Analysis Center be established that will address the need for CI protection and continuity.

In Section 105 of the USA PATRIOT Act, the Director of the US Secret Service was required to develop a national network of electronic crime task forces throughout the US that would work to prevent, detect, and investigate different types of electronic crimes, including potential terrorist attacks against CI and financial payment systems.

Homeland Security Act

Another bill passed during this session of Congress was HR 5005 (PL 107-296), the Homeland Security Act of 2002. This new law outlined the DHS' responsibilities for protecting the nation's CI. It established the DHS mission, which was to reduce the nation's vulnerability to terrorist attacks, major disasters, and other emergencies. The organization was also given the responsibility to evaluate potential vulnerabilities to assets and then create steps to protect them. Another critical part of the new law was entitled the Critical Infrastructure Information Act (CIIA) of 2002. In this part of the bill, CI information was defined as information that is not customarily in the public domain and related to the security of CI or protected systems.

In this part of the bill, the president and the Secretary of DHS were asked to exempt any CI information that was voluntarily submitted to the federal government from Freedom of Information Act (FOIA) disclosure requirements. The reason for this is many private groups share confidential or proprietary information with federal agencies in an effort to create more comprehensive plans to protect assets. The private companies are sometimes hesitant to share that information unless they have guarantees that it will not be shared. This new law ensures that shared information will not be disclosed, even if someone files an FOIA request. In this new law, Secretary of DHS was asked to establish procedures for the receipt, care, and storage of critical information that is shared as a way to protect the confidentiality of it.

Provisions within the CIIA detailed the circumstances under which the DHS may obtain, use, and disclose CI information as part of a CI protection program. The CIIA created several limitations on the disclosure of CI information voluntarily submitted to DHS (Section 214). If someone shared the protected information, they would face possible criminal penalties including a possible prison term of up to 1 year or fines, or both. In addition, they could be removed from their job.[1]

Section 214(e) of the bill requires that the Secretary of DHS create methods for the receipt and storage of CI information. To do this effectively,

117

the Secretary of DHS was to work collectively with the National Security Council and the Office of Science and Technology Policy to establish uniform procedures (see Note 1). The bill also had provisions to authorize the federal government to issue advisories, alerts, and warnings to relevant companies, targeted sectors, other governmental entities, or the general public regarding potential threats to critical infrastructure.

A new position, called an Under Secretary for Information Analysis and Infrastructure Protection (now the office for infrastructure Protection under the National Protection and Program Directorate), was made in the new law. This office was given the responsibility for the following:

1. Receiving and analyzing information and intelligence from law enforcement officials to help them understand the nature and scope of the terrorist threat made against the US homeland and to detect and identify potential threats of terrorism within the US.
2. Assessing the vulnerability of key resources and CIs found in the US.
3. Integrating relevant information and intelligence analyses, along with vulnerability assessments as a way to set priorities and fund protective measures.
4. Developing a comprehensive national plan for protecting critical resources and infrastructures.
5. Taking needed measures to protect critical resources and infrastructures.
6. Administering the Homeland Security Advisory System, being responsible for threat advisories, and providing specific warning information to state and local governments and the private sector, as well as providing suggestions regarding necessary protective actions and threat countermeasures.
7. Reviewing, analyzing, and recommending improvements in the policies that regulate sharing of law enforcement intelligence and other information related to the HS within and between federal agencies and state and local governments.

Maritime Transportation Security Act of 2002

Under the Maritime Transportation Security Act (MTSA) of 2002, ports and facilities were required to carry out vulnerability assessments of infrastructure and then develop security plans to keep them safe. The MTSA requires "an owner or operator of a vessel or facility ... [to] prepare and submit to the Secretary a security plan for the vessel or facility." The reach of this requirement can be quite broad. For example, because there are often chemical facilities located at or near ports (e.g., including petroleum refineries), chemical facilities were then required to comply with standards described in the MTSA. In order to maintain trade secrets, the MTSA did not require that any information developed under this statute be disclosed to the public. Information covered under this provision included "facility security plans, vessel security plans, and port vulnerability assessment; and other information related to security plans, procedures, or programs for vessels or facilities authorized under this chapter."

109TH CONGRESS (2005–2006)

In the 109th Congress, members passed the Post-Katrina Emergency Management Reform (PKEMR) Act of 2006. This new law amended the Homeland Security Act of 2002 to make changes to the role of Federal Emergency Management Agency (FEMA) and their ability to provide emergency response services to those affected by natural events. Members of Congress debated where FEMA should be located, but in the end they chose to keep FEMA as part of DHS. There were provisions in the law that clarified FEMA's mission, which included:

1. Leading the nation's efforts to prepare for, respond to, recover from, and mitigate the risks of, any natural and man-made disaster, including catastrophic incidents
2. Implementing a risk-based, all-hazards plus strategy for preparedness
3. Promoting and planning for the protection, security, resiliency, and postdisaster restoration of CI and key resources, including cyber and communications assets

There is also specific language in the PKEMR Act regarding the role, qualifications, authority, and responsibilities of the Administrator of FEMA, who should

1. Have not less than 5 years of executive leadership and management experience, significant experience in crisis management or another relevant field, and a demonstrated ability to manage a substantial staff and budget
2. Report to the Secretary of Homeland Security (HS) without being required to report through any other DHS official

119

3. Be the principal emergency preparedness and response advisor to the President, the Homeland Security Council, and the Secretary
4. Provide federal leadership necessary to mitigate, prepare for, respond to, and recover from a disaster
5. Develop a national emergency management system capable of responding to catastrophic incidents
6. Develop and submit to Congress each year an estimate of the resources needed for developing the capabilities of federal, state, and local governments necessary to respond to a catastrophic incident

The law created two new positions within FEMA: (a) a Director for Preparedness and (b) a Director for Response and Recovery. The changes also mandated the creation of 10 regional offices and area offices for the Pacific, for the Caribbean, and for Alaska. The personnel in these new offices were in turn asked to establish multiagency strike teams that would be prepared to respond to disasters, including catastrophic incidents, at a moment's notice. In addition, a National Advisory Council on Preparedness and Response was created whose task it would be to advise the FEMA Administrator on preparedness and emergency management. Members of the Council would be appointed by the administrator and should represent emergency management and law enforcement, general emergency response providers from state, local, and tribal governments, private sector, and nongovernmental organizations.

110TH CONGRESS (2007–2008)

The members of the 110th Congress continued to be concerned about protection of CI. In this session, they passed HR 1 (PL 110-53), or the Implementing Recommendations of the 9/11 Commission Act of 2007. In this law, new policies were established for protecting the nation's critical assets. Section 101 of the bill amended the Homeland Security Act of 2002 to create a Homeland Security Grant Program (specifically the Urban Area Security Initiative and a State Homeland Security Grant Program). The Secretary of HS and the FEMA Administrator were given the responsibility to decide who would be awarded the grants. The grant funding could be used for training, exercises, protecting CI, and/or purchasing equipment, among other reasons. The considerations for awarding the grants were provided in the bill, and they included things like the risk posed to the state, the degree of threat, vulnerability, and consequences related to CI or key resources, and the anticipated effectiveness of the state's proposed use of grant funds to improve interoperability.

Another Section of the bill, Section 409, made amendments to the Homeland Security Act so that Administrator of FEMA would establish model standards for credentialing CI workers. The administrator would then be asked to provide the standards, along with technical assistance to state, local, and tribal governments to aid them in protecting their assets.

Title X of the new law, Section 1001, was entitled "Improving Critical Infrastructure Security." In this section, the Secretary of DHS was asked to establish, maintain, and update a National Asset Database of each asset that the DHS determines to be a vital asset. Those assets were defined as those assets and services, if lost, interrupted, incapacitated, or destroyed, would have a negative or debilitating effect on the economic security, public health, or safety of the US, any state, or any local government. To help with this task, the bill required a National Infrastructure Protection Consortium be established that would advise DHS on the best way to identify assets and maintain the database. It was noted, however, that the Secretary should ensure that levees were included in the list of CI assets. The Secretary was also to maintain a classified and prioritized list of assets that the Secretary determines would, if destroyed or disrupted, cause national or regional catastrophic effects. The Secretary was asked to present annual reports on the database and the list to the Homeland Security Committees in both the House and Senate.

In Section 1519 of the law, DHS was asked to assess the methods that would likely be used in a deliberate terrorist attack against a railroad tank car used to transport toxic-inhalation-hazard materials. Included in that analysis was to be an estimate about the degree to which that method could cause death, injury, or serious health effects to victims, the environment, CI, national security, the national economy, or public welfare. Moreover, DHS was asked to conduct an analysis, with the assistance of the National Infrastructure Simulation and Analysis Center, on the analysis of a possible release of toxic-inhalation-hazard materials that might occur from a terrorist attack on a loaded railroad tank car that was loaded with such materials in urban and rural environments. This would help with the planning process for such an attack.

113TH CONGRESS (2013–2014)

A bill passed in the 113th Congress was HR 2952 (PL 113-246), also known as the Cybersecurity Workforce Assessment Act. Under this law, the Secretary of HS would conduct a yearly assessment of the cybersecurity workforce in DHS. For example, it would analyze the readiness of employees to meet its cybersecurity mission; the location of the cybersecurity workforce within DHS; a description of which positions are carried out by permanent full-time DHS employees, by independent contractors, by individuals employed by other federal agencies, or which positions are not filled; the percentage of individuals within certain specialty areas who have received essential training to perform their jobs; and any challenges that were confronted for that training.

In another bill (HR 3979: PL 113-291), the Carl Levin and Howard P. "Buck" McKeon National Defense Authorization Act for Fiscal Year 2015, one section (Sec. 1051) required the Department of Defense to report to Congress on the protection of top-tier defense-CI from electromagnetic pulse.

Amendments were made to the Homeland Security Act of 2012 in the National Cybersecurity Protection Act of 2014. The new law would establish a National Cybersecurity and Communications Integration Center within DHS that would help implement the responsibilities of the DHS Under Secretary for overseeing the protection of CI, cybersecurity, and other DHS programs. The new agency would work to ensure that information on cyber-risks and incidents would be shared with both federal and private groups. The agency would also work to ensure continuous coordination among all groups involved as well as assistance with training programs.

CONCLUSION

Protection of the nation's CI and assets is a top priority for the members of Congress, and they have passed many new laws to ensure that threats will be investigated and in the case of an event, damage will be kept to a minimum. For this reason, Congress has passed laws that attempt to increase communication among and between groups, and that have provided funding for protection efforts. In the future, Congress will continue to pass new laws to protect assets and save property and lives.

REVIEW QUESTIONS

1. What role did the USA PATRIOT Act play in CI protection?
2. What was the goal of the Homeland Security Act?
3. In the 109th Congress, members passed the PKEMR Act of 2006. What were the major elements of this bill as it pertains to CI protection?
4. Describe some of the bills that were not passed by Congress pertaining to CI protection.

APPENDIX

Bills Proposed Concerning Critical Infrastructure

106	S 2448	Internet Integrity and Critical Infrastructure (CI) Protection Act	Appointment of a Deputy Attorney General for Computer Crime and Intellectual Property to advise federal prosecutors and law enforcement on computer crime; to coordinate national and international activities for combating cybercrime; Provides criminal penalties for those who access protected computers when the offense causes losses of at least $5000 or when the offense causes the modification of medical records or when the offense causes a physical injury to any person or to the public's health or safety. Requires forfeiture of property used in committing such offenses or derived from proceeds. Requires the Director of the FBI to establish a National Cybercrime Technical Support Center to provide technical assistance for computer-related criminal activities. Requires the Director to develop at least 10 regional computer forensic laboratories, and to provide support for existing laboratories.
106	S 3188 HR 4246	Cybersecurity Enhancement Act	To facilitate the protection of CI in the US and to enhance the investigation and prosecution of computer-related crimes. Creates methods to ensure that information on CI and CI protection will not be made available under the Freedom of Information Act (FOIA) if the person submitting the information requests that the information not be made available.
107	HR 4	Energy Policy Act of 2002	Authorizes appropriations for a research and technology program pertaining to critical energy infrastructure protection; and provide funds to states for security to protect critical energy infrastructure facilities.

(Continued)

Bills Proposed Concerning Critical Infrastructure *(Continued)*

107	HR 1158; HR 4660	National Homeland Security Agency Act	Establishes a National Homeland Security Agency; transfers FEMA, Customs Service, Border Patrol, the Coast Guard, the CI Assurance Office, and the Institute of Information Infrastructure Protection of the Department of Commerce, the National Infrastructure Protection Center, and the National Domestic Preparedness Office of the FBI. Requires Director to be an advisor to the National Security Council.
107	HR 2435 S 1456	Cybersecurity Information Act	Prohibits the disclosure of cybersecurity information that is voluntarily provided to a federal entity. Such information shall be exempt from disclosure under FOIA; cannot be disclosed to a third party; and cannot be used in any civil action.
107	HR 2975	United and Strengthening America Act (USA ACT)	**Information Sharing for CI Protection—** Amends the Omnibus Crime Control and Safe Streets Act of 1968 to extend Bureau of Justice Assistance regional information sharing system grants to systems that enhance the investigation and prosecution abilities of participating federal, state, and local law enforcement agencies in addressing multijurisdictional terrorist conspiracies and activities.
107	HR 4660	National Homeland Security and Combating Terrorism act of 2002	To plan, coordinate, and integrate Government border security, CI protection, and emergency preparedness activities.
107	HR 5710	Homeland Security Information Sharing Act (CI Information Act)	Allows a CI Protection program to be formed by the President or the Secretary DHS.

(Continued)

124

Bills Proposed Concerning Critical Infrastructure *(Continued)*

			Exempts from the FOIA any CI information that is voluntarily submitted to a federal agency for use in the security of CI when accompanied by a statement that such information is being submitted voluntarily in expectation of nondisclosure protection. Requires that CI information that was voluntarily submitted to be stored so that it will not be made public. Sets criminal penalties for unauthorized disclosure of such information.
			Authorizes the federal government to issue advisories, alerts, and warnings to relevant companies, targeted sectors, other governmental entities, or the general public regarding potential threats to CI.
107	S 1407	CI Protection Act of 2001	Directs the National Infrastructure Simulation and Analysis Center (NISAC) to provide support for the activities of the President's Protection and Continuity Board for simulation and analysis of any CI systems (cyber and/or physical) as a way to get a better understanding of their complexity, and to facilitate changes that will mitigate any threats and to increase training, and to enhance the stability of CI. Requires the Board to provide information on the CI requirements of each federal agency.
107	S1419	Department of Defense Authorization Act	Authorizes funds for the Navy's CI protection initiative.
107	S1510	Uniting and Strengthening American Act	Requires the Director of the US Secret Service to develop a national network of electronic crime task forces throughout the US to prevent, detect, and investigate various forms of electronic crimes, including potential terrorist attacks against CI and financial payment systems.

(Continued)

Bills Proposed Concerning Critical Infrastructure *(Continued)*

			Amends the Omnibus Crime Control and Safe Streets Act of 1968 to extend Bureau of Justice Assistance regional information sharing system grants to systems that enhance the investigation and prosecution abilities of federal, state, and local law enforcement agencies in addressing multijurisdictional terrorist conspiracies and activities.
107	S 1534	Department of National Homeland Security Act	Establishes the Department of National Homeland Security. Among other agencies to be transferred here is the CI Assurance Office and the Institute of Information Infrastructure Protection of the Department of Commerce, and the National Infrastructure Protection Center and the National Domestic Preparedness Office of the FBI. Establishes within the Department: (a) separate Directorates of Prevention, CI Protection, and Emergency Preparedness and Response; and (b) an Office of Science and Technology (OST) to advise the Secretary with regard to research and development efforts and priorities for such directorates. Requires the Secretary to establish mechanisms for the sharing of information and intelligence with US and international intelligence entities.
107	S1593	Water Infrastructure Security and Research Development Act	Requires the Administrator of the EPA to establish a program of grants to research institutions to improve the protection and security of public water supply systems by carrying out projects concerning processes to address physical and cyberthreats to water supply systems. The projects should assess possible security issues and protect systems from potential threats by developing technologies, processes, guidelines, standards, procedures, real-time monitoring systems, and educational and awareness programs.

(Continued)

Bills Proposed Concerning Critical Infrastructure *(Continued)*

107	S 1766	Energy Policy Act: Energy Science and Technology Enhancement Act	Sets forth a national energy research and technology program that will encourage partnerships with industry, national laboratories, and institutions of higher learning. Each program will include research into critical energy infrastructure protection. Authorizes the Secretary of Energy to establish security enhancement programs for critical energy infrastructure. Instructs the Secretary of the Interior to establish the Outer Continental Shelf (OCS) Energy Infrastructure Security Program to provide financial assistance for State security plans against threats to critical OCS energy infrastructure facilities; and provide support for activities needed to maintain the safety and operation of critical energy infrastructure activities.
107	S2077	Securing Our States Act of 2002	Requires the Director of FEMA to make grants to States to improve CI protection.
107	S2452	Energy Science and Technology Enhancement Act of 2002	Sets forth a national energy research and technology program that operates in partnership with industry, the national laboratories, and institutions of higher learning. Includes within the program a focus on critical energy infrastructure protection research and development. Directs the Energy Secretary to plan Government activities relating to border security, CI protection, and emergency preparedness and to act as the focal point regarding crises and emergency planning and response. Transfers the CI Assurance Office of the Department of Commerce and the National Infrastructure Protection Center of the FBI to the Treasury Department.

(Continued)

127

Bills Proposed Concerning Critical Infrastructure *(Continued)*

			Establishes within the Department: (a) Directorates of Border and Transportation Protection, (b) CI Protection, and (c) Emergency Preparedness and Response. Provides that the Director of OST assist the Directorate of CI Protection.
107	S 2509/ S 2515	Transparent and Enhanced Criteria Act	Amends the Defense Base Closure and Realignment Act of 1990 to add the following to the selection criteria for the 2005 round of defense base closures and realignments: the costs and effects of relocating CI.
107	S Amdt 1812		To set aside funds for the CI protection initiative of the Navy.
107	S Amdt 2363		To set aside funds of the CI protection initiative of the Navy.
107	S Amdt 2514		To increase the amount provided for research for CI protection.
107	S Amdt 4422		To set aside $6,000,000 for operation and maintenance from the Navy for the CI Protection Program.
107	S Amdt 4552		To identify certain sites as key resources for protection by the Directorate of CI Protection.
108	HR 6	Energy Policy Act of 2003	Authorizes appropriations for a research and technology deployment program pertaining to critical energy infrastructure protection.
108	HR 10	9/11 Recommendations Implementation Act	Directs the Secretary of the Treasury to submit a report on public–private partnerships to protect critical financial infrastructure.
108	HR 3367 S 1230	To provide for additional responsibilities for the Chief Information Office of the DHS.	Directs the Chief Information Officer of DHS to establish a program to provide for efficient use of geospatial information. This will include providing geospatial information as necessary to implement the CI protection programs; and providing leadership in managing databases used by those responsible for planning, prevention, mitigation, assessment, and response to emergencies and CI.

(Continued)

Bills Proposed Concerning Critical Infrastructure *(Continued)*

108	HR 4852	DHS Authorization Act for FY 2005	Establishes within the Directorate for Information Analysis and Infrastructure Protection a National Cybersecurity Office. Establishes the Liberty Shield Award for Innovation and Excellence in CI Protection. Urges the DHS Homeland Security Operations Center to increase on-site participation of representatives from private sector CI sectors. Directs the Secretary of DHS to develop and distribute CI protection awareness and education materials for emergency response providers.
108	S 1229	Federal Employee Protection of Disclosures Act	Amends the Homeland Security Act of 2002 to prohibit disclosure of voluntarily shared CI information that is protected information.
108	S 2021	Domestic Defense Fund Act of 2004	Authorizes the Secretary of DHS to award grants to States, units of local government, and Indian tribes for homeland security development. The grants can be used to improve cyber and infrastructure security. Requires 70% of grant funds to be allocated among metropolitan cities and urban counties based on the Secretary's calculations of infrastructure vulnerabilities and threats such as proximity to international borders, nuclear, or other energy facilities, air, rail, or water transportation, and national icons and federal buildings. Allocates funds for discretionary grants for the protection of CI.
108	S Amdt 743		To set aside funds for the Collaborative Information Warfare Network at the CI Protection Center at the Space Welfare Systems Center.
108	S Amdt 1235		To make available from Research, Development, Test and Evaluation for the CI Protection Center.

(Continued)

129

Bills Proposed Concerning Critical Infrastructure *(Continued)*

109	HR 867/ S 394	Openness Promotes Effectiveness in our National Government Act (OPEN) government Act	Requires the Comptroller General to annually report on implementation of provisions to protect voluntarily shared CI information.
109	HR 1817	DHS Authorization Act for FY 2006	Requires the Comptroller General to annually report on implementation of provisions to protect voluntarily shared CI information.
109	HR 4881	National Defense CI Protect Act off 2006	Authorizes appropriations for DHS for FY 2006, including for CI grants. Amends the Homeland Security Act of 2002 requires the Under Secretary for Information Analysis and Infrastructure Protection to disseminate information relevant to CI sectors. Requires the Under secretary to assign Information Analysis and Infrastructure Protection functions to the Assistant Secretary for Information Analysis, the Assistant Secretary for Infrastructure Protection, and the Assistant Secretary for Cybersecurity. Subtitle D: CI Prioritization—Directs the Secretary of DHS to complete prioritization of the nation's CI according to the threat of terrorist attack; the likelihood that an attack would destroy or significantly disrupt such infrastructure; and the likelihood that an attack would result in substantial numbers of deaths and serious bodily injuries, a substantial adverse economic impact, or a substantial adverse impact on national security. Requires the Secretary of DHS, in coordination with federal agencies; state, local, and tribal governments, and the private sector, to review plans for securing CI. Protects certain CI information generated, compiled, or disseminated by DHS to be protected.

(Continued)

Bills Proposed Concerning Critical Infrastructure (*Continued*)

109	HR 5441	DHS Appropriations Act	Transfers to FEMA all functions of the Directorate of Preparedness except for the Office of Infrastructure Protection, the National Cybersecurity Division, and others. Establishes within FEMA a National Integration Center, a National Infrastructure Simulation and Analysis Center, a National Operations Center, and a Chief Medical Officer.
109	H Amdt 149		Required the DHS to coordinate its activities regarding CI protection with other relevant federal agencies.
109	S 494 S 2361 S 2766	Federal Employee Protection Act	Amends the Homeland Security Act of 2002 to provide that, for purposes of provisions regarding the protection of voluntarily shared CI information, a permissible use of independently obtained CI information includes any lawful disclosure an employee or applicant reasonably believes is credible evidence of waste, fraud, abuse, or gross mismanagement, without restriction as to time, place, form, motive, context, or prior disclosure.
109	S 2361	Honest Leadership and Accountability in Contracting Act	Amends the Homeland Security Act of 2002 to provide that, for purposes of provisions regarding the protection of voluntarily shared CI information, a permissible use of independently obtained CI information includes any lawful disclosure an employee or applicant reasonably believes is credible evidence of waste, fraud, abuse, or gross mismanagement, without restriction as to time, place, form, motive, context, or prior disclosure.

(*Continued*)

131

Bills Proposed Concerning Critical Infrastructure (*Continued*)

109	S 3721	Post-Katrina Emergency Management Reform Act of 2006	Sets forth provisions regarding FEMA's mission, which includes planning for the protection, security, resiliency, and restoration of CI and key resources, including cyber and communications assets. Directs the FEMA Administrator to establish at least two pilot projects to develop and evaluate strategies and technologies for capabilities in a disaster in which there is significant damage to CI.
110	1309	FOIA Amendments of 2007	Requires the Comptroller General to report on implementation of provisions for the protection of voluntarily shared CI information.
110	HR 1326 S 849	OPEN Government Act of 2007	Requires the Comptroller General to report on implementation of provisions for the protection of voluntarily shared CI information.
110	S 4	Improving America's Security Act of 2007	Establishes the State Homeland Security Grant Program to assist state, local, and tribal governments in preventing, preparing for, protecting against, responding to, and recovering from terrorist acts. The bill provides lists of permissible uses of grants, including the payment of personnel costs for protecting CI and key resources identified in the CI List. Lists considerations in awarding grants, including the nature of the threat, the location, risk, or vulnerability of CI and key national assets, and the extent to which geographic barriers pose unusual obstacles to achieving, maintaining, or enhancing emergency communications operability or interoperable communications. Directs the Administrator to create model standards that states may adopt in conjunction with CI owners and operators and their employees to permit access to restricted areas in the event of a natural disaster, terrorist act, or other man-made disaster.

(*Continued*)

Bills Proposed Concerning Critical Infrastructure *(Continued)*

Title XI: CI Protection: Directs the Secretary to establish a risk-based prioritized list of CI and key resources that: (a) includes assets or systems that, if successfully destroyed or disrupted through a terrorist attack or natural catastrophe, would cause catastrophic national or regional impacts; and (b) reflects a cross-sector analysis of CI to determine priorities for prevention, protection, recovery, and restoration. Requires the Secretary to include levees in the Department's list of CI sectors. Authorizes the Secretary to establish additional CI and key resources priority lists by sector.

Directs the Secretary to prepare a risk assessment of the CI and key resources of the nation. Authorizes DHS to rely on a vulnerability or risk assessment prepared by another federal agency that DHS determines is prepared in coordination with other DHS initiatives relating to CI or key resource protection and partnerships between the government and private sector.

Directs the Secretary to report to specified committees for each fiscal year detailing the actions taken by the government to ensure the preparedness of industry to: (a) reduce interruption of CI operations during a terrorist attack, natural catastrophe, or other similar national emergency; (b) provide sufficient financial assistance for the reasonable costs of the Information Sharing and Analysis Center (ISAC) for Public Transportation established to protect CI; (c) require public transportation agencies at significant risk of terrorist attack to participate in ISAC; and (d) encourage all other public transportation agencies to participate in ISAC.

(Continued)

133

Bills Proposed Concerning Critical Infrastructure (*Continued*)

109	S 274	Federal Employee Protection of Disclosures Act	Amends the Homeland Security Act of 2002 to provide that, for purposes of provisions regarding the protection of voluntarily shared CI, a permissible use of independently obtained CI information includes any lawful disclosure an employee or applicant reasonably believes is credible evidence of waste, fraud, abuse, or gross mismanagement, without restriction as to time, place, form, motive, context, or prior disclosure.
110	S606	Honest Leadership and Accountability in Contracting Act of 2007	Amends the Homeland Security Act of 2002 to provide that, for purposes of provisions regarding the protection of voluntarily shared CI, a permissible use of independently obtained CI includes any lawful disclosure an employee or applicant reasonably believes is credible evidence of waste, fraud, abuse, or gross mismanagement, without restriction as to time, place, form, motive, context, or prior disclosure.
110	S 1804	National Agriculture and Food Defense Act of 2007	States that the Secretary DHS shall lead federal, state, local, tribal, and private efforts to enhance the protection of US CI and key resources, including the agriculture and food system.
110	S 2215	Supporting America's Protective Security Advisor Act of 2007	Amends the Homeland Security Act of 2002 to establish the Protective Security Advisor Program Office within the Protective Security Coordination Division of the Office of Infrastructure Protection of DHS. Requires the office to have primary responsibility within DHS for encouraging state, local, and tribal governments and private sector owners and operators of CI and key resources to operate within the risk management framework of the National Infrastructure Protection Plan. The office should also coordinate national and intergovernmental CI and key resource activities with such governments, owners, and operators as well as conduct risk assessment analyses that enhance the preparedness of CI and key resources.

(*Continued*)

Bills Proposed Concerning Critical Infrastructure (*Continued*)

110	S Amdt 415		To amend title X, with respect to CI protection efforts by federal departments and agencies.
111	HR 6351	Strengthening Cybersecurity for CI Act	Grants the Secretary of DHS primary authority in the creation, verification, and enforcement of measures for the protection of critical information infrastructure, including practices applicable to critical information infrastructures that are not owned by or under the direct control of the federal government. It authorizes the Secretary to conduct audits to ensure that appropriate measures are taken to secure critical information infrastructure. Establishes a National Office for Cyberspace, headed by an Executive Cyber Director, who shall have authority to oversee interagency cooperation on security policies relating to the creation, verification, and enforcement of measures regarding the protection of critical information infrastructure.
111	S 946	Critical Electric Infrastructure Protection Act of 2009	Directs the Secretary of Homeland Security to conduct an investigation to determine if the security of federally owned programmable electronic devices and communication networks (including hardware, software, and data) essential to the operation of critical electric infrastructure have been compromised. Directs the Secretary to make ongoing assessments and provide periodic reports with respect to cyber vulnerabilities and cyberthreats to CI, including critical electric infrastructure and advanced metering infrastructure. Directs the Federal Energy Regulatory Commission (FERC) to establish mandatory interim measures to protect against known cyber vulnerabilities or threats to the operation of the critical electric infrastructure.

(*Continued*)

Bills Proposed Concerning Critical Infrastructure *(Continued)*

111	S 1462	American Clean Energy Leadership Act of 2009	Amends the Federal Power Act to require FERC to issue rules or orders to protect critical electric infrastructure from cybersecurity vulnerabilities. Makes such rules or orders expire when a standard is developed and approved to address the vulnerability. Authorizes the Secretary of Energy to require people to take action to avert or mitigate an immediate cybersecurity threat to critical electric infrastructure.
112	HR 1136	Executive Cyberspace Coordination Act of 2011	Requires the Director of the National Office for Cyberspace to review federal agency budgets relating to the protection of information infrastructures. Establishes in the Executive Office of the President the Office of the Federal Chief Technology Officer. The duties of the Officer are to advise the President and agency officials on information technology infrastructures, strategy; and to establish public–private sector partnership initiatives. Grants the Secretary of Homeland Security primary authority for the protection of the CI infrastructure.
112	HR 2658	Federal Protective Service (FPS) Reform and Enhancement Act	Revises provisions governing the FPS. Declares FPS's mission to be to secure all facilities and surrounding federal property under its protection and to safeguard all occupants. Requires the Director of FPS to report to the Under Secretary responsible for CI. Directs the Secretary to submit a strategy for cooperation between the Under Secretary responsible for CI protection and the Under Secretary for Science and Technology regarding research, development, and deployment of security technology.

(Continued)

Bills Proposed Concerning Critical Infrastructure *(Continued)*

112	HR 3674	Promoting and Enhancing Cybersecurity and Information Sharing Effectiveness (PRECISE) Act of 2012	Amends the Homeland Security Act of 2002 to direct the Secretary of DHS to perform necessary activities to facilitate the protection of federal systems and to assist CI owners and operators, upon request, in protecting their CI information systems. Directs the Secretary, in carrying out cybersecurity activities, to coordinate with relevant federal agencies, state, and local government representatives, CI owners and operators, suppliers of technology for such owners and operators, academia, and international organizations and foreign partners; and develop and maintain a strategy that articulates DHS actions that are needed to assure the readiness, continuity, integrity, and resilience of federal systems and CI information systems. Directs the Secretary to make appropriate cyberthreat information available to appropriate owners and operators of CI on a timely basis.
112	H Amdt 326		To coordinate federal information security policy through the creation of a National Office for Cyberspace, and establishing measures for the protection of CI from cyberattacks.
112	S 1342	Grid CyberSecurity Act	Amends the Federal Power Act to direct the FERC to determine whether certain reliability standards are adequate to protect critical electric infrastructure from cybersecurity vulnerabilities, and order the Electric Reliability Organization (ERO) to submit a proposed reliability standard that will provide adequate protection of critical electric infrastructure from cybersecurity vulnerabilities.

(Continued)

137

Bills Proposed Concerning Critical Infrastructure (*Continued*)

			Authorizes the Secretary of Energy to: require persons subject to FERC jurisdiction to take immediate action that will best avert or mitigate the cybersecurity threat if necessary to protect critical electric infrastructure. Applies specified disclosure restrictions to critical electric infrastructure information submitted to FERC or DOE, or developed by a federal power marketing administration or the Tennessee Valley Authority, under this Act to the same extent as they apply to CI information voluntarily submitted to DHS. Authorizes FERC to require the ERO to develop and issue emergency orders address vulnerabilities and take immediate action to protect critical electric infrastructure if necessary. Directs the Secretary of Energy to assess the susceptibility of critical electric infrastructure to electromagnetic pulse (EMP) events and geomagnetic disturbances, and determine whether and to what extent infrastructure affecting the transmission of electric power in interstate commerce should be hardened against such events and disturbances.
112	S 1546	DHS Authorization Act	Applies specified disclosure restrictions to critical electric infrastructure information submitted to FERC or DOE, or developed by a federal power marketing administration or the Tennessee Valley Authority, under this Act to the same extent as they apply to CI information voluntarily submitted to the DHS. Requires FERC and DOE to establish information sharing procedures on the release of CI information to entities subject to this Act.

(*Continued*)

Bills Proposed Concerning Critical Infrastructure (*Continued*)

112	S 3414	Cybersecurity Act of 2012	Establishes a National Cybersecurity Council, to be chaired by the Secretary of DHS, to: identify categories of critical cyber infrastructure (CCI); establish a voluntary cybersecurity program for CI to encourage owners of CI to adopt such practices; develop procedures to inform owners and operators of CI of cyberthreats, vulnerabilities, and consequences.
			Directs the Council to designate an agency to conduct top-level cybersecurity assessments of cyber risks to CI with voluntary participation from private sector entities.
			Directs the Council to identify CCI within each sector of CI and CI owners within each category, and establish a procedure for owners of critical cyber infrastructure to challenge the identification.
			Directs the Council to identify CCI categories only if damage or unauthorized access could reasonably result in (a) the interruption of life-sustaining services sufficient to cause a mass casualty event or mass evacuations; (b) catastrophic economic damage to the US, including financial markets, transportation systems, or other systemic, long-term damage; or (c) severe degradation of national security.
			Requires the Council to establish procedures under which owners of critical cyber infrastructure shall report significant cyber incidents affecting critical cyber infrastructure.
			Provides for congressional review of critical cyber infrastructure determinations.
			Requires private sector coordinating councils (PSCC) within CI sectors established by the National Infrastructure Protection Plan to propose cybersecurity practices to the Council.

(*Continued*)

139

Bills Proposed Concerning Critical Infrastructure (*Continued*)

			Permits federal agencies with responsibilities for regulating the security of CI to adopt such practices as mandatory requirements. Directs the Council to establish the Voluntary Cybersecurity Program for CI under which owners of CI who are certified to participate in the Program select and implement cybersecurity measures of their choosing that satisfy such cybersecurity practices in exchange for (a) liability protection from punitive damages; (b) expedited security clearances; and (c) prioritized technical assistance, real-time cyberthreat information, and public recognition. Prohibits any of the above provisions relating to the CI public–private partnership from limiting the ability of a federal agency with responsibilities for regulating the security of CI from requiring that the cybersecurity practices adopted by the Council be met. Directs the Secretary to establish a CI Cybersecurity tip line. Requires the DHS and DOD to jointly establish academic and professional Centers of Excellence to protect CI in conjunction with international academic and professional partners.
113	HR 3032	Executive Cyberspace Coordination Act	Establishes the National Office for Cyberspace to serve as the principal office for coordinating issues relating to cyberspace. Requires the Director of the National Office for Cyberspace to review federal agency budgets relating to the protection of information infrastructures. Grants the Secretary of Homeland Security authority for the protection of the CI infrastructure, as defined by this Act.

(*Continued*)

Bills Proposed Concerning Critical Infrastructure *(Continued)*

113	HR 3410	CI Protection Act (CIPA)	Amends the Homeland Security Act of 2002 to require the Secretary of Homeland Security to conduct outreach to educate owners and operators of CI of the threat of EMP events. Directs the Secretary to conduct research to mitigate the consequences of EMP Attack events, including an analysis of the risks to CI from a range of EMP events and available technology options to improve the resiliency of CI to such events.
113	HR 3696	National Cybersecurity and CI Protection Act	Directs the Secretary of DHS to coordinate with federal, state, and local governments, national laboratories, CI owners and operators, and other cross-sector coordinating entities to facilitate a national effort to strengthen and maintain CI from cyberthreats; and ensure that DHS policies enable CI owners and operators to receive appropriate and timely cyberthreat information. In addition, the Secretary is to ensure that the allocation of federal resources is cost-effective and reduces burdens on CI owners and operators. Directs the Secretary to oversee federal efforts to support the efforts of CI owners and operators to protect against cyberthreats; to help share cyberthreat information with owners and operators of CI; and to facilitate cyber incident response assistance by providing analysis and warnings related to threats to, and vulnerabilities of, CI information systems. Requires the Secretary to: (a) designate CI sectors; and (b) recognize, for each sector, a previously designated Sector-Specific Agency (SSA), a Sector Coordinating Council (SCC), and at least one ISAC.

(Continued)

Bills Proposed Concerning Critical Infrastructure (*Continued*)

			Permits to be included as CI sectors: chemical; commercial facilities; communications; critical manufacturing; dams; Defense Industrial Base; emergency services; energy; financial services; food and agriculture; government facilities; healthcare and public health; information technology; nuclear reactors, materials, and waste; transportation systems; and water and wastewater systems. Directs the Secretary to implement procedures for continuous, collaborative, and effective interactions between DHS and CI owners and operators. Directs the National Institute of Standards and Technology (NIST) to facilitate the development of a voluntary, industry-led set of standards and processes to reduce cyber risks to CI.
113	HR 5712	DHS Private Sector Office Engagement Act of 2014	Amends the Homeland Security Act of 2002 with provisions establishing a Private Sector Office within DHS. Gives the Assistant Secretary the responsibility to promote best practices regarding cybersecurity and CI protection to the private sector.
113	S2519	National Cybersecurity Protection Act	Amends the Homeland Security Act of 2002 to establish a national cybersecurity and communications integration center (NCCIC) in DHS that will be responsible for overseeing CI protection programs. Directs the Under Secretary to develop, maintain, and exercise adaptable cyber incident response plans to address cybersecurity risks to CI.

(*Continued*)

Bills Proposed Concerning Critical Infrastructure (*Continued*)

114	HR 85	Terrorism Prevention and CI Protection Act	

Requires the Secretary to make the application process for security clearances relating to a classified national security information program available to SCCs, sector information sharing and analysis organizations, and owners and operators of CI.

Prohibits this Act from being construed to grant the Secretary any authority to promulgate regulations or set standards relating to the cybersecurity of private sector CI that was not in effect on the day before the enactment of this Act.

Directs the Secretary of Homeland Security to work with CI owners and operators and state, local, tribal, and territorial entities to take necessary steps to manage risk and strengthen the security and resilience of the nation's CI against terrorist attacks. DHS should also establish terrorism prevention policies with international partners to strengthen the security and resilience of domestic CI and CI located outside of the US. DHS is to establish a task force to conduct research into the best means to address the security and resilience of CI to reflect the interconnectedness and interdependency of CI. The security and resiliency of CI will be furthered by the establishment of the Strategic Research Imperatives Program. Finally, DHS should make research findings available and provide guidance to federal civilian agencies for the identification, prioritization, assessment, and security of their CI.

(*Continued*)

143

Bills Proposed Concerning Critical Infrastructure (*Continued*)

			Authorizes the Secretary to consult with other federal agencies on how best to align federally funded research and development activities that seek to strengthen the security and resilience of the nation's CI.
			Requires the Secretary to: develop a description of the functional relationships within DHS and across the federal government related to CI security and resilience, and demonstrate a near real-time situational awareness, research-based pilot project for CI.
114	HR 1073	CI Protection act	Amends the Homeland Security Act of 2002 to require DHS to conduct a campaign to educate owners and operators of CI, emergency planners, and emergency responders at all levels of government about EM threats. Directs DHS to conduct research to mitigate the consequences of EM threats, including (a) a scientific analysis of the risks to CI from EM threats; (b) a determination of the CI that are at risk from EM threats; (c) an analysis of available technology options to improve the resiliency of CI to EM threats; and (d) the restoration and recovery capabilities of CI under differing levels of damage and disruption from various EM threats.
	HR 1560	Cyber Networks Act	Requires the NCCIC to be the lead federal civilian agency for cross-sector sharing of information related to cyberthreat indicators and cybersecurity risks for federal and non-federal entities. Expands the NCCIC's functions.
			Directs the Under Secretary for Science and Technology to provide to Congress an updated strategic plan to guide the overall direction of federal physical security and

(*Continued*)

144

Bills Proposed Concerning Critical Infrastructure *(Continued)*

			cybersecurity technology research and development efforts for protecting CI. Requires the plan to identify CI security risks and any associated security technology gaps. Requires the Under Secretary to produce a report on the feasibility of creating a risk-informed prioritization plan in the case that multiple CIs experience cyber incidents simultaneously.
114	HR 1731	National Cybersecurity Protection Advancement Act	Amends the Homeland Security Act of 2002 to require DHS's NCCIC to oversee information sharing across CI sectors, with state and major urban area fusion centers and with small and medium-sized businesses. Redesignates DHS's National Protection and Programs Directorate as the Cybersecurity and Infrastructure Protection. Directs the Under Secretary for Science and Technology to provide an updated strategic plan to guide the overall direction of federal physical security and cybersecurity technology research and development efforts for protecting CI. The plan should identify CI security risks and any associated security technology gaps and identify programmatic initiatives for the advancement and deployment of security technologies for CI protection, including public–private partnerships, intragovernment collaboration, university centers of excellence, and national laboratory technology transfers.
114	HR 2271	Critical Electric Infrastructure Protection Act	Amends the Federal Power Act to authorize the Department of Energy (DOE) to issue orders for emergency measures to protect the reliability of either the bulk-power system or the defense critical electric infrastructure whenever the President issues a written directive identifying an imminent grid security emergency.

(Continued)

145

Bills Proposed Concerning Critical Infrastructure (*Continued*)

			Instructs DOE, before issuing an order for such emergency measures, to consult with governmental authorities in Canada and Mexico, regarding implementation of the emergency measures.
			Requires DOE to identify facilities in the US and its territories that are critical to the defense of the US, and vulnerable to a disruption of the supply of electric energy provided by an external provider.
			Exempts critical electric infrastructure information from mandatory disclosure requirements under the FOIA.
			Directs the FERC to designate critical electric infrastructure information, and prescribe regulations and orders prohibiting its unauthorized disclosure but also authorizing appropriate voluntary sharing with federal, state, local, and tribal authorities.
			Shields a person or entity in possession of critical electric infrastructure information from any cause of action for sharing or receiving information that was done in accordance with this Act.
114	HR 2402	Protecting CI Act	This bill amends the Federal Power Act to exempt protected electric security information from mandatory public disclosure under the FOIA. It also prohibits any state, local, or tribal authority from disclosing such information pursuant to state, local, or tribal law.

NOTE

1. Stevens, G. M., and Tatelman, T. B. September 27, 2006. *Protection of Security-Related Information. Congressional Research Service.* Retrieved from: http://fas .org/sgp/crs/secrecy/RL33670.pdf.

8

DHS Perspective on Risk

INTRODUCTION

The events of September 11, 2001, catapulted the concept of "risk" to the lips of every public policy maker and public official. Long regarded as a private sector term it is often found in the fields of science and engineering, the notion of managing risks associated with the safety, security, and resilience of our nation became the central focus for the newly formed Department of Homeland Security (DHS). The myriad of risks faced by the US has increased with each crisis, regardless of whether they are natural hazards, technological hazards, or terrorist events. The Joplin, Missouri, tornados from 2011; the 2015 Union Pacific train derailment in Texas during the remnants of Hurricane Patricia flooding; and the terrorist attack in San Bernardino, California, are just a few recent examples of hazards that caused loss of life, injuries, and loss of economic activity.

As these events illustrate, we live in a dynamic and uncertain world where previous events do not always shed light on the future. The San Bernardino attacks clearly were a game changer with the realization that social media has a "dark side" where encryption and radicalization has gone undetected by the best of our counterterrorism professionals. Once again, calculating risk morphs into a new reality.

While these events were not predicted, the managing of risks associated with the likelihood of such crises is the responsibility of the DHS and its partners. In this role, DHS must understand and manage these myriad homeland security risks.[1] As threats and hazards change, the challenge for DHS is to maintain the capability and capacity to identify, understand, and address all risks. It is the responsibility of the Office of Risk

147

Management and Analysis (RMA) to manage the advancement of risk management efforts by the homeland security enterprise.[2] In this capacity, RMA provides risk analysis, enhances risk management capabilities of partners, and integrates homeland security risk management approaches (see Note 2). It is in this latter role that policy initiatives for risk are generated. Establishing a common framework for homeland security risk management by developing policy, doctrine, guidance, and governance is essential to the RMA mission.

Three key documents have been produced which support this common framework: the *DHS Risk Lexicon*, *DHS Risk Management Process*, and the Fundamentals of *Risk Management Fundamentals* (see Note 2). These documents serve as doctrine to define the principles, process, and operational practices of effective homeland security risk management. They were created with the express intent to be used by DHS organizations and personnel. This chapter details these doctrines and their significance in defining the DHS perspective on risk.

DHS RISK LEXICON

To support the goal of building an integrated risk management (IRM) framework, the DHS Risk Steering Committee (RSC) produced a document with definitions and terms that are fundamental to the practice of homeland security RMA. Initiated in 2008, the DHS Risk Lexicon provides a common language to improve the capability of the DHS to assess and manage homeland security risk. Initially, the DHS Risk Lexicon contained 23 terms developed by an RSC working group known as the Risk Lexicon Working Group (RLWG). Validated against glossaries used by other countries and professional associations, the definitions serve as a tool to improve capabilities of DHS to assess and manage homeland security risk. In 2010, the second edition of the DHS Risk Lexicon was published with an additional 50 new terms and definitions.[3] These definitions are developed through a three-phase process and include:

- **Collection**—terms are collected from across DHS and the risk community.
- **Harmonization**—a single meaning for each term is produced by taking multiple, and often conflicting definitions, and synthesizing them.
- **Validation, Review, and Normalization**—non-DHS sources are used for validating harmonized definitions to guarantee that the

definitions produced for use in DHS are consistent with those used by the larger risk community. The entire RLWG is provided with proposed definitions for comment, which are debated and standardized for grammar and format.[4]

Among the key terms are definitions of risk, risk assessment, risk analysis, and risk-based decision making. The student of risk management policy would benefit from reviewing all the terms described in the document. The DHS Risk Lexicon provides a definition, sample usage of the term, and an annotation that describes in more detail how the term is used. For example, the definition of *risk-based decision making* is described as follows:

> **Definition:** determination of a course of action predicated primarily on the assessment of risk and the expected impact of that course of action on that risk.
>
> **Sample Usage:** After reading about threats and vulnerabilities associated with vehicle explosives, she practiced risk-based decision making by authorizing the installation of additional security measures.
>
> **Annotation:** Risk-based decision making uses the assessment of risk as the primary decision driver, while risk-informed decision making may account for multiple sources of information not included in the assessment of risk as significant inputs to the decision process in addition to risk information. Risk-based decision making has often been used interchangeably, but incorrectly with risk-informed decision making" (see Note 4, p. 33).

The DHS Risk Lexicon is used by DHS risk practitioners, decision makers, stakeholders, and state, local, tribal, and territorial government partners, as well as academia (see Note 4, p. 43). It is important to note that the DHS Risk Lexicon has helped in the development of institutional policy and technical guidelines, training and educational materials, as well as communications throughout the Homeland Security Enterprise (see Note 4, p. 43). A challenge of the DHS Risk Lexicon is that it must be constantly updated and maintained. This is accomplished through a partnership between the RLWG and DHS Lexicon program. Overseeing the maintenance of existing terms and the addition of new terms is a major focus. In addition, consistency with related federal interagency efforts must also be established. The Office of RMA continually collects information on risk-related lexicons and glossaries as they become available throughout the federal government (see Note 4, p. 42).

149

RISK MANAGEMENT GUIDELINES

These guidelines were published to serve as technically accurate primers for DHS risk analysis practitioners on key homeland security RMA processes and techniques. The first set of these guidelines were published in 2009 and included the following:

- Defining the decision context
- Developing scenarios
- Designing risk assessments
- Analyzing consequences
- Assessing indirect consequences in risk analysis
- Developing and evaluating alternative risk management strategies
- Communicating risk analysis results to decision makers

RISK MANAGEMENT FUNDAMENTALS

In 2011, an authoritative statement regarding the principles and process of homeland security risk management and what they mean to homeland security planning and execution was published. The release of this capstone document, Risk Management Fundamentals, was a major step forward in establishing a comprehensive homeland security risk doctrine.[5] The intent was to help develop a framework to make risk management an essential part of planning, preparing, and executing organizational missions. Homeland security leaders, supporting staffs, program managers, analysts, and operating personnel make use of this document in their efforts to promote risk management (see Note 1, p. 5). *Risk Fundamentals* is not a blueprint for homeland security action, but rather a doctrine to support homeland security practitioners and their own experiences. Specifically, the doctrine offers these five areas of purpose:

1. Promote a common understanding of, and approach to, risk management
2. Establish organizational practices that should be followed by DHS components
3. Provide a foundation for conducting risk assessments and evaluating risk management options

4. Set the doctrinal underpinnings for institutionalizing a risk management culture through consistent application and training on risk management principles and practices
5. Educate and inform homeland security stakeholders in risk management applications, including the assessment of capability, program, and operational performance, and the use of such assessments for resource and policy decisions (see Note 1, pp. 5–6)

POLICY FOR IRM

The Policy for IRM was established in May 2010, by then Secretary of Homeland Security, Janet Napolitano. Entitled, *DHS Policy for Integrated Management*, this document formalized many of the organizational aspects of the DHS risk effort. Specifically, it assigned lead responsibility to the National Protection and Programs Directorate and coordination authority to the Director of RMA. In addition, it established a number of key committees and processes to standardize risk across the DHS.[6] The policy supports the premise that security partners can most effectively manage risk by working together, and that management capabilities must be built, sustained, and integrated with federal, state, local, tribal, territorial, nongovernmental, and private sector homeland security partners (see Note 1, p. 1).

HOMELAND SECURITY RISK: TENETS AND PRINCIPLES

As suggested previously, the guidelines presented in the *Risk Management Fundamentals* are not designed to promote one way of doing risk management; rather, they offer broad guidelines that each organization may use to tailor to their own needs. The doctrine discourages a "one-size-fits-all" approach, but does suggest that all DHS risk management programs be based on two key tenets:

- Risk management should enhance an organization's overall decision-making process and maximize its ability to achieve its objectives.
- Risk management is used to shape and control risk, but cannot eliminate all risk (see Note 1, p. 11).

In addition to these two key tenets, DHS identifies five key principles for effective risk management which include:

- **Unity of Effort**—reiterates that homeland security risk management is an enterprise-wide process and should promote integration and synchronization with entities that share responsibility for managing risks.
- **Transparency**—establishes that effective homeland security risk management depends on open and direct communications.
- **Adaptability**—includes designing risk management actions, strategies, and processes to remain dynamic and responsive to change.
- **Practicality**—acknowledges that homeland security risk management cannot eliminate all uncertainty nor is it reasonable to expect to identify all risks and their likelihood and consequences.
- **Customization**—emphasizes that risk management programs should be tailored to match the needs and culture of the organization, while being balanced with the specific decision environment they support (see Note 1, pp. 11–12).

A COMPREHENSIVE APPROACH

Supporting the DHS Policy for IRM requires a comprehensive approach. According to the doctrine, *Risk Fundamentals*, a comprehensive approach improves decision making by allowing organizations to identify and balance internal and external sources of risk. Internal sources of risk include financial stewardship, personnel reliability, and systems reliability. External sources of risk may be identified as those that are caused by external factors. Global, political, and societal trends, as well as hazards from natural disasters, terrorism, cybercrimes, pandemics, and so forth are some examples (see Note 1, p. 13). Applying a comprehensive approach to risk management ensures that all risks are considered in a holistic manner. Risks should be managed as a system, while at the same time considering the underlying factors that directly impact organizational effectiveness and mission success (see Note 1, p. 13). DHS identifies three organizational risk categories which demonstrate the holistic nature of a comprehensive approach: (a) strategic risks, (b) operational risks, and (c) institutional risks. These categories are described in Table 8.1.

Table 8.1 DHS Organizational Risk Categories

	Strategic Risks	**Operational Risks**	**Institutional Risks**
Definition	Risk that affects an organization's vital interests or execution of a chosen strategy, whether imposed by external threats or arising from flawed or poorly implemented strategy.	Risk that has the potential to impede the successful execution of operations with existing resources, capabilities, and strategies.	Risk associated with an organization's ability to develop and maintain effective management practices, control systems, and flexibility and adaptability to meet organizational requirements.
Description	These risks threaten an organization's ability to achieve its strategy, as well as position itself to recognize, anticipate, and respond to future trends, conditions, and challenges. Strategic risks include those factors that may impact the organization's overall objectives and long-term goals.	Operational risks include those that impact personnel, time, materials, equipment, tactics, techniques, information, technology, and procedures that enable an organization to achieve its mission objectives.	These risks are less obvious and typically come from within an organization. Institutional risks include factors that can threaten an organization's ability to organize, recruit, train, support, and integrate the organization to meet all specified operational and administrative requirements.

Source: Department of Homeland Security. 2011. *Risk Management Fundamentals.*

Key Practices

Included in this comprehensive approach are three key requirements. According to the DHS, effective management of risk is fostered and executed through the following:

1. A commitment and active participation by an organization's leadership.
2. A consistent approach across the organization.
3. The ability to view risk on a comprehensive, enterprise-wide basis (see Note 1, p. 14).

DHS RISK MANAGEMENT PROCESS

The DHS Policy for IRM (Figure 8.1) directs DHS organizations to employ a standardized risk management process. It is the expressed purpose of this approach to encourage comparability and shared understanding of information and analysis in the decision-making process (see Note 1, p. 15). Comprised of seven planning and analysis efforts, the DHS risk management process is as follows:

1. **Defining and framing the context** of decisions and related goals and objectives

DHS risk management process

Figure 8.1 DHS risk management process. (From Department of Homeland Security. 2011. *Risk Management Fundamentals*. Washington, DC: US DHS.)

2. **Identifying the risks** associated with the goals and objectives
3. **Analyzing and assessing** the identified risks
4. **Developing alternative actions** for managing the risks and creating opportunities, and analyzing the costs and benefits of those alternatives
5. **Making a decision** among alternatives and implementing that decision
6. **Monitoring** the implemented decision and comparing observed and expected effects to help influence subsequent risk management alternatives and decisions
7. **Risk communications** underpinning the entire risk management process

Define and Frame the Context

This initial stage will inform and help to shape the successive stages of the risk management cycle. An organization is likely to pull together a risk analysis and management team to tackle complex risk issues. These are often referred to as planning teams, a workforce, or working group. To establish the context of risk, analysts must gain a strong understanding of the requirements and the environment in which the risks are to be managed. Among the considerations are policy concerns, goals and objectives, mission needs, decision makers and stakeholder interests, time frame, resources, and risk tolerance (see Note 1, p. 16).

Identify Potential Risk

The homeland security enterprise covers a wide array of risks and as such makes identifying them complicated. As mentioned previously, there are three organizational risk categories which can help sort out and identify potential risks: (a) strategic, (b) operational, and (c) institutional. Some of the techniques that DHS suggests include making a list according to "unusual," "unlikely," and "emerging" risks (see Note 1, p. 18). The scenarios are also used as a tool in the identification of potential risks. These are hypothetical situations that comprised of a hazard, an entity impacted by that hazard, and are associated conditions including consequences when appropriate (see Note 1, p. 19).

155

Assess and Analyze Risk

Assessing and analyzing risk includes the following components: determining a methodology, gathering data, executing the methodology, validating and verifying the data, and analyzing the outputs. It is interesting to note that risk practitioners will often move back and forth between these various components. Rarely will they occur in a linear fashion. Specifically, these components include the following:

Methodology—when choosing a risk assessment methodology, it is important to stay within the organization's capabilities. DHS defines "methodology" in its *Risk Fundamentals Doctrine* as "any logical process by which the inputs into an assessment are processed to produce outputs that inform the decision" (see Note 1, p. 20). According to DHS, the most important aspect to consider in selecting a methodology is the decision the assessment must inform. In other words, the methodology should be appropriate to inform the decision (see Note 1, p. 20). Complex methods should be avoided unless they are necessary to assess the risk. It is also a good strategy to look at similar assessments which have already been completed. Other considerations are data availability, time, financial, and personnel constraints. Homeland security risks are also assessed in terms of *likelihood* and *consequences* (see Table 8.2).

It is important to note, however, that there is no single methodology that is appropriate for measuring the likelihood of consequences of every risk. Furthermore, each methodology requires independent judgment regarding its design, and in some cases likelihood and consequences may not be necessary for the assessment.

Methodologies also might include considering homeland security risks as a function of *threats, vulnerabilities, and consequences* (TVC).

Table 8.2 Homeland Security Risks: Likelihood and Consequences

Likelihood is the chance of something happening, whether defined, measured, or estimated in terms of general descriptors, frequencies, or probabilities.

Consequences (or impact) include the loss of life, injuries, economic impacts, psychological consequences, environmental degradation, and inability to execute essential missions.[a]

Source: Department of Homeland Security. 2011. *Risk Management Fundamentals.* Washington, DC: US DHS.

[a] US DHS. 2011. *Risk Management Fundamentals.* Washington, DC: US DHS, p. 20.

This can be especially useful when assessing critical infrastructure protection. The TVC framework will be discussed in the next chapter.

As stated earlier, simple methodologies are preferred and most are sorted into qualitative and quantitative categories. Overall, the methodology that best meets the decision maker's needs is generally considered the best choice (see Note 1, p. 21).

Gathering Data—Sources for collecting data on risk information may come from a variety of places including historical records, models, simulations, and elicitations of experts in the field. It is necessary to consider all aspects of the decision, regardless of whether they can be quantified. For example, psychological impacts might be considered along with loss of life and financial losses. Sometimes there may be pieces of data that are unknown. These may be expressed as uncertainty in the outputs (e.g., a major earthquake in California might be estimated to fall within a range, with some values being more likely than others). Hence, it might be useful to consider the impact of the uncertainty along with the other pieces of data which have been collected (see Note 1, p. 21).

Validating and Presenting the Data—DHS suggests that throughout the risk assessment process, the gathered data and evidence should be carefully studied and compared with previous work. The data and evidence should be analyzed to identify relevant and interesting features to the decision maker, who may have a specified area they wish to focus (see Note 1, p. 22).

Developing Alternative Actions

In the risk assessment process, the ultimate objective is to provide decision makers with a structured way to recognize and select risk management actions. Developing viable alternatives provides leaders with a clear image of the potential benefits and costs of specific risk assessment options. According to DHS, the development of alternative risk management actions should:

- Be understandable to participants of the process, including decision makers and stakeholders
- Match and comply with the organization's relevant doctrine, standards, and plans
- Provide documentation with assumptions explicitly detailed
- Allow for future refinements

- Include planning for assessment of progress toward achieving desired outcomes (see Note 1, p. 22)

Additionally, DHS has outlined specific approaches that may be used to develop and evaluate alternatives (see Table 8.3).

Make Decision and Implement Risk Management Strategies

When a decision maker determines which alternatives are best for managing a specific risk, he or she can either decide to implement a new plan of action, or maintain an existing policy. In this process, the decision maker must consider the feasibility of implementing the options and how various alternatives will affect and ultimately reduce the risk. Other considerations include sufficient resources, capabilities, time, policies, legal issues, as well as the potential impact on stakeholders. Additionally, the possibility of the action creating new risks for the organization must also be taken into account (see Note 1, p. 24).The strengths and weaknesses of the alternatives should be clearly articulated so the decision is made on sound judgment. Implementing the decision needs to include proper leadership and a comprehensive project management approach.

Evaluation and Monitoring

This phase focuses on evaluating and monitoring the performance of the risk option to determine whether it has achieved the state goals and objectives. DHS warns that in addition to assessing performance, organizations

Table 8.3 DHS Methods for Developing and Evaluating Alternatives

- Reviewing lessons learned from relevant past incidents
- Consulting subject matter experts, best practices, and government guidelines
- Brainstorming
- Organizing risk management actions
- Evaluating options for risk reduction and residual risk
- Developing cost estimates for risk management actions
- Comparing the benefit of each risk management action with its associated cost
- Eliminating potential options.[a]

Source: Department of Homeland Security. 2011. *Risk Management Fundamentals.* Washington, DC: US DHS.
[a] US DHS. 2011. *Risk Management Fundamentals.* Washington, DC: US DHS, p. 24.

should guard against unintended adverse impacts such as creating additional risk or failing to recognize changes in risk characteristics (see Note 1, p. 25). While the implementation of the risk management program must be measured and improved, the action risk reduction measures must also be assessed. According to DHS, the evaluation should be conducted in a way that is commensurate with both the level of risk and the scope of the mission (see Note 1, p. 25). Effectiveness criteria are often used in this phase. This consists of tracking and reporting on performance results with concrete, realistic measures. For example, in situations where the decision maker decided to do nothing, the continued appropriateness of accepting the risk may be the best possible measure. In other situations, the best measure is often the reduction of the likelihood or consequences associated with a risk (see Note 1, p. 26). Some methods used in this evaluation phase include red teaming (scenario role-playing), exercises, external review, and surveys (see Note 1, p. 26).

Risk Communications

Central to the DHS risk management process are risk communications. For each element of the risk management process, effective communications with stakeholders, partners, and customers are critical. According to DHS, there must be a consistent, two-way communication throughout the process to ensure that decision makers, analysts, and officials in charge are able to implement any decision and share a common understanding of what the risk is and what factors may contribute to managing it (see Note 1, p. 15). It is important to note that communication requirements will differ according to the audience and time frame. DHS states that typically, risk communication is divided between internal and external audiences and between incident and standard time frames (see Note 1, p. 26). Table 8.4 illustrates these concepts.

According to DHS, an incident does not represent a break in the risk management process, but rather a temporary acceleration after which the process continues as normal (see Note 1, p. 26). Furthermore, risk communications will be most effective if guided by the following:

- Plan for communications
- Maintain trust
- Use language appropriate to the audience
- Be both clear and transparent
- Respect the audience concerns
- Maintain integrity of information (see Note 1, p. 28)

Table 8.4 Department of Homeland Security Risk Communication Audiences

Internal Risk Communications—Some risk communications are internal to an organization, for example between analysts and decision makers.

External Risk Communications—Occur when the public and cross-agency nature of homeland security risk necessitates that DHS communicate with external stakeholders, partners, and the public.

Incident Communications (also referred to as "crisis communications")—This takes place under different conditions than standard communications. During a crisis the need to explain the situation clearly becomes a priority. Public officials must operate under extraordinary time constraints to get out factual and potentially lifesaving information.

Standard Communications—After a crisis event, standard communications should resume so that all stakeholders build a common understanding of what has happened, why certain decisions were made, and how to move forward.[a]

[a] US DHS. 2011. *Risk Management Fundamentals*. Washington, DC: US DHS, p. 27.

CONCLUSION

An understanding of the DHS perspective on risk management is an important objective for the student of risk policy. Essential to this understanding are three key documents: the DHS Risk Lexicon, DHS Risk Management Process, and Risk Management Fundamentals. Promoting the understanding of sound risk management principles, and establishing and sustaining a risk management culture across DHS and its partners is the major focus of this perspective. Furthermore, applying consistent doctrine is a critical step toward creating a cohesive approach to homeland security.

REVIEW QUESTIONS

1. How does the DHS define risk?
2. Explain the documents Risk Management Fundamentals, the DHS Risk Lexicon, and the DHS Risk Management Process.
3. Discuss the IRM approach. Why has DHS adopted it and what is the significance for critical infrastructure protection?
4. List and describe the four risk communications audiences. Give an example for each one.

NOTES

1. US DHS. April 2011. *Risk Management Fundamentals: Homeland Security Risk Management Doctrine.* Washington, DC: US DHS, p. 1, pp. 5–6, pp. 11–16, pp. 18–22, pp. 24–26, p. 28.
2. US DHS. http://www.dhs.gov/office-risk-management-and-analysis-mission.
3. US DHS. http://www.dha.gov/dhs-risk-lexicon.
4. US DHS. 2010. *DHS Risk Lexicon.* Washington, DC: US DHS, p. 2, p. 33, p. 42, p. 43.
5. US DHS. 2011. *Strategies and Methods for Informing Risk Management: An Alternative Perspective,* A White Paper. Washington, DC: US DHS, p. 10.
6. Napolitano, J. May 27, 2010. *DHS Policy for Integrated Risk Management,* memorandum. Washington, DC: US DHS.

9
Methods of Risk Assessment

INTRODUCTION

As presented in Chapter 8, the Department of Homeland Security (DHS) has made strides to standardize risk and vulnerability assessment through an integrated risk management (IRM) approach. Prior to DHS implem enting the IRM approach, a myriad of methods, from cost–benefit analyses to evaluations, have been used to assess risk. Over the years, a considerable amount of money has been spent on various methods and software approaches to managing risk. Programs such as Risk Analysis and Management for Critical Asset Protection (RAMCAP™), CARVER Target Analysis and Vulnerability Assessment, and The Partnership for Safe and Secure Communities (PASCOM) have been used at the federal, state, and local levels. The current system in place is the Threat and Hazard Identification and Risk Assessment (THIRA) method. The National Infrastructure Protection Plan (NIPP) 2013 calls for employing the THIRA process as a method to integrate human, physical and cyber elements of critical infrastructure risk. In this chapter, we will briefly examine these earlier methods of risk assessment and focus on the current approach favored by the DHS and the Federal Emergency Management Agency (FEMA).

BRIEF DISCUSSION OF EARLIER RISK ASSESSMENT METHODS

Enhancing the security of our nation's CI has advanced tremendously since 9/11. Along the way there have been numerous approaches to assessing and managing risk. Many of these methods were borrowed from the private sector and have their roots in the fields of engineering, science, and the military. However, the transfer of these techniques to the public sector has not been seamless. Risk management can mean something different to everyone and the quest to standardize a common risk approach has been a major goal of DHS. The current approach favored by the DHS and the FEMA, is the "IRM" approach. The goal of the IRM is to identify, evaluate, prioritize, counter, and monitor the likelihood, vulnerability, and consequences of threats, natural hazards, and natural disasters to local people, property, infrastructure, and environment.[1] This approach serves as the basis of the THIRA, as described in *Comprehensive Preparedness Guide (CPG) 201: Threat and Hazard Identification and Risk Assessment Guide*.[2]

RAMCAP, CARVER, AND PASCOM

Before THIRA, other methodologies were used by state and local governments in conjunction with the DHS in their efforts to standardize risk assessment. One of these, RAMCAP, is a framework for analyzing and managing risks associated with terrorist attacks against CIs. The purpose is to provide government decision makers with essential information about consequences and vulnerabilities in the private sector, which owns 85% of the nation's CI.[3] The program is a seven-step process for assets analysis (asset characterization, threat characterization, consequence analysis, vulnerability analysis, threat assessment, risk assessment, and risk management). It is unique in that it facilitates the comparison of risks within a sector and across multiple sectors by employing a common terminology and standardized measurement metrics (see Note 3). This methodology is sector-specific in application, meaning the process is tailored to specific aspects of the 16 CI sectors. These are compiled in documents called sector-specific guidance (SSGs) documents. These SSGs assist companies to identify and report on the vulnerabilities and potential consequences of terrorism by providing guidance on how to complete both preliminary and in-depth assessments.

CARVER was originally developed by the US military to identify areas within critical or military infrastructures that may be vulnerable to an attack by the US Special Forces. It is a six-step approach to conducting security vulnerability assessments on CI. It identifies the following critical component of an asset that meets that requirement:

- Critically
- Accessibility
- Recuperability

- Effect
- Recognizability

Later, it was adopted by the FDA and the US Department of Agriculture for the food and agriculture CI sectors. The approach allows food companies to analyze and identify critical areas that are most likely targets of an attack.[4] CARVER + Shock will be discussed in greater detail in Chapter 10.

As part of the Partnerships for Safe and Secure Communities, PASCOM was developed as a process for communities to systematically identify critical assets, conduct community vulnerability assessments, and develop executive preparedness programs in a manner that is tailored to the individual community's profile. PASCOM is an assessment tool that communities may use to identify its critical assets, create threat scenarios, assess vulnerabilities, and analyze risk.[5]

FEDERAL GUIDELINES FOR RISK ASSESSMENT

Current methods of risk assessment must begin with a discussion of federal guidelines. On March 30, 2011, President Barack Obama signed Presidential Policy Directive 8 (PPD-8): National Preparedness. This directive was a result of the realization that first responders cannot do it all by themselves and began a new chapter with the intent and scope of national preparedness.[6] The new policy theme that emerged was that capabilities required a whole community approach—from the federal government to individual citizens. In this approach, leaders at all levels of government, private industry, nonprofit organizations, and the public must work together in a systematic effort to keep the nation safe and resilient when struck by catastrophic events such as natural disasters, acts of terrorism, cyberthreats, technological incidents, and pandemics.[7] The goal of the policy directive is to ensure that federal departments and agencies work with the whole community to develop a national preparedness goal and a system to guide and track activities toward that preparedness goal. Within this framework there are five mission areas of national preparedness: *prevention, protection, mitigation, response,* and *recovery.* By far, the most significant of these missions is prevention. Methods of risk assessment are embodied in the idea that prevention is the key to thwarting future catastrophic events. If you prevent an event from happening—it cannot occur.

Within the National Preparedness Goal are 31 core capabilities categorized by the five mission areas (see Table 9.1). The core capabilities are essential elements that are needed to achieve the National Preparedness Goal.[8]

Table 9.1 Core Capabilities by Mission Area

Prevention	Protection	Mitigation	Response	Recovery
		Planning **Public Information and Warning** **Operational Coordination**		
Forensics and attribution	Access control and identity verification	Community resilience	Critical transportation	Economic recovery
Intelligence and information sharing	Cybersecurity	Long-term vulnerability reduction	Environmental response/health and safety	Health and social services
Interdiction and disruption	Intelligence and information sharing	Risk and disaster resilience assessment	Fatality management services	Housing
Screening, search, and detection	Interdiction and disruption	Threats and hazard identification	Infrastructure systems	Infrastructure systems
	Physical protective measures		Mass care services	Natural and cultural resources
	Risk management for protection programs and activities		Mass search and rescue operations	
	Screening, search, and detection		On-scene security and protection	
	Supply-chain integrity and security		Operational communications	
			Public and private services and resources	
			Public health and medical services	
			Situational assessment	

Source: FEMA. October 2014. *Jurisdictional Threat and Hazard Identification and Risk Assessment Training Support Package,* pp. 1–8.

In order to meet the National Preparedness Goal, the National Preparedness System (NPS) was developed to provide an integrated set of guidance, programs, and processes. The NPS provides an all-of-nation approach for building and sustaining a cycle of preparedness activities over time. The following are six essential parts to this system:

- Identifying and assessing risk
- Estimating capability requirements
- Building and sustaining capabilities
- Planning to deliver capabilities
- Validating capabilities
- Reviewing and updating (see Note 7, pp. 1–9)

These six components of the NPS include specific resources and tools to assist communities in building strong preparedness programs. In support of these components, National Planning Frameworks were established to set the strategy and doctrine for building, sustaining, and delivering the 31 core capabilities identified in the National Preparedness Goal. These frameworks cover all five mission areas and are built to be scalable, flexible, and adaptable. They also provide a common terminology and overall approach. The strength of the National Planning Frameworks is that they are movable—and easily adapted to various jurisdictions. Things tend to change quickly and the frameworks have the ability to be expanded or contracted based upon need. The frameworks address the roles of individuals, nonprofit entities and governments, nongovernmental organizations (NGOs), the private sector, communities, CI, governments, and the nation as a whole (see Note 7, pp. 1–11). In terms of developing a risk assessment plan, the National Planning Frameworks are crucial—especially when creating a THIRA. The frameworks contain detailed information about the 31 core capabilities, which are needed to properly define desired outcomes, set capability targets, and specify appropriate resources (see Note 7, pp. 1–11).

THIRA PROCESS

The DHS/FEMA THIRA process is a framework that provides a comprehensive approach for identifying risks and associated impacts. This process helps a community to understand which risks it faces by providing a common assessment in which they can identify threats and hazards of greatest concern (see Note 7, pp. 1–20). Such threats and hazards would

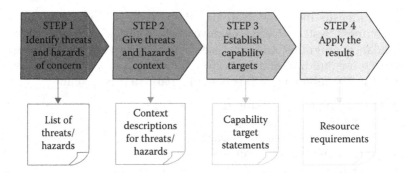

Figure 9.1 Four-step threat and hazard identification and risk assessment (THIRA) process. (From US DHS. 2013. *Threat and Hazard Identification and Risk Assessment Guide [CPG-201]*, 2nd ed., p. 2).

most stress the core capabilities of the community. The process is completed in four steps (see Figure 9.1):

1. Identify threats and hazards of concern
2. Give the threats and hazards context
3. Establish capability targets
4. Apply the results

Step 1: Identify Threats and Hazards of Concern

In Step 1 of the THIRA process, communities develop a list of community-specific threats and hazards. These will be unique to your own jurisdiction, therefore community leaders and first responders will need to collaborate on identifying the specifics of these threats and hazards of concern. Three categories must be taken into consideration (see Table 9.2):

- Natural hazards
- Technological hazards
- Human-caused incidents

Additionally, there are two factors which must be considered when selecting threat and hazards for inclusion in the THIRA:

1. The likelihood of the incident
2. The significance of the threat/hazard effects (see Note 7, pp. 1–22)

Table 9.3 shows an example of what Step 1 looks like in the THIRA process.

Table 9.2   Threat and Hazard Examples

Natural	Technological	Human-Caused
Avalanche	Airplane crash	Biological attack
Animal disease	Dam failure	Chemical attack
outbreak	Levee failure	Cyber incident
Drought	Mine accident	Explosives attack
Earthquake	Hazardous materials	Radiological attack
Epidemic	release	Sabotage
Flood	Power failure	School and workplace
Hurricane	Radiological failure	violence
Landslide	Train derailment	
Pandemic	Urban conflagration	
Tornado		
Tsunami		
Volcanic eruption		
Wildfire		
Winter storm		

Source: FEMA. October 2014. *Jurisdictional Threat and Hazard Identification and Risk Assessment Training Support Package*, pp. 1–22.

Table 9.3   Step 1 Examples

Natural	Technological	Human-Caused
Resulting from acts of nature	Involves accidents or the failures of systems and structures	Caused by the intentional actions of an adversary
Earthquake	Accidental chemical releases	Improvised explosive device (IED)

Source: FEMA. October 2014. *Jurisdictional Threat and Hazard Identification and Risk Assessment Training Support Package.* pp. 1–21.

Step 2: Give Threats and Hazards Context

In Step 2 of the THIRA process, context descriptions are given which outline the conditions, including time and location, under which a threat or hazard might occur. Essentially the question asked is, "How will the threat or hazard affect your community?" It is suggested that during this step communities seek out experts or analyze statistics to better inform their descriptions (see Note 7, pp. 1–23). It is important that communities consider only those threats that would affect them. For example, if you live in Cleveland, Ohio and are developing a THIRA, you would not add a context to the natural hazard of an avalanche. However, you would add context to the threat of a winter storm or tornado.

Step 3: Establish Capability Targets

Once you have established your context descriptions in Step 2, you will use them in Step 3 to assess each threat and hazard in context and develop a specific capability target for each of the 31 core capabilities identified in the National Preparedness Goal (see Table 9.1; Note 7, pp. 1–24). This is an important step as the capability targets define what it would take for the community to successfully meet the challenge of the threat (see Note 7, pp. 1–24). In this step, communities can also begin to identify preparedness activities. This might include establishing a list of resources and venues in the community where shelters could be established in the event the threat or hazard does occur.

Step 4: Apply the Results

The results of the THIRA are then applied by creating a list of resources needed to successfully manage the risk. In this step, communities will consider specific activities that will reduce the need for extra resources in the future. For example, suppose the power goes out due to a winter ice storm. You have established that you will need to provide 72 hours of power to shelter in a local high school. You might need to consider generators, food services, water, and volunteers. Other resource requirements can be created to support resource allocation decisions, operations planning, and mitigation activities. The goal here is to consider activities that you can handle at the local level which would reduce the risk for extra resources in the future (see Note 7, pp. 1–25). Table 9.4 illustrates a short example of what a partial THIRA might look like.

Benefits of Conducting a THIRA

There are a number of benefits for using the THIRA method of risk assessment in your community. These include the following:

- Long-term strategy and risk-based decision making
- Gap analysis and shortfall planning
- Standardized process/risk management aid
- Tie to National Preparedness Report (NPR) Findings
- Compliance with grant requirements (see Note 7, pp. 1–27)

Table 9.4 Example of a Partial Threat and Hazard Identification and Risk Assessment (THIRA)

Threat/Hazard	Earthquake
Context description	A magnitude 7.8 earthquake along the mainline fault occurring at approximately 2:00 p.m. on a weekday with ground-shaking and damage expected in 19 counties, extending from Alpha County in the south to Tau County in the north, and into the Zeta Valley.
Core capability: mass search and rescue operations	
Capability target	Within 72 hrs, rescue: 5000 people in 1000 completely collapsed buildings 1000 people in 2000 noncollapsed buildings 20,000 people in 5000 buildings 1000 people from collapsed light structures
Resource requirements	
Resources	Number required
Type I US&R task forces	10
Type II US&R task forces	38
Collapse search and rescue (S&R) type III teams	100
Collapse S&R type IV teams	20
Canine S&R type I teams	20

Source: FEMA. October 2014. *Jurisdictional Threat and Hazard Identification and Risk Assessment Training Support Package,* pp. 1–26.

Long-Term Strategy and Risk-Based Decision Making

A major goal of the THIRA is to get communities thinking in terms of strategies that are long term and specific. It is an economic reality that most jurisdictions are not fully equipped with the resources necessary to meet the challenges that a major disaster would present. The THIRA process empowers communities to plan for the long term by encouraging the whole community to focus on those likely threats and hazards that would have a significant impact on them (see Note 7, pp. 1–27). The ability to identify future trends and challenges, and then meet them with the appropriate resources is a critical aspect of this long-term strategy. Decisions must be risk based in order to avoid implementing an unsound strategy.

Gap Analysis and Shortfall Planning

The THIRA does not include a process for measuring gaps—it only identifies capability targets and resource needs. However, by performing additional analyses and comparing them to previous ones, planners can determine if gaps exist. In their shortfall planning, communities may have to rely on mutual aid agreements, memorandums of understanding (MOUs) with private and nonprofit sector partners, or other formalized processes to meet the capabilities they lack (see Note 7, pp. 1–28). Strategies to build the capabilities they lack may be part of the long-term planning process and may include such things as planning, personnel, equipment, training, exercise needs, and ways to resource these needs (see Note 7, pp. 1–28).

Standardized Process/Risk Management Aid

The THIRA process provides a common framework for identifying community-specific threats and hazards. It is also a means by which jurisdictions can learn from each other as they consider threats and hazards and develop preparedness activities. This standardized process also serves as an excellent risk management tool for all stakeholders. By participating in the THIRA process, communities begin to understand their particular risks. Once the THIRA is completed, they are able to make smart, information-based decisions on how to manage those risks and develop needed capabilities (see Note 7, pp. 1–28).

Tie to NPR Findings

In addition to informing individual communities of specific threats and hazards and the capabilities and resources needed to address them, the THIRA helps to inform and develop the NPR. If you recall, the NPR is required annually by PPD-8 and it summarizes progress in building and sustaining, and delivering the 31 core capabilities. It provides a national perspective on critical preparedness trends and is used to inform program priorities, allocate resources, and to communicate with stakeholders on common issues (see Note 7, pp. 1–28).

Compliance with Grant Requirements
In order to receive some types of federal assistance through the various DHS grant programs, many local, tribal, and state entities have been required to develop and maintain a THIRA to support their State Preparedness Report (SPR). Some of the programs that require THIRA are the Homeland Security Grant Program (HSGP), the Tribal Homeland Security Grant Program (THSGP), and the Emergency Management Performance Grants (EMPG). The requirements usually mandate that the THIRA be updated annually, and that they include a capability estimation process for a subset of the core capabilities.

Implementation of the Four-Step THIRA Process

In order to understand how the THIRA process is implemented, it is useful to take a deeper look at these four steps, and examine the specific factors that must be included.

Step 1: Identify Threats and Hazards of Concern
In this first step, communities must identify jurisdictional threats and hazards by considering threat and hazard groups, sources of information, and essential key factors. Here, communities will develop a list of specific threats and hazards that would overwhelm the community's core capabilities (Table 9.1). Throughout this step, communities should consider all of the different types of threats and hazards and the likelihood and significance of possible threats before including them in the actual THIRA document (see Note 7, pp. 2–4). Remember, the THIRA process considers three different types of threats and hazards: *natural, technological,* and *human-caused*. Developing an understanding of which threats and hazards pose the greatest risk, is the goal. As such, it would be helpful to review what significant threats and hazards have occurred in the past. Considering whether the previous incident could happen again and have the same impact on the community should also be debated. For example, a city in the Midwest might consider the effect of flash flooding after a significant amount of rainfall in a short period of time. The history of this natural threat should be researched to determine the likelihood of it occurring again. Has anything been done to mitigate the effects of a similar incident occurring again? If so, the community should explore the state of their current flood control measures, such as dams and levees (see Note 7, pp. 2–8). Additionally, local leaders

173

should be included in this first step to help build community support and to appropriate and or request necessary resources (see Note 7, pp. 2–7). It may also be beneficial to consider the threats and hazards of similar communities and how they have responded. The following is a list of some of the sources communities can access to help identify threats and hazards in this first step:

- State and local homeland security and emergency management laws, plans, policies, and procedures
- Existing hazard and risk assessments
- Local regional and neighboring community THIRAs
- After-action reports from community exercises
- Analysis of CI interdependencies
- Fusion Centers—bulletins and assessments

Whole community partners such as:

- Emergency management/homeland security agencies
- Local and state hazard mitigation offices
- Local or Regional National Weather Service offices
- Tribal governments
- FEMA Regional Offices
- Private sector partners
- Local/state fire, police emergency medical services, and health departments
- DHS Protective Services Advisors
- DHS Regional Cybersecurity Analysts
- Volunteer Organizations Active in Disasters
- Colleges/universities and other research organizations (see Note 7, pp. 2–8)

While completing the first step of the THIRA process, communities should only consider those threats and hazards which are deemed to be of greatest concern. The DHS recommends the two key factors tobe used to assist in identifying those threats and hazards of major concern: likelihood of the incident and the significance of the threat/hazard effects on the community (see Note 7, pp. 2–9). Likelihood is explained as the chance of something happening, whether defined, measured, or estimated objectively or subjectively. It is best determined by focusing on only those threats and hazards that could plausibly occur. While historical information is useful in this analysis, future likelihood should also be considered. A good example is the notion that a terrorist attack will never occur in a particular jurisdiction. Recent events have shown that a terrorist event can occur almost anywhere. Communities should not assume that since a terrorist attack has not occurred in their jurisdiction that it will not happen in the future. Rather, they need to consult with local law enforcement and other intelligence gathering agencies (such as the Joint Terrorism Task Force [JTTF], and fusion centers) to determine the likelihood of an attack happening. Similarly, natural disasters may be evaluated based off of past occurrences, but changing weather patterns should also be studied. The unpredictability of earthquakes, tornados, hurricanes, and flooding, and the devastation they bring, should be considered along with the historical data of the jurisdiction (see Note 7, pp. 2–8).

The second factor to consider is what effects will the threats or hazards have on the community? DHS advises that communities only consider those threats and hazards that would pose a serious strain on the community's ability to respond; that would cause operational coordination problems, or those that would cause great economic or social challenges (see Note 7, pp. 2–10). A good strategy is for communities to focus on threats beyond which they are currently prepared to manage. They should also consider the effects of other factors that may make a given threat or hazard worse (see Note 7, pp. 2–10). These might include shifting demographics toward coastal areas prone to natural disasters, systemic failures of CI (such as power grid failure and loss of potable water system), and reliance on technology. In some cases, these may adversely impact the disaster management services the community can activate, making a minor threat much worse (see Note 7, pp. 2–10).

Step 2: Give Threats and Hazards Context
Adding context to the local threats and hazards identified in Step 1 allows jurisdictional leaders and stakeholders to define the circumstances under which the threats or hazards might occur. This allows a more robust description of specific situations and gives planners a sense of scale for the impacts of the threat and hazards. The key is to develop context descriptions that are both detailed and relevant. DHS describes seven threat and hazard description factors: *time, place, adverse conditions, demographics, climate, built environment,* and *community infrastructure* (see Table 9.5); (Note 7, pp. 3–6). It is critical to bring these potential events into reality for your jurisdiction. You want this stage of the planning process to be outside of your current capabilities.

Table 9.5 Threat and Hazard Description Factors

Time

Jurisdictional leaders and stakeholders should look at the impact an incident would have at a particular time of day and whether the jurisdiction would be able to manage it. Some examples are a shopping mall on Black Friday, day versus weekdays, holidays, or annual festivals. The season of the year should also be considered as to which would have the greatest impact on the jurisdiction's ability to respond.

Place

Where is the location that the incident may occur? Is it a heavily populated area, in a commercially zoned location, or in a business district of the community? Do adequate entrance and exit routes exist to allow first responders to quickly contain the incident, and to provide for a well-ordered evacuation?

Adverse Conditions

Are there other circumstances that could influence the jurisdiction's ability to manage the incident? Has the impact of atmospheric conditions been considered, such as wind direction and speed or relative humidity, which might accelerate the harmful impact of a threat? What if there are multiple incidents occurring at the same time? Is the jurisdiction able to manage more than one event?

Demographics

What are the demographics of the jurisdiction? Is there a large retirement population living in special housing? Will they require assistance in the event of an evacuation? What percentage of the community is lesser than the age of 18 years of age? Do you have a population consisting of non-English-speaking citizens? How will you help them understand the nature of the incident and instructions for their safety?

Climate

Climate is important to consider, especially during a response. Does the jurisdiction exist in an area where severe summer heat or harsh winter cold is the norm? Is the jurisdiction located in an area of climate change where, for example, coastal areas will be at risk due to rising sea levels and the potential for more intense storms?

Built Environment

All of the man-made structures within a geographical space that humans use for work, residences, or for leisure activities make up the built environment. Leaders must consider how the built environment impacts the jurisdiction's ability to manage the incident. Is there a need for more emergency medical services (EMS) due to a large retirement community? Is the community rural with limited built environment to support an adequate response process? Are there volunteer services (police, fire, and EMS)? Does the community need to rely on support from outside the community for these services, thus lengthening the time for response?

(Continued)

Table 9.5 (*Continued*)   Threat and Hazard Description Factors

Community Infrastructure

A community's infrastructure includes all the assets and organizations in the public and private sector that are part of normal life and economic activity in the area. A jurisdiction may begin defining the community infrastructure in the 16 different critical sectors:

- Chemical
- Commercial facilities
- Communications
- Critical manufacturing
- Dams
- Defense industrial base
- Emergency services
- Energy
- Financial services
- Food and agriculture
- Government facilities
- Healthcare and public health
- Information technology
- Nuclear reactors, materials, and waste
- Transportation systems
- Water and wastewater systems

Community infrastructure consists of not only local CI, but also secondary local assets that might be relied on in the event that the critical assets are affected by a threat or hazard. Such assets include interconnecting links, such as roads, rail, bridges, phone lines, power lines, and broadcast towers; natural resources (i.e., water); places of local cultural significance; and any other unique assets or facilities.[a,b]

Source: FEMA. October 2014. *Jurisdictional Threat and Hazard Identification and Risk Assessment Training Support Package.*
[a] FEMA. October 2014. *Jurisdictional Threat and Hazard Identification and Risk Assessment Participant Guide,* pp. 3–8, 3–9, and 3–10.
[b] FEMA. October 2014. *Jurisdictional Threat and Hazard Identification and Risk Assessment Participant Guide,* p. 4–1.

Step 3: Establish Capability Targets

In this third step of the THIRA process, jurisdictions will focus on the core capabilities, estimate the consequences of a threat or hazard, determine the desired outcomes, and finally develop capability target statements. Capability targets are best described as what the community wants to achieve in a particular area of preparedness (see Note 7, pp. 4–8).

These should be both measurable and specific in content. The impacts of the threats and hazards identified in Step 2 of the THIRA process should be used here to develop the capability targets. Essentially, communities must identify the core capabilities that will be needed (Table 9.1), and consider both the *impacts* of threats and the *desired outcomes* of community threat management. Impacts describe how a threat or hazard will affect core capability and is linked to the size and complexity of the incident (see Note 7, pp. 4–9). It is essential that community planners be able to interpret the impacts an incident could have on a jurisdiction. These impacts can be expressed in a variety of ways, such as the following:

- Size
- Complexity
- Casualties
- Disruption of CI
- Communications
- Economic impacts

Estimating impacts should involve whole community partners as well as local experts. Modeling software can be used to allow planners to better estimate the breadth and seriousness of the impacts of a given threat. One of these is HAZUS-MH—a geographic information system for natural hazards used by FEMA. It is a multihazard risk assessment tool that can model four types of hazards: (a) flooding, (b) hurricanes, (c) coastal surges, and (d) earthquakes. Another notable tool is the John Hopkins University Hospital's National Center for the Study of Preparedness and Catastrophe Event Response (PACER) suite. This includes three interactive modeling tools to help communities estimate human impacts: Emergency Mass Casualty Planning Scenarios (EMCAPS) 2.0, Surge, and Flucast. EMCAPS 2.0 allows local disaster management planners, hospitals, and medical planners to model different disaster scenarios in order to better estimate the human impacts of incidents. Surge supports medical planners to assess current hospital surge capacity, and Flucast is a tool for hospitals to determine weekly flu cases based upon historical data (see Note 7, pp. 4–15).

The *desired outcomes* are those standards to which a community will have successfully managed the incident. These may be expressed as level of effort in percentages and time frame of service delivery (see Note 7, pp. 4–18). Measurable percentages are most often used for the prevention, protection, and mitigation mission areas. For example, if the desired outcome is screening for threats, the outcome description might be to screen 100% of baggage, mail, and targeted cargo (see Note 7, pp. 4–19). The time frame is most often used for response and recovery mission areas. Success is often measured by communities delivering capabilities within a stated time frame. For example, recovering all fatalities within 24 hours of the incident, setting up warming shelters for displaced populations within 48 hours, and or completing search and rescue operations with 72 hours. Tables 9.6 and 9.7 illustrate some examples of desired outcomes expressed as measurable percentages and as time frames.

The next step is to create capability target statements. These are concise definitions of success that include both detailed, capacity-specific

Table 9.6 Example of Percentage-Based Desired Outcomes

Outcome Type	Example Outcome Description
Screening for threats	Screen 100% of targeted cargo, conveyances, mail, baggage, and people associated with an imminent terrorist threat or act using technical, nontechnical, intrusive, or nonintrusive means.
Verifying identity	Ensure 100% verification of identity to authorize, grant, or deny physical and cyber access to specific locations, information, and networks.

Source: FEMA. October 2014. *Jurisdictional Threat and Hazard Identification and Risk Assessment Training Support Package*, pp. 4–19.

Table 9.7 Example Time-Based Desired Outcomes

Outcome Type	Example Outcome Description
Completing operations	Complete evacuation of neighborhood within 4 hr.
Establishing services	Establish feeding and sheltering operations for displaced populations within 24 hr.
Service duration	Maintain behavioral screening checks for affected population for 1 mo.
Combination	Establish feeding and sheltering operations within 24 hr and maintain services for a period of 2 wk.

Source: FEMA. October 2014. *Jurisdictional Threat and Hazard Identification and Risk Assessment Training Support Package*, pp. 4–20.

impacts of an incident; and the measurable desired outcomes to which consequences must be managed. Capability target statements are starting points for communities to estimate the resources they will need. This is essentially why communities do the THIRA process. Capability target statements may be simple or complex depending upon how the community is assessing the threat. A simple example may come from combining the largest impacts with the corresponding desired outcomes. A complex example would go deeper and look at how different threats and hazards affect the same core capability in different ways (see Note 7, pp. 4–22). The advantages of developing a complex capability target is that it will account for the desired outcomes for delivering service during the worst impacts and allow for a more accurate view of given incidents and the resources needed to successfully manage them (see Note 7, pp. 4–23).

Step 4: Apply the Results

In this final step of the THIRA, communities will estimate the resources they will require to manage the threats and hazards, which were identified in Steps 1 through 3. This is the resource estimation process, and it begins with communities identifying the mission-critical activities needed to manage an incident. Mission-critical tasks are those which are critical to achieving the desired outcome. These are usually drawn from existing community-level plans or from the Nation Planning Frameworks (see Note 7, pp. 5–6). It is important to note that these are not on-the-scene, emergency responder tasks. Rather, these involve efforts of the whole community at a much larger, more strategic level. As part of this process, communities develop a list of resources they will need to effectively manage the incident. These resource requirements are the lists of critical items (plans, organization, equipment, training, and exercises) which will be needed to manage and resolve the effects of a disaster event. They can also be used in mitigation efforts (see Note 7, pp. 5–7).

A key consideration here is the use of existing plans and capabilities. Communities may have current plans in place that may be useful in identifying the resources they will need. Plans should be written to provide assistance on how to best use the resources on hand or those that will be provided through mutual aid or other agreements. Existing capabilities should also be determined. Communities must know what capabilities and resources they currently have and can deploy in response to an incident occurring within their jurisdiction (see Note 7, pp. 5–7).

Finally, resources may be categorized through a process known as *resource typing*. Resource typing is defining and categorizing, by

Table 9.8   Tier I and Tier II Type Resources

Tier I

National Incident Management System (NIMS).

The complete list of typed resources may be found at: https://rtlt.preptoolkit
.org/Public.

Tier II

State, tribal, and local-typed standardized, deployable, resources.

No FEMA-involved in defining or inventorying of these resources.

Includes: mutual aid resources and Emergency Management Assistance
Compact (EMAC) resources.

Source: FEMA. October 2014. *Jurisdictional Threat and Hazard Identification and
Risk Assessment Training Support Package,* pp. 5–9.

capability, the resources requested, deployed, and used in incidents. These
definitions establish a common language and defines a resource's (for
equipment, teams, and units) minimum capabilities. FEMA is responsible
for the development and maintenance of National Incident Management
System (NIMS) resource typing definitions that are national in scope.[9]
Here the resources are categorized by the level of service they are capable
of providing during response and recovery operations. Resource typing
includes requesting Tier I NIMS—typed assets as well as those localized,
Tier II, and other standardized resources (see Note 7, pp. 5–7). Table 9.8
illustrates these various types of resources.

Capacity/Capability Calculations

Jurisdictional leaders must learn how to calculate and develop written
resource requirements for any situation. Calculating the resource requirements for a community may be accomplished by looking at their existing and required capabilities, and the threat or hazard of concern. By
using the identified capability targets (Step 3), the operational capacities
of resources, and available time, communities can best determine what
resources they will need to manage an incident. A simple calculation
example is as follows:

Simple Calculation Example

- Mission critical activity: search buildings for survivors
- Identified Resource: Urban Search and Rescue (US&R) Task Forces
  (see Note 7, pp. 5–11)

Table 9.9 Calculation Example

Capability Target	Search 42 Type 1 Structures in 72 hr
Resource	Type 1 US&R task force.
Operational capacity	Type 1 US&R task force can search two Type 1 structures a day.
Time available	3 days (72 hr).
Calculated resource requirement	Seven Type 1 US&R task forces.

Source: FEMA. October 2014. *Jurisdictional Threat and Hazard Identification and Risk Assessment Training Support Package*, pp. 5–12.

The calculation process should be approached carefully with emphasis placed on finding the most appropriate resources for achieving the capability targets. In addition, the typical performance characteristics of those resources and how they might fare on local conditions should be considered. The level of detail should be kept to a minimum. DHS recommends using Tier I resource types, when possible. Table 9.9 illustrates a full calculation example.

Example of a Completed THIRA

Table 9.10 shows a completed THIRA from the State of New Mexico.[10] Notice the progression from capability target to resource requirement for the Critical Transportation Core Capability. Four different threats/hazards are identified: earthquake, terrorism, wildfire, and mass migration. In this example, notice the use of detail, and the inclusion of key points from each of the four steps in the THIRA process.

APPLYING THIRA RESULTS TO POLICY DECISIONS

Once the final calculations have been completed, communities may use the results of the THIRA to make critical decisions about how the community can achieve its capability targets through the allocation of resources. The results may indicate that the community must either sustain current capabilities or it may expose capability shortfalls and gaps (see Note 7, pp. 5–16). Conducting the THIRA is also beneficial in that community planners can use it achieve buy-in from government leaders, and the whole community to support making the necessary investments to build new or expand current capabilities (see Note 7, pp. 5–17). The THIRA is scalable, meaning it can be adjusted to fit the needs and profile

Table 9.10 Example of a Completed THIRA: State of New Mexico

Critical Transportation Core Capability

Desired Outcomes and Impacts

Threat/ Hazard	Desired Outcomes	Impacts
Earthquake	During the first 4 hr, Department of Homeland Security and Emergency Management (DHSEM) will coordinate with local Emergency Management to establish physical access by air for search and rescue and emergency lifesaving equipment and personnel. Within the first 4 hr, DHSEM in coordination with ESF #1 and ESF # 13 will assist local Emergency Management programs in identifying traffic control packages necessary to secure the affected area. During the first 24 hr, DHSEM will assist Local Emergency Management to establish full and unrestricted physical access by land to the affected area(s) for the delivery of required resources to save lives and to evacuate citizens at risk, special needs population, and animals from the affected area(s). During the first 24 hr, coordinate activities to acquire resources for local Emergency Management programs to meet the critical sustainment needs of citizens and emergency response personnel in the impacted area(s) for 2 weeks.	Extensive rockslides and debris are blocking major transportation and evacuation routes on Highways 502, 501, and 4. There is damage to two bridges on major roadways that has made them impassable. The need to maximize available ground transportation for movement of resources, personnel, and nonlife-threatening medical issues and evacuees is essential.

(Continued)

183

Table 9.10 (*Continued*) Example of a Completed THIRA: State of New Mexico

Critical Transportation Core Capability

Desired Outcomes and Impacts

Threat/ Hazard	Desired Outcomes	Impacts
Terrorism		Downtown area will be impassable. Debris removal will have to be completed to regain use of roadway. Roadways are within the perimeter of the incident. A large number of roadblocks will be needed to control access. Busses will be needed to transport people from the area.
Wildfire		Debris from burned vegetation, trees, and homes could be blocking roadways hindering evacuation from the area. Security concerns exist throughout incident area, so the need for security road blocks exist to keep criminal elements from entering area, and ensure evacuees do not return to area before it is rendered safe.
Mass migration		Six buses will be needed to move 2000 evacuees from approximately five collection points. Anticipate need for wreckers to move stranded cars blocking roadways; ESF 1 will coordinate this.

(Continued)

Table 9.10 (*Continued*)   Example of a Completed THIRA: State of New Mexico

Critical Transportation Core Capability

Desired Outcomes and Impacts

Threat/Hazard	Desired Outcomes	Impacts

Capability Targets

During the first 4 hr of the incident, DHSEM will coordinate with local Emergency Management to establish physical access by air for search and rescue and emergency lifesaving equipment and personnel. Within the first 4 hr, DHSEM in coordination with ESF # 1 and ESF # 13 will assist local Emergency Management programs in identifying traffic control equipment necessary to secure the affected area. Needed resources are 5–10 programmable directional signs, 100 road barriers, and over 1000 traffic cones. During the first 24 hr, DHSEM will assist Local Emergency Management to establish full and unrestricted physical access by land to the affected area(s) for the delivery of required resources to save lives and to evacuate citizens at risk, special needs population, and animals from the affected area(s). Support is needed for 3000 injured citizens, 6250 displaced citizens, 625 at risk and special needs population, and 250 animals in the affected area(s). During the first 24 hr, coordinate activities to acquire resources for local Emergency Management programs to meet the critical sustainment needs of citizens and emergency response personnel in the impacted area(s) for 2 weeks.

Resource Requirements: NIMS Tier I Resources

Group	Resource	Type	Number Required
Public Works	Buses	Type I	12
Animal Health Emergency	Large Animal Transport Team	Type I	2
Animal Health Emergency	Small Animal Transport Team	Type I	10
EMS	Air Ambulance (Rotary-Wing)	Type II	2
EMS	Air Ambulance (Fixed-Wing)	Type II	2
Incident Management	Evacuation Liaison Team (ELT)	Type I	1
Incident Management	Airborne Transport Team (Fixed-Wing)	Type II	2

(Continued)

185

Table 9.10 (*Continued*) Example of a Completed THIRA: State of New Mexico

Critical Transportation Core Capability

Desired Outcomes and Impacts

Threat/ Hazard	Desired Outcomes	Impacts	
Law Enforcement	Mobile Field Force Law Enforcement (Crowd Control Teams)	Type II	150
EMS	Ambulance Strike Team	Type II	20
EMS	Ambulance Strike Team	Type IV	20
Public Works	Civil/Field Engineer	Type I	10
Fire and Hazardous Materials	HazMat Entry Team	Type II	5

Resource Requirements: Other Resources

Resource	POETE	Number Required
National Guard search and rescue helicopters (Medivac)	Equipment	2
National Guard soldiers for traffic control along evacuation/reentry routes	Team	100
New Mexico Department of Transportation (NMDOT) directional road signs	Equipment	10
NMDOT jersey barriers	Equipment	100

Source: New Mexico Department of Homeland Security and Emergency Management. 2013. *State of New Mexico THIRA.* http://www.nmdhsem .org/local-thira-guidance.aspx.

of a particular community or jurisdiction. In that sense, the results can inform policy decisions at the smallest of levels (i.e., local, rural, tribal). THIRA is strategic planning which may assist communities to develop better preparedness and mitigation activities, and ultimately reduce the amount of resources needed in the future. It also fosters communications between policy makers, state and local authorities, emergency managers, and other stakeholders, ultimately contributing to policy decisions for emergency preparedness and disaster plans.

CONCLUSION

DHS has made significant strides to standardize risk and vulnerability assessment through an IRM. While previous methods have been used, DHS now supports the THIRA process and encourages its use by communities to identify capability targets and resource requirements necessary to address anticipated and unanticipated risks. Consistent application of the THIRA provides an important tool for integrating the whole community and for policy makers to make informed decisions on CI protection.

CLASS ACTIVITIES: DEVELOP A SAMPLE THIRA

Activity 1: Identify Threats and Hazards

Break into teams and create a list of jurisdictional threats and hazards. Each team will be assigned a local jurisdiction, and should choose three threats and three hazards, one from each category (natural, technological, and human-caused). Present your findings to the class.

Activity 2: Contextualize Threats and Hazards

Identify Community Infrastructure: Each team will be assigned a critical infrastructure (CI) sector from the list of 16 categories created by DHS. Within that sector, each team should identify as many specific examples of CI as they can that exist within their jurisdiction. Next, prioritize your identified specific examples (by which ones are most critical to the jurisdiction) and add up to two other characteristics, elements, events, or other factors important to the jurisdiction that might be useful in evaluating the significance of threats or hazards. Present your findings to the class.

Develop Context Descriptions for Jurisdictional Threats and Hazards: Each team will then chose *one* incident from the list of three threats and hazards of significant concern identified in activity one and create a context description. This should include the conditions (at a minimum time and location) most relevant to the community. Use Table 9.5 Threat and Hazard Description factors to develop your context descriptions. Present your findings to the class.

Activity 3: Establish Capability Targets

Estimate Impacts of a Threat of Hazard: Using the context descriptions developed in Activity 2, choose five core capabilities, one from each of the five mission areas (prevent, protect, mitigation, response, and recovery) that would pertain to managing the threat or hazard (see Table 9.1). Next, estimate impacts of the threat or hazard on the chosen capabilities. Present your findings to the class.

Develop Desired Outcomes and Capability Target Statements: Using all of the information created in the previous activities, each team will develop one desired outcome for each of the five core capabilities identified in the *Estimate Impacts of a Threat of Hazard* activity (mentioned earlier). Use the estimated impacts and the desired outcomes to develop one capability target statement for each of the core capabilities. Present your findings to the class.

Activity 4: Apply the Results

Using the capability target statements from each of the core capabilities previously identified in Activity 3, identify the necessary resources needed to request, deploy, and use to manage your incident. Your team will need to use the FEMA resource typing source found at https://rtlt .preptoolkit.org/Public. Calculate the resource requirements by considering the capability targets, operational capacities of resources, and time available. Present your final THIRA results to the class.

NOTES

1. US DHS. 2011. *Risk Management Fundamentals*. Washington, DC: US DHS.
2. DHS, FEMA. 2013. *Comprehensive Preparedness Guide (CPG) 201: Threat and Hazard Identification and Risk Assessment Guide*. Washington, DC: US DHS.
3. Aiding the Fight against Terrorism, ASME-ITI Gets Contract to Develop RAMCAP™ Guidelines to Protect Critical Infrastructure. *Business Wire*. 2006.
4. Government Training, Inc. 2006. *CARVER+Shock Vulnerability Assessment Tool*.
5. Eastern Kentucky University Justice and Safety Center. Retrieved from: http://jsc.eku.edu/pascom.

6. Caudle, S. 2012. Homeland security: advancing the national strategic position. *Homeland Security Affairs*, Vol. xiii.

7. DHS, FEMA. October, 2014. *Jurisdictional Threat and Hazard Identification and Risk Assessment Participant Guide*. Washington, DC: US DHS, pp. 1–28.

8. FEMA. October 2014. *Jurisdictional Threat and Hazard Identification and Risk Assessment Training Support Package*, pp. 1–26.

9. DHS, FEMA. October 2014. *Resource Management and Mutual Aid*. Retrieved from: https://www.fema.gov/resource-management-mutual-aid#.

10. New Mexico Department of Homeland Security and Emergency Management. 2013. *State of New Mexico THIRA*. Retrieved from: http://www.nmdhsem.org/local-thira-guidance.aspx

10

Sector-Specific Agencies'
Approaches to Risk
Food and Agriculture Sector, Water and Wastewater Sector, and Energy Sector

INTRODUCTION

In early 2013, President Obama announced Presidential Policy Directive 21 (PPD-21), *Critical Infrastructure Security and Resilience*, thus setting the stage for the next era in critical infrastructure protection policies. With this new plan, the number of critical sectors was reduced from 18 to 16, and a reorganization of a number of the Sector-Specific Agencies (SSAs) and their sectors took place. Each SSA develops a Sector-Specific Plan (SSP) through a coordinated effort involving its public and private sector partners. These plans detail how the National Infrastructure Protection Plan (NIPP) risk management framework is implemented within the context of the unique characteristics and risk environment of each sector.[1] SSPs are updated every 4 years to ensure that each sector is meeting evolving threats.

The most recent updates occurred in the year 2015 and address the increasing nexus between cyber and physical security, as well as the continued interdependence between various sectors, risks associated with

191

climate change, and an aging and outdated infrastructure.[2] These newer risks present continued challenges to critical infrastructure protection and the management of risk. The following chapters will explore the roles and responsibilities of these SSAs, each sector's own approach to risk management, as well as the policy implications. The sectors covered will serve as an example of the varied approaches and how each SSP tailors national strategic guidance to the unique operating conditions and risk landscape of its respective sector.

FOOD AND AGRICULTURE SECTOR PROFILE

Protecting the nation's food and agriculture infrastructure is a complex undertaking with responsibilities that extend beyond the boundaries of the US. The Food and Agriculture (FA) sector is comprised of systems that are almost entirely owned by private interests, which operate in highly competitive global markets.[3] The FA sector covers more than 935,000 restaurants and institutional food service establishments and an estimated 114,000 supermarkets, grocery stores, and other food retailers. With an estimated 2.1 million farms, and more than 200,000 registered food manufacturing, processing, and storage facilities, this sector accounts for roughly one-fifth of the nation's economic activity (see Note 3). As with all of the sectors, the FA sector has critical interdependencies with many sectors but specifically with the following sectors:

- Water and Wastewater sector—for clean irrigation and processed water
- Transportation sector—for movement of products and livestock
- Energy sector—to power the equipment needed for agriculture production and food processing
- Chemical sector—for fertilizers and pesticides used in the production of crops (see Note 1).

Some of these sector risks include food contamination and disruption (accidental or intentional), disease and pests, severe weather (droughts, floods, and climate variability), and cybersecurity. Under PPD-21, the US Department of Agriculture (USDA) and Department of Health and Human Services (HHS) were designated as the SSAs for the FA sector. The HHS has delegated this responsibility to the Food and Drug Administration (FDA) (see Note 3, pp. 5–7).

GOALS AND PRIORITIES OF THE FA SECTOR

The goals outlined in the FA SSA for the years 2015 to 2019 include the following:

- **Goal 1:** Continue to promote the combined federal, state, local, tribal, and territorial (SLTT), and private sector capabilities to prevent, protect against, mitigate, respond to, and recover from man-made and natural disasters that threaten the national FA infrastructure.
- **Goal 2:** Improve sector situational awareness through enhanced intelligence communities and information sharing among all sector partners.
- **Goal 3:** Assess all-hazards risks, including cybersecurity, to the FA sector.
- **Goal 4:** Support response and recovery at the sector level.
- **Goal 5:** Improve analytical methods to bolster prevention and response efforts, as well as increase resilience in the FA sector (see Note 3, p. 14).

The FA sector outlines five priorities to support the furtherance of these goals:

- **Priority 1:** Improve the ability to prevent, detect, and respond to animal and plant disease outbreaks and food contamination, whether naturally occurring or intentional, through the expansion of laboratory systems and qualified personnel.
- **Priority 2:** Enhance and integrate existing information sharing approaches.
- **Priority 3:** Raise awareness of and evaluate potential cyber risks, and encourage FA sector members to use the National Institute of Standards and Technology (NIST) Cybersecurity Framework.
- **Priority 4:** Continue to resolve decontamination and waste management–related issues.
- **Priority 5:** Engage all levels of the FA sector in national planning efforts and goals (see Note 3, p. 14).

FA SECTOR: ASSESSING RISK

As discussed in earlier chapters, the NIPP risk management framework calls for critical infrastructure partners to assess risk from any scenario as a function of consequence, vulnerability, and threat: $R = f(C,V,T)$. When conducting a risk assessment, the FA sector generally focuses on systems and networks as well as individual assets (see Note 3, p. 23). Remember, the purpose of conducting a risk assessment is to decide where to put limited resources while having the greatest impact. In the FA sector, risk assessments of food safety are conducted to determine the quantitative or qualitative value of risk attributed to exposure of food contamination by either a biological or chemical hazard (see Note 3, p. 23). The FA sector uses a number of different methodologies to identify and determine each component of risk (consequence, vulnerability, and threat). The following discussion outlines the methods used for each of these three components.

Reportable Data (Consequence)

This first component of risk is assessed through the accumulation of reportable data (i.e., illness and death and economic impact). The USDA and FDA both have structures in place to monitor adverse events. Data are then collected to produce a clear picture of the consequence for each type of disaster (see Note 3, p. 24).

CARVER Plus Shock Method (Vulnerabilities)

Vulnerability assessments are useful to assist SSAs identify the products of highest concern, threat agents likely to be used, points in the production process where intentional contamination is most likely to occur, laboratory testing and research needs, and potential countermeasures that may be taken (see Note 3, p. 24). The CARVER plus Shock methodology is used by the FA sector to determine the vulnerabilities in its assets, systems, and networks. This is accomplished by encompassing the consequences and threats.

It is important to note the relationship between the opportunity (vulnerability) and outcome (consequence) of an attack in the FA Sector. The definition of vulnerability, as stated in the NIPP, presents a challenge for application to the FA sector. The NIPP defines vulnerability as a physical feature or operational attribute that renders an entity open to exploitation or susceptible to a given hazard. However, many of the FA sector's interdependent systems are not physical structures like buildings, bridges, or dams. Rather, they are open areas such as farms, ranches, or livestock transport areas (see Note 3, p. 25).

These systems are susceptible to natural threats like disease and food-borne pathogens and as a result, it may not be feasible to prevent the introduction of threat agents. In response, the FA sector supports timely awareness by veterinarians, agriculture producers, and nationally coordinated disease surveillance programs that have the ability to target different threat agents in its systems (see Note 3, p. 25). Moreover, because the interdependent relationships within and among other sectors presents additional vulnerabilities for the FA sector, there is a need to clearly identify these points of dependence on critical partner sectors. Coordination with those SSAs must be established to address, mitigate, and strengthen these vulnerabilities.

As stated earlier, vulnerability and consequence assessments must be conducted together in order to determine risk in the FA sector. The CARVER plus Shock method has been adapted from the military version (CARVER) for use in the food industry. It is an offensive targeting prioritization tool that allows the user to think like an attacker to identify the most attractive targets for an attack. A food production facility or process may be assessed using this method to determine the most vulnerable points and focus resources on protecting those weaknesses in their infrastructure (see Note 3, p. 26). CARVER is an acronym for the following six attributes used to evaluate the attractiveness of a target for an attack:

- Criticality—measure of public health and impacts of an attack
- Accessibility—ability to physically access and egress from target
- Recuperability—ability of system to recover from an attack
- Vulnerability—ease of accomplishing attack
- Effect—amount of direct loss from an attack as measured by loss in production
- Recognizability—ease of identifying target

CARVER plus Shock is a modified version that evaluates a seventh attribute, the combined health, economic, and psychological impacts of an attack, or the SHOCK attributes of a target.[4] The scales have been developed for each of the seven attributes which may be used to rank the attractiveness of a target. While these scales were developed with the mind-set that mass mortality is a goal of terrorist organizations, it is important to remember that any intentional food contamination could also have a major psychological and economic impacts on the affected industry (see Note 4, p. 2). Tables 10.1 through 10.6 illustrate these attributes and the scales used by agencies for scoring each one.

Table 10.1 CARVER Plus Shock Attributes and Scale for Criticality

Example Metrics of Criticality Criteria	Scale
Loss of over 10,000 lives OR loss of more than $100 billion. (*Note:* if looking on a company level, loss of >90% of the total economic value for which you are concerned.[a])	9–10
Loss of life is between 1000 and 10,000 OR loss of between $10 billion and $100 billion. (*Note:* if looking on a company level, loss of between 61% and 90% of the total economic value for which you are concerned.[a])	7–8
Loss of life between 100 and 1000 OR loss of between $1 and $10 billion. (*Note:* if looking on a company level, loss of between 10% and 30% of the total economic value for which you are concerned.[a])	5–6
Loss of life less than 100 OR loss of between $100 million and $1 billion. (*Note:* if looking on a company level, loss of between 10% and 30% of the total economic value for which you are concerned.[a])	3–4
No loss of life OR loss of less than $100 million. (*Note:* if looking on a company level, loss of <10% of the total economic value for which you are concerned.[a])	1–2

Source: FDA. 2009. Protecting and Promoting Your Health. *CARVER + Shock Primer: An Overview of the CARVER Plus Shock Method for Food Sector Vulnerability Assessments.*

Criticality: A target is critical when introduction of threat agents into food at this location would have significant health or economic impact.

[a] The total economic value for which you are concerned depends upon your perspective. For example, for a company this could be the percentage of a single facility's gross revenues, or percentage of a single facility's gross revenues, or percentage of a company's gross revenues lost from the effect on a single product line. Likewise, a state could evaluate the effect of the economic loss caused by an attack of a facility or farm by the proportion of the state's economy contributed by that commodity.

Table 10.2 CARVER Plus Shock Attributes and Scale for Accessibility

Example Metrics of Accessibility Criteria	Scale
Easily Accessible (e.g., target is outside building and no perimeter fence). Limited physical or human barriers or observation. Attacker has relatively unlimited access to the target. Attack can be carried out using medium or large volumes of containment without undue concern detection. Multiple sources of information concerning the facility and the target are easily available.	9–10
Accessible (e.g., target is inside building, but in unsecured part of facility). Human observation and physical barriers limited. Attacker has access to the target for an hour or less. Attack can be carried out with moderate to large volumes of containment, but requires the use of stealth. Only limited specific information is available on the facility and the target.	7–8
Partially Accessible (e.g., inside building, but in a relatively unsecured, but busy, part of facility). Under constant possible human observation. Some physical barriers may be present. Contaminant must be disguised, and time limitations are significant. Only general, nonspecific information is available on the facility and the target.	5–6
Hardly Accessible (e.g., inside building in a secured part of facility). Human observation and physical barriers with an established means of detection. Access generally restricted to operators or authorized persons. Containment must be disguised and time limitations are extreme. Limited general information available on the facility and the target.	3–4
Not Accessible. Physical barriers, alarms, and human observation. Defined means of intervention in place. Attacker can access target for <5 minutes with all equipment carried in pockets. No useful policy available information concerning the target.	1–2

Source: FDA. 2009. Protecting and Promoting Your Health. *CARVER + Shock Primer: An Overview of the CARVER Plus Shock Method for Food Sector Vulnerability Assessments.*

Accessibility: A target is accessible when an attacker can reach the target to conduct the attack and egress the target undetected. Accessibility is the openness of the target to the threat. This measure is independent of the probability of successful introduction of threat agents.

Table 10.3 CARVER Plus Shock Attributes and Scale for Recuperability

Example Metrics of Recuperability Criteria	Scale
>1 year	9–10
6 months to 1 year	7–8
3–6 months	5–6
1–3 months	3–4
<1 month	1–2

Source: FDA. 2009. Protecting and Promoting Your Health. *CARVER + Shock Primer: An Overview of the CARVER Plus Shock Method for Food Sector Vulnerability Assessments.*

Recuperabilty: A target's recuperability is measured in the time it will take for the specific system to recover productivity.

Table 10.4 CARVER Plus Shock Attributes and Scale for Effect

Example Metrics of Effect Criteria	Scale
>50% of the system's productive impacted	9–10
25%–50% of the system's production impacted	7–8
10%–25% of the system's production impacted	5–6
1%–10% of the system's production impacted	3–4
<1% of system's production impacted	1–2

Source: FDA. 2009. Protecting and Promoting Your Health. *CARVER + Shock Primer: An Overview of the CARVER Plus Shock Method for Food Sector Vulnerability Assessments.*

Effect: Effect is a measure of the percentage of system productivity damaged by an attack at a single facility. Thus, effect is inversely related to the total number of facilities producing the same product.

Table 10.5 CARVER Plus Shock Attributes and Scale for Recognizability

Example Metrics of Recognizability Criteria	Scale
The target is clearly recognizable and requires little or no training for recognition.	9–10
The target is easily recognizable and requires only a small amount of training for recognition.	7–8

(Continued)

Table 10.5 (Continued) CARVER Plus Shock Attributes and Scale for Recognizability

Example Metrics of Recognizability Criteria	Scale
The target is difficult to recognize or might be confused with other targets or target companies and requires some training for recognition.	5–6
The target is difficult to recognize. It is easily confused with other targets or components and requires extensive training for recognition.	3–4
The target cannot be recognized under any conditions, except by experts.	1–2

Source: FDA. 2009. Protecting and Promoting Your Health. *CARVER + Shock Primer: An Overview of the CARVER Plus Shock Method for Food Sector Vulnerability Assessments.*

Recognizabilty: A target's recognizability is the degree to which it can be identified by an attacker without confusion with other targets or components.

Table 10.6 CARVER Plus Shock Attributes and Scale for Shock

Example Metrics of Shock Criteria	Scale
Target has major historical, cultural, religious, or other symbolic importance. Loss of over 10,000 lives. Major impact on sensitive subpopulations, e.g., children or the elderly. National economic impact more than $100 billion.	9–10
Target has high historical, cultural, religious, or other symbolic importance. Loss between 1000 and 10,000 lives. Significant impact on sensitive subpopulations, e.g., children or the elderly. National economic impact between $10 and $100 billion.	7–8
Target has moderate historical, cultural, religious, or other symbolic importance. Loss of life between 100 and 1000. Moderate impact on sensitive subpopulations, e.g., children or the elderly. National economic impact between $1 and $10 billion.	5–6

(Continued)

199

Table 10.6 (*Continued*) CARVER Plus Shock Attributes and Scale for Shock

Example Metrics of Shock Criteria	Scale
Target has little historical, cultural, religious, or other symbolic importance. Loss of life <100. Small impact on sensitive subpopulations, e.g., children or the elderly. National economic impact between $100 million and $1 billion.	3–4
Target has no historical, cultural, religious, or other symbolic importance. Loss of life <10. No impact on sensitive subpopulations, e.g., children or the elderly. National economic impact less than $100 million.	1–2

Source: FDA. 2009. Protecting and Promoting Your Health. *CARVER + Shock Primer: An Overview of the CARVER Plus Shock Method for Food Sector Vulnerability Assessments.*

Shock: Shock is the final attribute considered in the methodology. Shock is the combined measure of health, psychological, and collateral national economic impacts of a successful attack on the target system. Shock is considered on a national level. The psychological impact will be increased if there are a large number of deaths or the target has been historical, cultural, religious, or other symbolic significance. Mass casualties are not required to achieve widespread economic loss or psychological damage. Collateral economic damage includes such items as decreased national economic activity, increased unemployment in collateral industries, etc. Psychological impact will be increased if victims are members of sensitive subpopulations such as children or the elderly.

There are five essential steps to the CARVER plus Shock process. These are as follows:

Step 1—Establishing Parameters
Step 2—Assembling Experts
Step 3—Detailing Food Chain Supply
Step 4—Assigning Scores
Step 5—Applying What Has Been Learned (see Note 4, pp. 1–2)

Step 1—Establishing Parameters
Prior to scoring, the scenarios and assumptions you plan to use in the analysis must be determined. Initially, you need to decide what you are

trying to protect and what you are trying to protect it from. This should include the following:

- What food supply chain you are going to assess? (e.g., hot dog production versus deli meat production versus chicken nugget production, overall assessment based on generic process from farm to table versus post-slaughter processing in a specific facility)
- What is the endpoint of concern? (e.g., foodborne illness and death versus economic impacts)
- What type of attacker and attack you are trying to protect against? Attackers could range from disgruntled employees to international terrorist organizations. Different attackers have different capabilities and different goals. One example is a major assumption used by Food Safety and Inspection Service (FSIS) and FDA in their vulnerability assessments is that one of the goals of terrorist organizations is to cause mass mortality by adding acutely toxic agents to food products (see Note 4, p. 2). That assumption has a major impact on the scoring of the various parts of the supply chain.
- What agent(s) might be used? The agent used in your scenario will impact the outcome of the assessment. Potential agents include biological, chemical, or radiological agents (see Note 4, pp. 1–2).

Step 2—Assembling Experts
The assessment team should consist of subject matter experts from the following industries: food production, food science, toxicology, epidemiology, microbiology, medicine (human and veterinarian), radiology, and risk assessment. Once the team has been assembled, the CARVER-Shock method should be applied to each element of the food system infrastructure. Using the scenario and assumptions detailed in Step 1, values from one to ten for each attribute should be assigned (see Note 4, pp. 1–2).

Step 3—Detailing Food Supply Chain
In this step, the system under evaluation should first be described. The analysis should include a graphical representation (flow chart) of the system and its subsystem, complexes, components, and nodes (its smaller

structural parts). For example, if you are evaluating hot dog production, the food system is hot dog production, which can be broken down into subsystems (production of live animals subsystem, slaughter/processing subsystem, distribution subsystem). Those subsystems can be further broken down into complexes (e.g., slaughterhouse facility and processing facility), which can then be broken down into components and include the raw materials (receiving area, processing area, storage area, shipping area, etc.), and to the smallest possible nodes (e.g., individual pieces of equipment) (see Note 4, p. 2).

Step 4—Assigning Scores
Once the infrastructure has been broken down into its smallest parts (i.e., components and nodes), these can be ranked or scored for each of the seven CARVER-Shock attributes to calculate an overall score for that node. The nodes with the higher overall scores are those that are potentially the most vulnerable nodes (i.e., most attractive targets for an attacker). The rationale for a particular consensus score should be captured (see Note 4, p. 2).

Step 5—Applying What Has Been Learned
In this final step, you have already identified the critical nodes of the system and are now ready to develop a plan to establish countermeasures that minimize the attractiveness of the nodes as targets. Countermeasures might include enhancements to physical security, personnel security, and operational security that help to reduce an attacker's access to the product or process (see Note 4, p. 2).

Final Calculations and Interpretation

Once the attribute scales have been completed for a given node within the food supply system, the ranking on all of the scales can be totaled to give an overall value for that node. This process should be repeated for each node within a food supply system. A comparison of the overall values for all the nodes can be made to rank the vulnerability of the different nodes relative to each other. Nodes with the highest total rating have the highest potential vulnerability and should be the focus of countermeasure efforts (see Note 4, p. 5).

Federal Policy on Vulnerability Assessments

Federal guidelines Homeland Security Presidential Directive 9 (HSPD-9) require the USDA and FDA to conduct vulnerability assessments of the FA sector and to update them every 2 years. This includes efforts by the Strategic Partnership Program for Agroterrorism (SPPA) Initiative which, between the years 2005 and 2008, conducted over 50 vulnerability assessments on a variety of food and agricultural products, processes, or commodities under the regulatory authority of the FDA and USDA (see Note 3, p. 27). Additionally, USDA has conducted more than 30 vulnerability assessments and updates including products and factors such as deli meats, establishment size, ground beef, hot dogs, imported food products, liquid eggs, ready-to-eat meals, National School Lunch Program, ready-to-eat chicken, threat agents, transportation, and water used in food. The FDA also conducted 18 vulnerability assessments and updated 16 of its original assessments conducted under the SPPA Initiative (see Note 3, p. 27).

National Counterterrorism Center and Threat and Hazard Identification and Risk Assessment

The final component of a risk assessment is to determine the threat. The National Counterterrorism Center (NCTC) is the lead entity in determining this final component for the FA sector. All FA sector threats deemed credible by law enforcement agencies are investigated further with the help from FA sector partners. The DHS and the Intelligence Community provide critical information to the FA sector that helps in determining the criticality of known risks.

As presented in Chapter 9, the Threat and Hazard Identification and Risk Assessment (THIRA) also assists the FA sector in risk assessment by helping government and private sector partners (i.e., any entity receiving federal grants for preparedness activities) understand the risks within their community and estimate capability requirements. Those critical infrastructures within the FA sector are largely privately owned and operated, which requires a community approach to risk assessments as outlined by THIRA. Efforts such as those outlined in the SPPA and in FSIS's cybersecurity vulnerability initiative, are central to securing the vast and open network of systems that comprise the FA sector (see Note 3, p. 24).

WATER AND WASTEWATER SYSTEMS SECTOR PROFILE

With more than 153,000 public drinking water systems and approximately 16,500 publicly owned treatment works in the US, the water and wastewater sector infrastructure is one of the most critical to protect them. Safe drinking water and properly treated wastewater are vital for human consumption and activity, the prevention of disease, and the health of the environment. The water and wastewater sector infrastructure consists of drinking water and wastewater systems, most of which are found in local municipalities, and has a long history of implementing programs that provide for clean and safe water.[5] Under the guidance of the Safe Drinking Water Act (SDWA) and Clean Water Act (CWA), drinking water and wastewater utilities have been conducting routine, daily, weekly, and monthly water quality monitoring for over 30 years (see Note 5, pp. 1–5).

Today, research continues to advance ways to improve the quality of water and the safety of these systems. Under Homeland Security Presidential Directive 7 (HSPD-7), the US Environmental Protection Agency (EPA) is designated as the SSA for this critical infrastructure. The sector is susceptible to risks associated with malicious acts, natural disasters, and denial of service attacks. These could result in a large number of illnesses or casualties, as well as negative economic impacts. Additionally, critical services such as firefighting and healthcare (hospitals), and other dependent and interdependent sectors such as energy, transportation, and FA, would suffer damaging effects from a denial of potable water or properly treated wastewater (see Note 5, p. 1).

Drinking Water and Wastewater

Safe drinking water is essential to the life of an individual and society as a whole. The effects of a drinking water contamination would be devastating and far-reaching with significant consequences to public health, the economy, and the environment. Likewise, a disruption of a wastewater treatment utility or service can cause loss of life, economic impacts, and severe public health and environmental impacts. Both drinking water and wastewater systems can be divided into three elements: (a) physical, (b) cyber, and (c) human (see Note 5, pp. 8–11). Table 10.7 shows the elements contained in both water and wastewater components.

Table 10.7   Drinking Water and Wastewater Elements

	Physical Elements	Cyber Elements	Human Elements
Drinking Water	Water source Conveyance Raw water storage Treatment Finished water storage Distribution system Monitoring system	Supervisory Control and Data Acquisition (SCADA) system	Employees and contractors
Wastewater	Collection Raw influent storage Treatment Treated wastewater storage Effluent/ discharge Monitoring system	Supervisory Control and Data Acquisition (SCADA) system	Employees and contractors

Source: US DHS. 2010. *Water and Wastewater Sector-Specific Plan,* pp. 8–11.

GOALS AND PRIORITIES OF THE WATER AND WASTEWATER SECTOR

Table 10.8 illustrates the vision and mission statements of both the water and wastewater sector and the EPA. These statements guide the sector and are the foundation for its goals.

The water and wastewater SSP includes four goals, each with a set of objectives, which guide the strategic planning process for sector protection and resilience. Table 10.9 shows these specific goals and objectives.

Table 10.8 Vision and Mission Statements of the Water and Wastewater Sector and Environmental Protection Agency

Water and Wastewater Sector Vision Statement

A secure and resilient drinking water and wastewater infrastructure that provides clean and safe water as an integral part of daily life, ensuring the economic vitality of and public confidence in the nation's drinking water and wastewater service through a layered defense of effective preparedness and security practices in the sector.

EPA's Water Security Mission Statement

To provide national leadership in developing and promoting programs that enhance the sector's ability to prevent, detect, respond to, and recover from all hazards.

Source: DHS. 2010. *Water and Wastewater Sector-Specific Plan*, p. 15.

Table 10.9 Water and Wastewater Sector Goals and Objectives

Goal 1	Sustain Protection of Public Health and the Environment

The nation relies on sustained availability of safe drinking water and on treatment of wastewater to maintain public health and environmental protection. To better protect public and environmental health, the water and wastewater sector works to ensure the continuity of both drinking and wastewater services.

Objective 1	Encourage integration of security concepts into daily business operations at utilities to foster a security culture.
Objective 2	Evaluate and develop surveillance, monitoring, warning, and response capabilities to recognize and address all-hazards risks at water sector systems that affect public health and economic viability.
Objective 3	Develop a nationwide laboratory network for water quality protection that integrates federal and state laboratory resources and uses standardized diagnostic protocols and procedures, or develop a supporting laboratory network capable of analyzing threats to water quality.

(Continued)

Table 10.9 (*Continued*) Water and Wastewater Sector Goals and Objectives

Goal 2	Recognize and Reduce Risk

With an improved understanding of the vulnerabilities, threats, and consequences, owners and operators of utilities can continue to thoroughly examine and implement risk-based approaches to better protect, detect, respond to, and recover from all hazards.

Objective 1	Improve identification of vulnerabilities based on knowledge and best available information, with the intent of increasing the sector's overall protection posture.
Objective 2	Improve identification of potential threats through knowledge base and communications—with the intent of increasing overall protection posture of the sector.
Objective 3	Identify and refine public health and economic impact consequences of man-made or natural incidents to improve utility risk assessments and enhance the sector's overall protection posture.

Goal 3	Maintain a Resilient Infrastructure

The water and wastewater sector will investigate how to optimize continuity of operations to ensure the economic vitality of communities and the utilities that serve them. Response and recovery from an incident in the sector will be crucial to maintaining public health and confidence.

Objective 1	Emphasize continuity of drinking water and wastewater services as it pertains to utility emergency preparedness, response, and recovery planning.
Objective 2	Explore and expand implementation of mutual aid agreements/compacts in the water and wastewater sector. The sector has significantly enhanced its resilience through agreements among utilities and states; increasing the number and scope of these will further enhance resilience.

(Continued)

207

Table 10.9 (*Continued*) Water and Wastewater Sector Goals and Objectives

Goal 3	Maintain a Resilient Infrastructure
Objective 3	Identify and implement key response and recovery strategies. Response and recovery from an incident in the sector will be crucial to maintaining public health and confidence.
Objective 4	Increase understanding of how the sector is interdependent with other critical infrastructure sectors. Sectors such as healthcare and public health and emergency services are largely dependent on the water and wastewater sector for their continuity of operations, while the water and wastewater sector is dependent on sectors such as chemical and energy for continuity of its operations.
Goal 4	**Increase Communication, Outreach, and Public Confidence**
Safe drinking water and water quality are fundamental to everyday life. An incident in the water sector could have significant impacts on public confidence. Fostering and enhancing the relationships between utilities, government, and the public can mitigate negative perceptions in the face of the incident.	
Objective 1	Communicate with the public about the level of protection and resilience in the water and wastewater sector and provide outreach to ensure the public's ability to be prepared for and respond to a natural disaster or man-made incident.
Objective 2	Enhance communication and coordination among utilities and federal, state, and local officials and agencies to provide information about threats.
Objective 3	Improve relationships among all water and wastewater sector partners through a strong public–private partnership characterized by trusted relationships.

Source: DHS. 2010. *Water and Wastewater Sector-Specific Plan*, pp. 16–17.

WATER AND WASTEWATER SECTOR: ASSESSING RISK

There are a diversity of assets in the water and wastewater sector, such as size, treatment complexity, disinfection practices, and geographic locations. As such, a multitude of all-hazard risk assessment methodologies have been developed. These are used by sector owners and operators and address a full range of utility components, including the physical plant (physical); employees (human); information technology/supervisory control and data acquisition (SCADA) and communications (cyber); and customers (see Note 5, p. 23). As with all sectors, the water and wastewater sector conducts full risk assessments using the formula: Risk (R) = f (Consequence [C], Threat [T], Vulnerability [V]) (see Note 5, p. 24). Risk assessments are conducted at the asset level by owners and operators, and are based on local conditions, threats, and other factors; approaches to and the results of an assessment may vary for each type of asset (see Note 5, p. 24).

The EPA partners with DHS and water sector partners to come up with risk assessment documents and tools in order to assist owners and operators in conducting local assessments. These initiatives are ongoing to improve the security of the sector. There are three risk assessment tools which have been widely used across the water and wastewater sector:

1. Risk Assessment Methodology—Water (RAM-W)
2. Security and Environmental Management Systems (SEMS) emergency response checklist
3. Vulnerability Self-Assessment Tool (VSAT) (see Note 5, p. 27)

In 2010, the ASME Innovative Technologies Institute (ASME ITI) and the American Water Works Association (AWWA) developed a risk and resilience standard for the water and wastewater sector based on Risk Analysis and Management for Critical Asset Protection (RAMCAP) Plus. RAMCAP Plus establishes a common terminology and measurement metrics for analyzing risk and resilience. This process originally consisted of a seven-step methodology that enables asset owners to perform analyses of their risks and risk reduction options.[6] RAMCAP was first identified by DHS as a model for sector-specific guidance in 2005 and used it for various national assets including nuclear power plants, petroleum refineries, and water and wastewater systems (see Note 6, pp. 34–36). When the water and wastewater sector developed its first version of its SSP, the goals included improving identification of vulnerabilities, threats, and consequences to utility owners and operators could implement risk-based approaches to enhance security and resilience of their assets. ASME ITI, under the sponsorship of DHS,

Table 10.10 Seven Analytic Steps of RAMCAP Plus

Step 1: Asset Characterization: What are the critical assets?

Step 2: Threat Characterization: What reasonably possible event can harm or disrupt them?

Step 3: Consequence Analysis: What would the event cost in terms of human suffering or economic loss?

Step 4: Vulnerability Analysis: Where are the assets most open to harm from an event?

Step 5: Threat Assessment: What is the likelihood that an event will occur?

Step 6: Risk/Resilience Assessment: Risk = Consequences × (Vulnerability × Threat). Resilience = Service Outage × (Vulnerability × Threat).

Step 7: Risk/Resilience Management: What are the options to reduce risks and increase resilience? What is the benefit/cost ratio of the options?

Source: Morely, K., and Brashear, J. January 2010. Protecting the water supply. *Mechanical Engineering, 132*, 1, pp. 34–36.

initiated discussion with the water and wastewater sector to consider the development of sector-level guidance based on RAMCAP Plus, and hence it was put in place (see Note 6, pp. 34–36).

RAMCAP Plus is a process for analyzing and managing the risks and resilience associated with malicious attacks and natural disasters against critical infrastructures. The standard proposes specific threat scenarios and is comprised of seven interrelated analytic steps. Table 10.10 lists these steps and a brief overview of what they each entail. These steps provide a foundation for owners and operators to collect, interpret, and analyze data, and use those results in their decision-making processes for managing risk and resilience.

WATER AND WASTEWATER SECTOR–SPECIFIC INITIATIVES/POLICIES

The water and wastewater sector has made significant progress to address the all-hazards risk environment of today. Some of the sector's accomplishments include the following:

- The formation of specialized working groups and the development of quality products such as the *Roadmap to a Secure & Resilient Water Sector* and the *Roadmap to Secure Control Systems in the Water Sector* (the latter addressed activities to mitigate cybersecurity risk over the next 10 years).

- Water security initiative pilots which were implemented in five US cities (Cincinnati, Dallas, New York City, Philadelphia, and San Francisco). Information gathered from the initial pilot was used to publish three interim guidance documents to advise utilities regarding the design, development, and use of contaminant monitoring and warning systems.
- Establishment of intrastate mutual aid and assistance agreements, such as Water and Wastewater Agency Response Networks within 47 states to foster a utilities-helping-utilities approach to response and recovery efforts following incidents or events (see Note 5, Preface).

Finally, in compliance with HSPD-7, all SSAs provide DHS with annual reports that serve as a primary tool for assessing performance and reporting on progress in the sector. The water and wastewater sector must also provide data to support this report. The sector annual report accomplishes the following purposes:

1. Provides a common vehicle across all sectors to communicate critical infrastructure and key resource (CIKR) protection performance and progress to CIKR partners and other government entities
2. Establishes a baseline of existing sector-specific CIKR protection programs and initiatives
3. Identifies plans for SSA resource requirements and budget
4. Determines and explains how sector efforts support the national effort
5. Provides an overall progress report for the sector
6. Provides feedback to DHS, sectors, and other government entities to illustrate the continuous improvement of CIKR protection activities
7. Helps identify and share beneficial practices from successful programs (see Note 5, p. 38)

ENERGY SECTOR PROFILE

PPD-21 identifies the energy sector as uniquely critical because it provides an "enabling function" across all critical infrastructure sectors. With over 80% of the country's energy infrastructure owned by the private sector, protecting the energy sector requires a strong partnership between government and industry partners. The energy infrastructure is divided into three interrelated segments: electricity, oil, and natural gas. These segments are widely diverse, geographically dispersed, and are often interdependent of one another.[7]

According to the DHS, the US electricity segment alone contains more than 6413 power plants and approximately 1075 (GW) of installed generation. Additionally, about 48% of electricity is produced by combusting coal (primarily transported by rail), 20% is found in nuclear power plants, and 22% by combusting natural gas. Hydroelectric plants (6%), oil (1%), and renewable sources (solar, wind, and geothermal) (3%), make up the remaining generation. Furthermore, the heavy reliance on pipelines to distribute products across the nation emphasizes the interdependencies between the energy and transportation systems sector.[8] The energy sector is subject to regulation in various forms, as they are often overseen under numerous jurisdictions. The complexities of the operating structure, along with the evolving threat, make this sector especially challenging to protect. The Department of Energy is the SSA for this sector (see Note 7, p. 3).

ENERGY SECTOR GOALS AND PRIORITIES

As with other critical infrastructure sectors, the energy sector has developed a sector vision, goals, and priorities which are aligned and in support of the NIPP critical infrastructure security and resilience goals. Table 10.11 provides an overview of the national vision, goals, and priorities for the energy sector.

Table 10.11 National and Energy Sector Critical Infrastructure Vision, Goals, and Priorities

Vision Statement
A nation in which physical and cyber critical infrastructure remain secure and resilient, with vulnerabilities reduced, consequences minimized, threats identified and disrupted, and response and recovery hastened.

National and Energy Sector Critical Infrastructure Goals
- Assess and analyze threats to, vulnerabilities of, and consequences to critical infrastructure to inform risk management activities.
- Secure critical infrastructure against human, physical, and cyberthreats through sustainable efforts to reduce risk, while accounting for the costs and benefits of security investments.
- Enhance critical infrastructure resilience by minimizing the adverse consequences of incidents through advance planning and mitigation efforts, as well as effective responses to save lives and ensure the rapid recovery of essential services.

(Continued)

Table 10.11 (*Continued*)   National and Energy Sector Critical Infrastructure Vision, Goals, and Priorities

- Share actionable and relevant information across the critical infrastructure community to build awareness and enable risk-informed decision making.
- Promote learning and adaptation during and after exercises and incidents.

Electricity Subsector Priorities	Oil and Natural Gas Subsector Priorities
Tools and Technology—Deploying tools and technologies to enhance situational awareness and security of critical infrastructure. Deploying the propriety government technologies on utility systems that enable machine-to-machine information sharing and improved situational awareness of threats to the grid. Implementing the National Institute of Standards and Technology (NIST) Cybersecurity Framework. **Information Flow**—Making sure actionable intelligence and threat indicators are communicated between the government and industry in a time-sensitive manner. Improving the bidirectional flow of threat information. Coordinating with interdependent sectors. **Incident Response**—Planning and exercising coordinated responses to an attack. Developing playbooks and capabilities to coordinate industry-government response and recovery efforts. Ongoing assessments of equipment-sharing programs.	The Oil and Natural Gas Subsector Coordinating Council strives to provide a venue for industry owners and operators to mutually plan, implement, and execute sufficient and necessary sector-wide security programs; procedures and processes; information exchange; accomplishment assessment; and progress to strengthen the security and resilience of its critical infrastructure. Priorities are placed in the following: • Partnership coordination • Implementation and communication • Identification of sector needs/gaps and/or best practices • Information sharing • Business continuity

Source: US DHS. 2015. *Energy Sector-Specific Plan*, pp. 3–4.

ENERGY SECTOR: ASSESSING RISK

The energy sector consists of highly diverse assets, systems, functions, and networks. It also has a considerable amount of experience in risk management. Over the years, the industry has responded to the increased need for enterprise-level security efforts and business continuity plans, and continues to assess the security vulnerabilities of single-point assets such as refineries, storage terminals, and power plants, as well as networked features such as pipeline, transmission lines, and cyber systems (see Note 7, p. 13). It is interesting to note that the types of threats faced by the electricity, oil, and natural gas industries vary widely, as does the meaning of "risk" as perceived by each organization. A discussion of these is important before we delve into the overall sector efforts.

Electricity Subsector Risks and Threats

Risk assessments of the electricity subsector are conducted by a wide variety of organizations. For example, the North American Reliability Corporation (NERC) assesses risks in terms of the potential impact to the reliability of the bulk power system. The question asked here might be, "did an event result in the loss or interruption of service to customers?" On the other hand, private companies and utilities examine risks and threats as they relate to the operational and financial security of each company. The question here might be, "could a threat negatively impact the company's financial health?" (see Note 7, p. 5). While there are differences across the subsector as to what constitutes risk, the electricity subsector has identified several issues as the key risks and threats to its infrastructure. These include:

- Cyber and physical security threats
- Natural disasters and extreme weather conditions
- Workforce capability ("aging workforce") and human errors
- Equipment failure and aging infrastructure
- Evolving environmental, economic, and reliability regulatory requirements
- Changes in the technical and operational environment, including changes in fuel supply (see Note 7, p. 5).

214

Oil and Natural Gas Subsector Risk and Threats

The oil and natural gas subsector has a worldwide geographic presence and as such, faces a diverse risk environment. Key risks in the oil and natural gas industry are as follows:

- Natural disasters and extreme weather conditions
- Regulatory and legislative changes—including environmental and health—as well as increased cost of compliance
- Volatile oil and gas prices and demands
- Operational hazards, including blowouts, spills, and personal injury
- Disruption due to political instability, civil unrest, or terrorist activities
- Transportation infrastructure constraints impacting the movement of energy resources
- Inadequate or unavailable insurance coverage
- Aging infrastructure and workforce
- Cybersecurity risks, including insider threats (see Note 7, p. 6)

Cybersecurity

A growing and evolving security challenge for the energy sector is that of cybersecurity. A common framework is needed to guide the public–private partnerships that the energy sector encompasses. As discussed in previous chapters, policies to address evolving cyberthreats were outlined by President Obama in the 2013 Executive Order (EO) 13636, "Improving Critical Infrastructure Cybersecurity," one of which directed the NIST to work with stakeholders to develop a cybersecurity framework (see Note 7, p. 14). To comply with this standard, the Department of Energy (DOE) collaborated with industry partners to develop the Energy Sector Cybersecurity Framework Implementation Guidance. As mentioned previously, the energy sector organizations have a strong track record of working together to develop cybersecurity standards, tools, and processes that ensure uninterrupted services. The DOE worked with the Electricity Subsector and Oil & Natural Gas Subsector Coordinating Councils along with other SSAs to develop this Framework Implementation Guidance specifically for energy sector owners and operators.[9] This was designed to assist energy sector organizations in four specific areas to:

- Characterize their current and target cybersecurity posture
- Identify gaps in their existing cybersecurity risk management programs, using the framework as a guide, and identify

215

areas where current practices may exceed the framework implementation

- Effectively demonstrate and communicate their risk management approach and use of the framework to both internal and external stakeholders

There are a myriad of cybersecurity risk management tools, processes, standards, and guidelines widely used by energy sector organizations. An example of one of these tools is the Cybersecurity Capability Maturity Model (C2M2). Developed in 2011, this program is a public–private partnership effort to improve energy sector cybersecurity capabilities and to understand the cybersecurity posture of the industry (see Note 9, p. 1). In 2014, two distinct C2M2s were developed—one for the electricity subsector and another for the oil and natural gas subsector. Other notable tools include the Cyber Resilience Review (CRR) and the Cyber Security Evaluation Tool (CSET). Table 10.12 describes an example of cybersecurity risk management approaches used across the energy sector.

In addition to approaches used cross-sector, the electricity subsector and the oil and natural gas subsector each have tailored standards or cybersecurity approaches that many organizations may use either voluntarily or by requirement (see Note 9, p. 6). Tables 10.13 and 10.14 illustrate examples of risk management approaches that are applicable only to specific subsectors.

Table 10.12 Example Cybersecurity Risk Management Approaches Used in Energy Sector

Name	Summary	Additional Information
Cybersecurity Capability Maturity Model (C2M2), both Electricity Subsector and Oil and Natural Gas Subsector-specific versions	Used to assess an organization's cybersecurity capabilities and prioritize their actions and investments to improve cybersecurity.	http://energy.gov /oe/cybersecurity-capa bility-maturity-model -c2m2
Cyber Resilience Review (CRR)	Evaluates an organization's operational resilience and cybersecurity practices across ten domains.	https://www.us-cert .gov/ccubedvp/ self-service-crr

(Continued)

Table 10.12 (*Continued*)   Example Cybersecurity Risk Management
Approaches Used in Energy Sector

Name	Summary	Additional Information
Cyber Security Evaluation Tool (CSET)	Guides users through a step-by-step process to assess their control system and information technology network security practices against recognized industry standards.	http://ics-cert.us-cert .gov/Assessments
Electricity Subsector Cybersecurity Risk Management Process (RMP) Guideline	Enables organizations to apply effective and efficient risk management processes and tailor them to meet their organizational requirements.	http://energy.gov/oe /downloads /cybersecurity-risk -management-process -rmp-guideline-final -may-2012

Source: US Department of Energy. 2015. *Energy Sector Cybersecurity Framework Implementation Guidance*, p. 5.

Table 10.13   Examples of Electricity Subsector Cybersecurity Risk Management
Approaches

Name	Summary	Additional Information
Critical Infrastructure Protection (CIP) Standards	The North American Electric Reliability Corporation (NERC) CIP Standards provide a set of regulatory cybersecurity requirements to assist in securing the energy system assets that operate and maintain the bulk electric grid.	http://www.nerc.com /pa/Stand/Pages /CIPStandards.aspx

(*Continued*)

217

Table 10.13 (*Continued*) Examples of Electricity Subsector Cybersecurity Risk Management Approaches

Name	Summary	Additional Information
Interagency Report (IR) 7628, Guidelines for Smart Grid Cyber Security	The National Institute of Standards and Technology (NIST) guidelines present an analytical framework to develop effective cybersecurity strategies tailored to their particular smart grid-related characteristics, risk, and vulnerabilities.	http://csrc.nist.gov /publications /PubsNISTIRs .html#NIST-IR-7628

Source: US Department of Energy. 2015. *Energy Sector Cybersecurity Framework Implementation Guidance,* p. 6.

Table 10.14 Examples of Oil and Natural Gas Cybersecurity Risk Management Approaches

Name	Summary	Additional Information
Control Systems Cyber Security Guidelines for the Natural Gas Pipeline Industry	The Interstate Natural Gas Association of America (INGAA) guideline assists operators of natural gas pipelines in managing their control systems cybersecurity requirements. It sets forth and details the unique risk and impact-based differences between the natural gas pipeline industry and the hazardous liquid pipeline and liquefied natural gas operators.	http://www.ingaa.org

(*Continued*)

Table 10.14 (*Continued*) Examples of Oil and Natural Gas Cybersecurity Risk Management Approaches

Name	Summary	Additional Information
RP 780 Risk Assessment Methodology	The American Petroleum Institute (API) document provides guidance on risk assessment for oil and natural gas operations.	http://www.api.org /Environment-Health -and-Safety /Environmental -Performance/~/link .aspx?_id=91E6E0827 3F24CE9B88D71A477 DF85AB&_z=z
Chemical Facilities Antiterrorism Standards	The risk-based performance standards (RBPS) from the Department of Homeland Security (DHS) provide guidance on physical and cybersecurity for organizations handling chemicals of interest. RBPS 8 specifically requires facilities regulated by CFATS to address cybersecurity in their facility security plan.	http://www.dhs.gov /chemical-facility-anti -terrorism-standards

Source: US Department of Energy. 2015. *Energy Sector Cybersecurity Framework Implementation Guidance*, p. 6.

Finally, energy sector organizations can map their current cybersecurity approach to the framework elements, using specific mappings as a guide. The framework implementation approach consists of seven steps which outline the activities that should be taken in a cybersecurity risk assessment. These are as follows:

- Step 1: Prioritize and Scope—organization decides how and where it wants to use the framework.
- Step 2: Orient—organization identifies in-scope systems and assets (i.e., people, information, technology, and facilities).

- Step 3: Create a Current Profile—organization identifies its current cybersecurity and risk management state.
- Step 4: Conduct a Risk Assessment—perform a risk assessment for in-scope portion of the organization.
- Step 5: Create a Target Profile—organization identifies goals that will mitigate risk commensurate with the risk to organizational and critical infrastructure objectives.
- Step 6: Determine, Analyze, and Prioritize Gaps—gaps should be identified in both the target profile and target tier.
- Step 7: Implement Action Plan—the organization implements the action plan and tracks its progress over time, ensuring that gaps are closed and risks are monitored (see Note 9, pp. 8–18).

The framework implementation should be included in an organization's risk management process. Intended as a continuous activity, it should be repeated according to organization criteria. Additionally, a plan to communicate progress to the appropriate stakeholders should also be implemented. Validation and feedback at each step is encouraged for process improvement and overall efficiency and effectiveness (see Note 9, p. 18).

CONCLUSION

Each critical infrastructure sector has distinctive characteristics, operating models, and risk profiles. To protect our nation's food supply, water systems and energy networks require strong policy proposals and methods that reflect an understanding of the current risk landscape. DHS and sector partners have worked together to address these security challenges and build resilience within unique risk management perspectives. The FA sector, water and wastewater sector, and energy sector illustrate not only the vastness of critical infrastructures, but also the variety of approaches and policies used to managing risk. CARVER, THIRA, and RAMCAP Plus are just some of the methods favored by these sectors. While some of the sectors share risk approaches, the extent to which risk can be estimated also varies by hazard. Therefore, adopting the appropriate policies and methods are critical for successful risk management.

REVIEW QUESTIONS

1. What is a SSA? Explain the SSP and how each is used by the individual sectors.

2. Describe the missions of the critical infrastructure sectors presented in this chapter.
3. Identify and explain the various methods each sector takes to managing risk. Is there an overlap in methods?
4. How do different hazards impact the various approaches taken by each sector to manage risk?

NOTES

1. DHS. *Food and Agriculture Sector.* Retrieved from: https://www.dhs.gov/food-and-agriculture-sector.
2. DHS. 2015. *Sector-Specific Plans.* Retrieved from: http://www.dhs.gov/2015-sector-specific-plans.
3. DHS. 2015. *Food and Agriculture Sector-Specific Plan*, pp. 5–7, p. 14, pp. 23–27.
4. FDA. 2009. Protecting and Promoting Your Health, *CARVER + Shock Primer: An Overview of the CARVER Plus Shock Method for Food Sector Vulnerability Assessments*, pp. 1–2, p. 5.
5. DHS. 2010. *Water Sector-Specific Plan*, Preface, pp. 1–5, pp. 8–11, p. 23, p. 24, p. 27, p. 38.
6. Morely, K., and Brashear, J. (2010). Protecting the water supply. *Mechanical Engineering, 132,* 1, 34–36.
7. DHS. 2015. *Energy Sector-Specific Plan*, p. 3, p. 5, p. 6, p. 13, p. 14.
8. DHS. *Energy Sector.* Retrieved from: https://www.dhs.gov/energy-sector.
9. US Department of Energy. January 2015. *Energy Sector Cybersecurity Framework Implementation Guidance*, p. 1, p. 6, pp. 8–18.

11

Sector-Specific Agencies' Approaches to Risk
Healthcare and Public Health Sector, Transportation Systems Sector, and Emergency Services Sector

INTRODUCTION

Many of the 16 critical infrastructure sectors are highly dependent on fellow sectors, meaning they rely on the services, systems, and processes to operate. An increased reliance upon information technology and telecommunications has increased the dependence of one sector upon another. The Healthcare and Public Health (HPH) Sector, Transportation Systems Sector, and Emergency Services Sector (ESS) are good examples of these interdependencies and the risks of cascading failures from a single disaster. A classic example is the September 11, 2001, terrorist attacks, which shut down our transportation networks, impaired emergency services, and challenged area hospitals. The sectors covered in this chapter each offer a unique policy framework and approach to risk management. It is important to note that a heavy reliance on cyber technologies permeate these sectors, creating newer risks and interdependencies.

HPH PROFILE

The HPH is a vast and diverse sector that employs about 13 million personnel and representing an estimated 16.2% ($2.2 trillion) of our nation's gross domestic product.[1] This sector includes acute care hospitals, ambulatory healthcare, and a sizeable and multifaceted public–private healthcare system. A large portion of private sector enterprises are also included with this sector such as those manufacturing, distributing, and selling drugs, vaccines, medical supplies, and equipment (see Note 1). The HPH protects all sectors of the economy from hazards such as terrorism, infectious disease outbreaks, and natural disasters. As with other critical sectors, the vast majority of the HPH Sector are privately owned and operated and therefore information sharing and collaboration with other sectors is essential.[2]

It is important to note that while healthcare tends to be delivered and managed locally, the public health component of the sector, focused primarily on population health, is managed across all levels of government (see Note 2). The Department of Health and Human Services (HHS) is designated as the Sector-Specific Agency (SSA) for this sector. Threats to the HPH Sector come not only from natural disasters and terrorism, but also from high costs, limited resources, and excessive demands on personnel, equipment, and systems.

GOALS AND PRIORITIES OF THE HPH

The HPH Sector vision promotes a resilient national healthcare and public health infrastructure by striving to protect its workforce and ensure its ability to respond to and recover from routine and emergency events (see Note 2). This vision, along with the HPH Sector mission and goals can be found in Table 11.1.

HPH: ASSESSING RISK

Conducting risk assessment in the HPH Sector is customary to achieve compliance with safety, physical security, and information security regulations. Meeting these regulatory requirements includes hospitals needing to achieve certification requirements for reimbursement by the Federal Medicare program; pharmaceutical companies meeting

Table 11.1   Healthcare and Public Health Sector (HPH) Vison, Mission, and Goals

---

HPH Sector Vision

The HPH Sector will achieve overall resilience against all hazards. It will prevent or minimize damage to, or destruction of, the nation's healthcare and public health infrastructure. It will strive to protect its workforce and preserve its ability to mount timely and effective responses (without disruption to services in unaffected areas) and to recover from both routine and emergency situations.

Mission Statement for the HPH Sector

To sustain the essential functions of the nation's healthcare and public health delivery system and to support effective emergency preparedness and response to nationally significant hazards by implementing strategies, evaluating risks, coordinating plans and policy advice, and providing guidance to prepare, protect, prevent, and, when necessary, respond to attacks on the nation's infrastructure, and support the necessary resilience in infrastructure to recover and reconstitute healthcare and public health services.

Goals for the HPH

Goal 1: Service Continuity—Maintain the ability to provide essential health services during and after disasters or disruption in the availability of supplies or supporting services such as water and power.

Goal 2: Workforce Protection—Protect the sector's workforce from the harmful consequences of all hazards that may compromise their health and safety and limit their ability to carry out their responsibilities.

Goal 3: Physical Asset Protection—Mitigate the risks posed by all hazards to the sector's physical assets.

Goal 4: Cybersecurity—Mitigate risks to the sector's cyber assets that may result in disruption to or denial of health services.

Source: DHS. 2010. *Healthcare and Public Health Sector-Specific Plan.*

regulations to safeguard the effectiveness of their products; and those aspects of the healthcare system which require data to comply with security and privacy rules as found in the Health Insurance Portability and Accountability Act (HIPPA) of 1996 (see Note 2). In addition to meeting regulatory requirements, the HPH Sector supports risk assessment to expose underlying vulnerabilities and potential points of failure in the system. The HPH Sector is vast and complex, and it is difficult to apply one risk analysis method to the entire sector. Organizations in the sector use a variety of tools and methods to assess vulnerabilities and consequences. The following discussion outlines some of them.

Strategic Homeland Security Infrastructure Risk Analysis

Strategic Homeland Security Infrastructure Risk Analysis (SHIRA) provides a common framework that sectors can use to assess the economic, loss of life, and psychological consequences resulting from terrorist incidents as well as natural hazards and domestic threats (see Note 2). It is a threat-based approach and is the result of an integrated "fusion" effort between the infrastructure protection and intelligence communities (ICs). SHIRA is similar to the military decision-making process where intelligence initiates the planning and all functional areas participate in the entire process.

The SHIRA model begins with the SSA working with the IC to rank the threat and define current themes. In this case, it is the HHS agency. Vulnerabilities and consequences are next assessed. Finally, the HITRAC calculates the risk ratings. The risk ratings are used to compare the risks faced by a sector or associated with an attack method or threat theme. The simple formula is: Risk = Threat × Vulnerability × Consequence.

On behalf of the HPH Sector, Risk Assessment Working Group (RAWG) uses the SHIRA methodology to develop scenarios of real-world events that could impact critical sector services, including the delivery of care and the medical supply chain (see Note 2). Some of the scenarios that have been developed include those relating to biological, cyber, and vehicle-borne explosive devices, and insider threats (see Note 2). The SHIRA analysis favors those events that are high consequence and have a possibility of occurring. Sample targets include laboratories handling biological select agents and toxins, manufacturing facilities, medical supply storage facilities, and cyber infrastructure (see Note 2).

HPH SECTOR AND CYBERSECURITY

As previously mentioned, under Presidential Policy Directive 21 (PPD-21), the HHS has SSA responsibility for the HPH Sector. HHS implements its SSA role for the HPH Sector through the Critical Infrastructure Protection (CIP) Program within the Office of the Assistant Secretary for Preparedness and Response (ASPR). Through this program, the HHS works in voluntary partnership with public and private sector entities to enhance their security and resilience with respect to all hazards, including cyberthreats.[3]

Cybersecurity in the HPH Sector is becoming more of a concern as medical devices have become increasingly linked to the Internet, hospital networks, and other medical devices. This reliance on technology for medical purposes has opened up a new set of vulnerabilities. Devices can malfunction, treatments can be interrupted, and there may be breaches to patient information. In light of PPD-21, the federal government has worked with the HPH Sector, including private entities, to manage risk and strengthen the security and resilience of this critical infrastructure against cyberthreats.

For example, in 2014, the Center for Devices and Radiological Health (CDRH) finalized its guidance for industry entitled, "Content of Premarket Submissions for Management of Cybersecurity in Medical Devices."[4] Additionally, the National Institute of Standards and Technology (NIST) published a voluntary risk-based framework focusing on enhanced cybersecurity. The cybersecurity framework is for organizations of any size in any of the 16 critical infrastructure sectors that either already have a mature cyber risk management and cybersecurity program, or that do not have such programs. Many of the sectors have adopted this framework in their sector-specific plans. The HPH sector has also utilized this framework to help manage and limit cybersecurity risks. The framework is comprised of three primary components: *core, implementation tiers,* and *profile,* and provides an assessment mechanism that enables organizations to determine their current cybersecurity capabilities. Additionally, organizations can set individual goals for a target state and establish a plan for improving and maintaining cybersecurity programs.[5] Table 11.2 illustrates the framework components.

The five elements of the framework core are considered essential to an effective cybersecurity program. These five core elements are further described in Table 11.3.

The framework implementation tiers provide context on how an organization views cybersecurity risk and the processes in place to manage that risk. Ranging from Partial (Tier 1) to Adaptive (Tier 4), each tier describes an increasing degree of rigor and sophistication in cybersecurity risk management practices. Further, each tier provides information as to the extent to which risk management is informed by business needs and is integrated into an organization's overall risk management practices (see Note 5). Table 11.4 illustrates these four tiers and specific components. Considered within the tier selection process are an organization's current risk management practices, threat environment, legal and regulatory requirements, business/mission objectives, and organizational constraints

Table 11.2 Cybersecurity Framework Components

Framework Core	Framework Implementation Tiers	Framework Profile
Cybersecurity activities and informative references, organized around particular outcomes.	Describes how cybersecurity risk is managed by an organization and degree the risk management practices exhibit key characteristics.	Aligns industry standards and best practices to the framework core in a particular implementation scenario
Enables communication of cyber risks across an organization.	Tiers are identified as: Tier 1: Partial Tier 2: Risk informed Tier 3: Repeatable Tier 4: Adaptive	Supports prioritization and measurement while factoring in business needs.
Comprises five elements: Identity Protect Detect Respond Recover		

Source: NIST. February 12, 2014. *Framework for Improving Critical Infrastructure Cybersecurity.*

(see Note 5). Furthermore, organizations should consider external guidance from federal government departments and agencies, Information Sharing and Analysis Centers (ISACs), existing maturity models, or other sources to determine which tier they should select. It is important to note that these tiers do not represent maturity levels, meaning successful implementation of the framework is not based upon tier determination, but rather on achievement of the outcomes described in the organization's target profile (see Note 5).

Finally, the framework profile enables an organization to establish a roadmap for reducing cybersecurity risk that is aligned with organizational and sector goals. Since many organizations are complex, there may be a need to create multiple profiles that are aligned with particular components and specific needs (see Note 5). Framework profiles can be used to describe current state or target state of cybersecurity activities. The current profile indicates the cybersecurity outcomes that are currently being achieved,

Table 11.3 Cybersecurity Framework Core Elements

Functions	Definitions	Categories
Identity	An understanding of how to manage cybersecurity risks to systems, assets, data, and capabilities.	Asset management, business environment, governance, risk assessment, and risk management strategy.
Protect	The controls and safeguards necessary to protect or deter cybersecurity threats.	Access control, awareness and training, data security, data protection processes, maintenance, and protective technologies.
Detect	Continuous monitoring to provide proactive and real-time alerts of cybersecurity related events.	Abnormalities and events, continuous monitoring, detection processes.
Respond	Incident-response activities.	Response planning, communications, analysis, mitigation, and improvements.
Recover	Develop and implement the appropriate activities to maintain plans for resilience and to restore any capabilities or services that were impaired due to a cybersecurity event.	Recovery planning, improvements, and communications.

Source: NIST. February 12, 2014. *Framework for Improving Critical Infrastructure Cybersecurity.*

and the target profile indicates outcomes which are needed to achieve the desired cybersecurity risk management goals. A comparison of the two profiles may be useful to reveal gaps in risk management actions that need to be addressed. Furthermore, organizations that make this comparison a priority are better prepared to gauge resource estimates, which are needed for such items as staffing and funding. Overall, this risk-based approach enables an organization to achieve cybersecurity goals in a cost-effective and prioritized manner (see Note 5).

Efforts to mitigate cybersecurity in the HPH Sector have been ongoing with sector members increasing their own cybersecurity activities. One example is the American Hospital Association (AHA), which has been working to increase awareness of cyberthreats among hospital

Table 11.4 Cybersecurity Framework Implementation Tiers

Tier 1: Partial	Tier 2: Risk Informed	Tier 3: Repeatable	Tier 4: Adaptive
Organizational cybersecurity risk management practices are not formalized, and risk is managed in an ad hoc manner with limited awareness of risk and no collaboration with other entities.	Risk-management processes and programs are in place but may not be established by organization-wide policy; collaboration is understood but organization lacks formal capabilities. Information is shared informally.	Formal policies for risk-management processes and programs are established and there is an organization-wide approach to managing cyber risk. The organization understands its dependencies and partners. External participation with partners enables collaboration and risk-based management decisions in response to events.	Risk-management processes and programs are based on lessons learned and is embedded in the organizational culture. The organization manages risk and actively shares information with partners to ensure accurate, current information is being shared.

Source: NIST. February 12, 2014. *Framework for Improving Critical Infrastructure Cybersecurity.*

executives by providing them with risk resources. The AHA has provided a series of threat briefings and teleconferences on cyberthreats to their members, which have been supported by presenters from the HHS Critical Infrastructure Protection Branch, DHS, National Security Council (NSC) Staff, and others (see Note 3).

In response to cybersecurity efforts for medical devices, the FDA has published a number of guidelines, including *Guidance for Industry: Cybersecurity for Networked Medical Devices Containing Off-the-Shelf Software* (issued January 14, 2005), *FDA Safety Communication: Cybersecurity for Medical Devices and Hospital Networks* (issued June 13, 2013), and *Draft*

Guidance for Industry and FDA Staff: Content of Premarket Submissions for Management of Cybersecurity in Medical Devices (issued June 14, 2013) (see Note 3). Another example is an internal agency program, the HHS Cybersecurity Program. This information security and privacy program helps to protect HHS against potential information technology threats and vulnerabilities and is dedicated to compliance with federal mandates and legislation. HHS also participates in CyberRx, a series of industry-wide exercises to stimulate cyberattacks on healthcare organizations (see Note 3).

HPH SECTOR: POLICY INITIATIVES

The HHS/ASPR's CIP supports key activities and policies for risk assessment including infrastructure risk analysis and prioritization, cybersecurity initiative coordination, emergency operation liaison with private sector partners during emergencies, and sector lead for developing, evaluating, and implementing all hazards critical infra-structure protection measures (see Note 3). The initiatives taken include the following:

1. The CIP can provide subject matter expert (SME) support for part-ners requesting guidance on best practices for both physical and cyber critical infrastructure protection. The HHS/ASPR's Critical Instructure Protection Program can tap into its private sector partners in the following healthcare and public health subsectors:
   a. Direct Healthcare
   b. Plans and Payers
   c. Mass Fatality Management
   d. Pharmaceuticals
   e. Public Health
   f. Labs
   g. Blood
   h. Medical Materials
   i. Health IT and Medical Technology (see Note 3).
2. Another key initiative includes opportunities for two-way shar-ing of information with national-level private sector partners. This includes a wide representation of experts in all aspects of healthcare and public health critical infrastructure protection. The CIP team partners in the exchange of critical expertise in

areas such as cybersecurity, physical security, workforce protection, and supply chain management (see Note 3).

3. The Homeland Security Information Network for the Healthcare and Public Health community (HSIN-HPH) is an infrastructure protection tool for the HPH Sector. It is the nation's primary web portal for public and private collaboration to protect critical infrastructure and key resources (CIKR). Through HSIN-HPH, sensitive but unclassified information can be shared with trusted partners. Specifically, users have access to the following:

    a. Timely, relevant, and actionable information about threats, vulnerabilities, security, policy, cybersecurity, and incident response and recovery activities affecting the healthcare and public health community
    b. Alerts and notifications of credible threats
    c. Best practices for protection and preparedness measures for HPH stakeholders
    d. CIKR preparedness and resilience analysis and research products
    e. Communication and collaboration with other SMEs (see Note 3)

In addition to these initiatives, the Office of Policy and Planning (OPP) advises HHS and ASPR leaders through policy options and strategic planning to support domestic and international public health emergency preparedness and response activities. Some of the activities are as follows:

1. Leads an integrated approach to policy development and analysis within ASPR
2. Analyzes proposed policies, presidential directives, and regulations, and develops short- and long-term policy objectives for ASPR
3. Serves as ASPR's focal point for the NSC policy coordination activities and represents the ASPR, as appropriate, in interagency policy coordination meetings and related activities
4. Studies public health preparedness and response issues, identifies gaps in policy, and initiates policy planning and formulation to fill identified gaps
5. Leads the implementation of the Pandemic and All Hazards Preparedness Act (PAHPA) and is responsible for developing the quadrennial national health security strategy (NHSS) and the NHSS Biennial Implementation Plan for public health emergency preparedness and response[6]

TRANSPORTATION SYSTEMS SECTOR PROFILE

The US transportation network is expansive, open, and easily accessible by land, sea, and air. This complex set of interconnected systems includes a wide variety of airways, road, tracks, terminals, and passages that provide essential services. The DHS identifies seven interconnected subsectors: *aviation, highway infrastructure and motor carrier, maritime, mass transit and passenger rail, pipeline systems, freight rail,* and *postal and shipping.* These systems transport not only people, but also transport food, water, fuel, and other supplies vital to public health, safety, security, and the economic well-being of our country.[7] The Department of Homeland Security (DHS) Transportation Security Administration (TSA), the United States Coast Guard (USCG), and the Department of Transportation (DOT) are the Co-SSA for the Transportation Systems Sector. Table 11.5 presents an overview of the seven key subsectors of the Transportation System Sector.

The Transportation Systems Sector-Specific Plan details how the NIPP risk management framework is implemented within the context of the distinct characteristics and environment of the sector. Under the 2013 PPD-21, the postal and shipping sector was consolidated within the Transportation Systems Sector.

Similar to other sectors, the vast majority of the transportation infrastructure is owned by the private sector and is composed of physical, human, and cyber components. All of the remaining 15 CIKR sectors are highly dependent on transportation services, which in turn are dependent on the energy, communications, information technology, chemical, and critical manufacturing sectors (see Note 7).

TRANSPORTATION SYSTEM SECTOR MISSION AND GOALS

The mission of the transportation system sector is to continuously improve the risk posture of the transportation system. This mission and stated goals are illustrated in Table 11.6.

TRANSPORTATION SYSTEM SECTOR: ASSESSING RISK

Risk assessments in the Transportation System Sector use the basic risk equation of Risk = f (Threat, Vulnerability, Consequence). Because risk assessments of the transportation system examine the probability and

Table 11.5   Seven Key Subsectors of the Transportation System Sector

Aviation: includes aircraft, air traffic control systems, approximately 450 commercial airports and 19,000 additional airports, heliports, and landing strips. This mode includes civil and joint use military airports, heliports, short takeoff and landing ports, and seaplane bases.

Highway Infrastructure and Motor Carrier: encompasses nearly 4 million miles of roadway, almost 600,000 bridges, and some 400 tunnels in 35 states. Vehicles include automobiles, motorcycles, and trucks carrying hazardous materials, other commercial freight vehicles, motor coaches, and school buses.

Maritime Transportation System: consists of about 95,000 miles of coastline, 361 ports, 25,000 miles of waterways, 3.4 million square miles of Exclusive Economic Zone, and intermodal landside connections, which allow the various modes of transportation to move people and goods, to, from, and on the water.

Mass Transit and Passenger Rail: includes service by buses, rail transit (commuter rail, heavy rail—also known as subways or metros—and light rail, including trolleys and streetcars), long distance rail—namely Amtrak and Alaska Railroad—and other, less common types of service (cable cars, inclined planes, funiculars, and automated guideway systems).

Pipeline Systems: consist of vast networks of pipeline that traverse hundreds of thousands of miles throughout the country, carrying nearly all of the nation's natural gas and about 65% of hazardous liquids, as well as various chemicals. These include approximately 2.2 million miles of natural gas distribution pipelines, about 168,900 miles of hazardous liquid pipelines, and more than 109 liquefied natural gas processing and storage facilities.

Freight Rail: consists of seven major carriers, hundreds of smaller railroads, over 140,000 miles of active railroad, over 1.3 million freight cars, and roughly 20,000 locomotives. Further, over 12,000 trains operate daily. The Department of Defense has designated 30,000 miles of track and structure as critical to mobilize and resupply of US forces.

Postal and Shipping: moves over 574 million messages, products, and financial transactions each day. Postal and shipping activity is differentiated from general cargo operations by its focus on letter or flat mail, publications, or small- and medium-size packages and by service from millions of senders to nearly 152 million destinations.

Source: DHS. 2010. *Transportation Systems Sector.* https://www.dhs.gov /transportation-systems-sector.

the consequence of an undesirable event affecting, or resulting from, sector assets, systems or networks, transportation risk is characterized in two fundamentally and nonmutually exclusive ways: (a) risk to the transportation system, and (b) risk from the transportation system (see

Table 11.6 Transportation Systems Sector Mission and Goals

Transportation Systems Sector Mission

To achieve a sustained reduction in the impact of incidents to the sector's critical infrastructure

Goals for the Transportation Systems Sector

Goal 1: Prevent and deter acts of terrorism using, or against, the transportation system.

Goal 2: Enhance the all-hazards preparedness and resilience of the global transportation system to safeguard US national interests.

Goal 3: Improve the effective use of resources for transportation security.

Goal 4: Improve sector situational awareness, understanding, and collaboration.

Source: DHS. 2010. *Transportation Systems Sector-Specific Plan.*

Note 7, p. 32). The information considered in an assessment of transportation assets and systems might include cargo or passenger volume, proximity to population centers, and system dependence on a particular asset.

There are three classes of risk assessments that may be used in the sector. These assessments may vary in methodology depending on their scope and purpose, and are depicted as (a) Mission, Asset, and System Specific Risk Assessments (MASSRA), (b) Modal Risk Assessments, and (c) Sector Cross-Modal Risk Assessments. Table 11.7 details these three classes of risk assessments used in the Transportation System Sector.

The primary risk assessment methods used by the transportation modes along the three class levels (as listed in Table 11.7) are the Transportation Sector Security Risk Assessment (TSSRA), the Baseline Assessment for Security Enhancement (BASE), and the Maritime Security Risk Analysis Model (MSRAM). The following is a brief discussion of each of these primary methods.

Transportation Sector Security Risk Assessment

TSSRA is an analytical technique that ranks the risks associated with multiple attack scenarios in each mode and compares these risks across the sector. It is an example of both a cross-modal (Class 3) and a modal risk assessment (Class 2). The TSSRA process allows the sector to evaluate those scenarios which present the highest relative risk. The focus is on a wide-ranging set of possible scenarios, including cyber incidents,

Table 11.7   Three Classes of Risk Assessments in the Transportation Systems Sector

Class 1: Mission, Asset, and System Specific Risk Assessments	Class 2: Modal Risk Assessments	Class 3: Cross-Modal Comparative Analysis
MASSRA focus on one or more of the risk elements or on scenario-specific assessments. An example is a blast effect analysis on a certain type of conveyance. These assessments generally do not cross jurisdictional lines and have a narrow, specific focus. They provide a detailed analysis of infrastructure vulnerabilities and can be used to determine which countermeasures should be used to mitigate risk.	These are used to identify how best to determine or validate high-risk focus areas within a mode of transportation. These modal risk assessments may also help to establish the sector's priorities for a specific mode. TSA's transportation sector security risk assessment (TSSRA) tool is used to conduct modal security risk assessments for each of the primary transportation modes, as well as sub-modal groups such as the school bus transportation system. Further, the USCG uses the Maritime Security Risk Analysis Model (MSRAM) and other inputs to provide the maritime risk information to TSSRA.	Class 3 assessments are cross-modal risk assessments focusing on two or more modes, or on the entire sector. TSSRA, is also an example of a cross-modal comparative analysis method. These analyses help identify strategic planning priorities and define long-term visions. Additionally, these inform key leadership decisions, including investments in countermeasures. A good example is a sector-wide assessment could identify an Improvised explosive device (IED) attack to underwater tunnels as a top threat.

Risk Assessment Classes: Summary
These three risk assessment types may be conducted concurrently and/or independently by various sector partners. Once the assessments take place and the results are analyzed and disseminated, they are sent to the sector's leadership as tools to aid in decision making processes.

Source: DHS. 2010. *Transportation Systems Sector-Specific Plan*, pp. 34–35.
[a] DHS. 2010. *Transportation Systems Sector-Specific Plan*, pp. 34–35.

for different arrangements of transportation assets, attack types, and targets. Fault tree analysis is used to determine the risk. Costs, benefits, and perceived effectiveness of current and proposed measures are then calculated. The final risk scores are presented to decision makers and stakeholders, who in turn make informed decisions on transportation systems sector priorities (see Note 7, p. 35).

Baseline Assessment for Security Enhancement

The BASE is a comprehensive security assessment program designed to evaluate posture in 17 Security and Emergency Management Action Items foundational to an effective security program. Some of these action items are the agency's security plan, background investigation of employees, security training, drills and exercises, public awareness, facility security and access control, and cybersecurity (see Note 7, p. 37). Conducting a BASE informs security priorities, the development of security enhancement programs, allows for the allocation of resources, and assists in the compilation of smart security practices for mass transit and passenger rail agencies (see Note 7, p. 36). Furthermore, BASE is an example of a mission-specific assessment that focuses on vulnerability and effective security implementation. In the BASE program, TSA takes responsibility for reviewing the implementation of security actions jointly developed by TSA, DOT's Federal Transit Administration (FTA), and sector partners from mass transit and passenger rail systems (see Note 7, p. 36).

Maritime Security Risk Analysis Model

The USCG uses MSRAM specifically for assessing maritime security and risks. MSRAM is an example of a scenario-based risk assessment that falls into both the modal risk assessment (Class 2) and mission-specific risk assessment categories (Class 1) (see Note 7, p. 37). The MSRAM methodology uses a combination of target and attack mode scenarios and assesses risk in terms of threat vulnerability and consequences. It is a powerful tool that allows the Federal Maritime Security Coordinators and Area Maritime Security Committees (AMSCs) to perform detailed scenario risk assessments on all of the maritime sectors (see Note 7, p. 37). Furthermore, MSRAM is used by all levels of government—federal, state, and local.

237

TRANSPORTATION SYSTEM SECTOR POLICIES AND PRIORITIES

Information gathered from an assessment in the Transportation System Sector is then analyzed in combination with other factors in the decision environment. Collectively, this enables stakeholders and decision makers to set policy priorities and strategies for the sector. By prioritizing specific areas of risk, the sector can also determine resource allocation and budget needs. Table 11.8 illustrates examples of some factors that the sector considers when developing policy priorities and strategies based on risk assessment.

ESS PROFILE

ESS includes a diverse array of disciplines and capabilities that supports a broad range services in the areas of prevention, preparedness, response, and recovery. The ESS serves as the primary protector of the other 15 critical infrastructures, operating as the first line of defense. The ESS is so critical, that a failure or disruption in the sector could result in substantial damage, loss of life, major public health problems, long-term economic loss, and cascading disruptions to the other critical sectors.[8] Potential risks to the ESS include natural disasters and extreme weather patterns;

Table 11.8 Factors Impacting Transportation Systems Sector Priorities and Policies

Intelligence and Risk Assessment	Legislative and Executive Requirements
Modal Assessments	DHS Priorities
Intelligence Reports	Presidential Directives
Unknown Risk Hedges	Congressional Mandates
Comprehensive Reviews	Government Accountability Office (GAO)
Sector Comparative Analysis	Recommendations
Mission and Asset Specific Assessments	
Safety, Privacy, and Stakeholder Concerns	**Budget and Implementation Constraints**
Transportation Flow	Sector Capabilities
Safety/Security Conflicts	Budget and Acquisition Cycles
Privacy/Security Conflicts	Federal Regulation Timelines
Unfunded Mandate Issues	Competing National Budget Priorities

Source: DHS. 2010. *Transportation Systems Sector-Specific Plan*, p. 6.

cyberattacks or disruptions, violent extremist and terrorist attacks; as well as chemical, biological, radiological, and nuclear events.

As with other critical sectors, the risk of cyberattacks continues to evolve, especially with the reliance on cyber systems for emergency operations. Communications, data management, biometric activities, telecommunications, and electronic security systems are just some of the ways in which technological advancements to the sector also present risk. Additionally, increased expectations from the public for emergency response, along with limited financial resources, create an environment where risk to the sector is a serious challenge (see Note 8). The DHS is designated as the SSA for the ESS.

ESS KEY OPERATING CHARACTERISTICS

Millions of trained personnel, both in paid and volunteer capacities, make up the ESS community. The majority of these come from state, local, tribal and territorial (SLTT) levels of government. Some examples include city police departments, fire and rescue services, county sheriff's offices, public works departments, and at the federal level the Department of Defense police and fire departments (see Note 8). With a focus on the protection of other sectors and the public, the ESS consists of key operating characteristics. The DHS 2015 ESS Specific Plan identifies these characteristics as follows:

- The ESS is the most geographically distributed sector with more than 2.5 million personnel serving every location in all 50 states, five territories, and the District of Columbia.
- First response can greatly affect the resulting severity and duration of emergency events.
- Adaptability and flexibility are hallmarks of ESS operations.
- Sector operations are personnel-driven, but highly dependent on communications, information technology, and transportation systems.
- ESS personal are operating in a limited resource environment (see Note 8).

The ESS is made up of five disciplines: (a) law enforcement, (b) emergency management, (c) fire and rescue services, (d) emergency medical services, and (e) public works. The sector consists of systems and networks composed of three components: (a) human, (b) physical, and (c) cyber. Table 11.9 shows these components in detail.

Table 11.9 Emergency Services Sector (ESS) Components and Disciplines

Three Components	Five Distinct Disciplines		
Human	**More than 2,500,000** career and volunteer ESS personnel in five disciplines.	**Law Enforcement** **Emergency Management**	**Fire and Rescue Services** **Emergency Medical Services** **Public Works**
Physical	**Facilities** for daily operations, support, training, or storage.	**Equipment** Specialized for discipline and capability (e.g., personal protective, communications, and surveillance).	**Vehicles** Specialized for disciplines and capability (e.g., ambulances, HazMat, aircraft, and watercraft).
Cyber	**Virtual Operations** Emergency operations communications, database management, biometric activities, and security systems are frequently operated in cyberspace.	**Internet** The Internet is widely used by the sector to provide information and distribute alerts, warnings, and threats relevant to the sector.	**Information Networks** Computer-aided dispatch and watch and warning systems, information-sharing portals, and social networking are leveraged to keep the ESS informed and connected.

Source: DHS. 2015. *Emergency Services Sector-Specific Plan.*

As noted earlier, the majority of ESS personnel are public employees in the SLTT levels of government. The private sector, however, also contributes to the ESS with private industrial fire departments, private security officers, and private EMS providers. While the sector as a whole is not regulated, there are numerous regulations which govern many emergency response functions at the SLTT level including hazardous materials, fire and rescue, and public utilities. Finally, the ESS has critical sector interdependencies with the energy, communications, transportation systems, water, healthcare and public health, and information sectors (see Note 8). Specialized emergency services are also provided through individual personnel and teams. The following are the specialized capabilities:

- Tactical teams
- Hazardous devices team/public safety bomb disposal
- Public safety dive teams/maritime units
- Canine units
- Aviation units
- Hazardous materials
- Search and rescue (SAR)
- Public safety answering points
- Fusion centers
- Private Security Guard Forces
- National Guard Civil Support (see Note 8)

ESS SECTOR CURRENT RISKS

It can be argued that the ESS has one of the most critical missions of all sectors. Risks to its operations and functions could have devastating impacts on public safety, the protection of other infrastructures, and to first responders and others working in the ESS. The DHS 2015 ESS Specific Plan identifies four of the most significant sector threats, and their associated risks: (a) cyber infrastructure attacks or disruptions, (b) natural disaster and extreme weather, (c) violent extremist and terrorist attacks, and (d) incidents involving chemical, biological, and nuclear agents (see Note 8, p. 8). Table 11.10 provides details on these four sector threats.

ESS Goals and Priorities

As part of the 2015 Sector-Specific Plan, the ESS identified goals and priorities to guide the sector's security and resilience efforts over the next 4 years. Specifically, these four goals are as follows:

- **Partnership Engagement**—collaborating with sector partners and encouraging continuous growth and improvement of these partnerships.
- **Situational Awareness**—support an information-sharing environment.

Table 11.10 Significant Emergency Services Sector (ESS) Risks

Cyber Infrastructure Attacks or Disruptions

Advancements in technology have increased the dependency of the ESS on cyber-based infrastructures and operations. These include emergency operations communications, data management, biometric activities, telecommunications (i.e., computer-aided dispatch), and electronic security systems. Reliance on these technologies put the sector at risk for cyberattacks from anywhere in the world.

Natural Disasters and Extreme Weather (Earthquakes, Hurricanes, Fires, and Floods)

Patterns of more extreme weather increase the geographic magnitude and severity of disasters. These events require huge amounts of resources from the ESS, often for extended periods of time. In addition, disasters present increased hazard to responders and often disrupt critical services needed for an effective response.

Violent Extremist and Terrorist Attacks

There is an increased risk to emergency services personnel from violent extremists. These individuals are characterized by those who support or commit ideologically motivated violence to further political goals. These individuals are increasingly targeting first responders, especially law enforcement, and soft targets. Threats of terrorism persist, and are becoming more diversified through a wide range of attack methods. Radicalization on the Internet, and other forms of social media, enable these individuals to connect with others and plan violent attacks.

Chemical, Biological, Radiological, and Nuclear Incidents

Incidents involving chemical, biological, radiological and nuclear agents (CBRN) present serious risks to emergency services personnel responding to and treating victims of such attacks. Biological agents or infectious disease can quickly spread through numerous jurisdictions and greatly strain emergency services resources. Responding to HazMat incidents also create risks as first responders may not be provided with accurate cargo information. All of these agents require extensive training and specialized equipment. Shortfalls in budgets and other resources may limit the capabilities of the sector to rapidly respond to and contain such incidents.

Source: DHS. 2015. *Emergency Services Sector-Specific Plan.*

- **Prevention, Preparedness, and Protection**—implement a risk-based approach to improve the preparedness and resilience of the sector's overall capacity to perform its mission through policy initiatives and decision making.
- **Recovery and Reconstitution**—improve the operational capacity, sustainability, and resilience of the sector and increase the speed

and efficiency of normal services and activities following an incident (see Note 8).

In support of these goals, sector partners developed priorities to focus their efforts, which include the following:

- Developing and utilizing processes and mechanisms to support sector partnerships and information sharing
- Sharing best practices
- Enabling sector partners to implement their missions
- A focus on technological solutions and cybersecurity
- Encourage cross-sector and cross-discipline collaborations
- Defining current sector risk assessment and information-sharing capabilities and requirements (see Note 8)

ESS: ASSESSING RISK

The ESS approaches risk with an emphasis on its reliance upon digital technologies and other cyber infrastructures. Two documents released by the sector establish a baseline national-level cyber risk and identify risk mitigation strategies—the 2012 *Emergency Services Sector Cyber Risk Assessment* (ESS-CRA) and the 2014 *Emergency Services Sector Roadmap to Secure Voice and Data Systems* (Roadmap) (see Note 8). The ESS-CRA evaluates risk to the sector by focusing on the five ESS disciplines. The ESS-CRA uses the DHS Cyber Assessment Risk Management Approach (CARMA), along with the Cybersecurity Framework, to assess risk in the sector. CARMA provides a methodology for sector stakeholders to define key business functions that must be protected, and identifies risks posed to their functional viability.[9]

Risk management in the ESS operates from a point of common understanding and terminology, despite the varying conceptualizations of infrastructure criticality across disciplines and jurisdictions. While the national level assessments, such as the Strategic National Risk Assessment (SNRA), are important to an overall understanding of national risk, the ESS conducts risk assessments primarily at the state and local levels (see Note 8, p. 16). According to the ESS 2015 Sector-Specific Plan, Assessments conducted by the ESS adhere to several risk assessment methodology guidelines:

- Documented—information used in the assessment and how it is synthesized to generate risk estimate is documented and transparent to the user and others using the results.

- Reproducible—despite variance in each discipline's facilities, capabilities, and personnel, the results are comparable and repeatable. Subjective judgments are minimized to allow for future policy and value judgments by owners and operators.
- Defensible—assessment components are logically integrated and ESS disciplines are used appropriately to the risk analysis with a parallel effort to accomplish assessment accuracy and transparency (see Note 8, p. 17).

The ESS uses a number of risk assessment tools to assess the threats, vulnerabilities, and consequences. These assessments are crucial to decision making and policy implementation throughout the sector. Table 11.11 provides a description of these assessment tools.

ESS: Policy and Emerging Issues

Changes in policy, resources, threat types, and public expectations have impacted the ESS risk profile and public policy decision making. The DHS ESS Specific plan outline eight specific trends and issues, key to security and resilience efforts (see Note 8, p. 7). The following list describes these in detail.

- **Increasing public expectations for ESS expertise, rapid response capabilities, and real-time information sharing.** The focus has shifted to an all-hazard incident response planning. The public expects ESS personnel to respond quickly and efficiently to all types of incidents and to communicate information in real time. Public information needs can drain response personnel. Moreover, reduced budgets, increased mandates, training requirements, and high costs associated with equipment maintenance can further hinder resources (see Note 8, p. 7).
- **Reduced grant funding constraining state and local resources.** The ability of the ESS to identify risk and make changes to the sector profile may be inhibited by reductions in grant monies and reduced state and local budgets. For example, such restrictions have forced the ESS community to choose between terrorist threat mitigation strategies and additional police activities for drug and gang enforcement. At the same time costs have increased for healthcare, personnel, and fuel and maintenance equipment (see Note 8, p. 7).

Table 11.11 Emergency Services Sector (ESS) Risk Assessment Tools

State, local, tribal and territorial (SLTT) Hazard Identification and Risk Assessment (HIRA)

SLTT ESS partners conduct HIRAs to understand and examine specific potential or existing circumstances that can generate a disaster or emergency incident at the SLTT level. HIRAs focus on quantitative assessment of hazards and consequences.

Threat and Hazard Identification and Risk Assessment (THIRA)

THIRA expands on HIRA by broadening what is considered through the risk assessment process. SLTT entities use the THIRA process to complete the following qualitative risk assessment steps: identify the threats and hazards of primary concern to the community, develop threat and hazard context, establish targets for each core capability within the National Preparedness Goal, and apply the results to estimate resources required.

Enhanced Critical Infrastructure Protection (ECIP)

This tool facilitates outreach to establish or enhance the relationship between DHS and critical infrastructure owners and operators. Voluntary security surveys are offered as a result of the outreach and are conducted by DHS PSAs to assess the overall security and resilience of the nation's most critical infrastructure sites.

Onsite Assessments

SLTT entities deploy onsite risk assessment teams that focus on high priority assets within their area of responsibility (AOR). Many risk assessment teams concentrate on critical infrastructure vulnerability and provide recommendations to the owner/operator to address potential threats and security vulnerabilities. An example of an available federal onsite assessment is the Cyber Resilience Review—a no-cost voluntary cyber risk assessment facilitated by DHS cybersecurity professionals.

Planning Efforts

Joint committees, such as local emergency planning committees (LEPCs), primarily comprise local emergency services representatives familiar with a variety of jurisdiction-specific risk factors. LEPC meeting are open to all emergency management stakeholders and enable the illumination of risk factors that may be inadvertently excluded from assessments. Some sector partners also rely on capital budgeting plans to determine if the organization's risk management investments are worth pursuing.

Cybersecurity Assessment and Risk Management Approach (CARMA)

Provides a strategic methodology to identify, assess, and manage cyber critical infrastructure risks in the sector.

Source: DHS. 2015. *Emergency Services Sector-Specific Plan.*

- **Extreme weather events.** In recent years, extreme weather events have become more frequent. Over time these increase response demands which may drain sector personnel, assets, and capabilities. Of particular concern are natural disasters which threaten key services that enable ESS response (see Note 8, p. 7).
- **Greater dependence on cyber infrastructure.** As with other critical sectors, the ESS has become increasingly dependent on cyber assets, systems, and disciplines to carry out its services. Newer technologies such as Next-Generation 9-1-1, the transition toward cloud-based information systems, and the usage of geospatial tools, have enabled the ESS to expand and improve its operations. The downside is these newer technologies present new risks which further test the sector's ability to swiftly and carefully respond to emergencies (see Note 8, p. 7).
- **Changing population dynamics.** The changes in population density and characteristics present another set of challenges for the ESS. As people live longer, the average age of the general population increases. Older adults often require more medical response. Language barriers and threats from global mobility (i.e., risks of biological agents and communicable diseases) are other issues of concern for the sector (see Note 8, p. 8).
- **Attacks targeting or compromising ESS personnel.** While the nature of the disciplines in the ESS present inherent risk, first responders may also become the target of attacks when responding to mass casualty, active shooter, or IED incidents. ESS personnel may also suffer from physical or emotional trauma due to incident response (see Note 8, p. 7).
- **Aging infrastructure.** The nations aging infrastructure includes electrical grids, water/wastewater systems, and roads and bridges—all of which increases the risk of failure. These risks create incidents that ultimately require ESS response while also hampering services critical to ESS functions (see Note 8, p. 7).
- **Loss of workforce expertise.** As the average age of personnel increases, the risk of losing quality people to retirement is a real concern. New recruits tend to be less experienced (see Note 8, p. 7).

CONCLUSION

The HPH Sector, Transportation Sector, and Emergency Service Sector are complex infrastructures. Each requires the use of a variety of methods and tools to assess and manage risk. Specific methods of risk include SHIRA in the Healthcare and Public Health Sector, TSSRA in the Transportation Systems Sector, and THIRA in the ESS. The increasing link between physical and cybersecurity in these sectors necessitates the development of policies and initiatives to address evolving threats. It also creates more interdependencies. All three sectors support efforts to implement the Cybersecurity Framework and a collection of tools are being developed to assess cyber risks. Chapter 12 presents the communications, information technology, and financial sectors, all of which are also subject to cyber intrusions.

REVIEW QUESTIONS

1. Discuss the mission statements, goals, and priorities of each of the three sectors presented in the chapter.
2. List and describe the various approaches to managing risk taken by each of the three sectors presented in the chapter. Is there an overlap of methods used?
3. What are some of the key operating characteristics of the ESS? What makes these different from the Healthcare and Public Health or Transportation Systems Sectors?
4. Explain what is meant by partnership engagement. Which of the three sectors embraces this concept and why? Do you think it is applicable to other sectors? Explain your answer using specific examples.

NOTES

1. US DHS. 2010. *Healthcare and Public Health Sector-Specific Plan*. Washington, DC: US DHS.
2. US DHS. *Healthcare and Public Health Sector*. Retrieved from: https://www.dhs .gov/healthcare-and-public-health-sector.
3. US Department of Health and Human Services. *Assistant Secretary for Preparedness and Response*. Retrieved from: http://www.phe.gov.
4. Hanson, C. 2015. CDRH Schedules January 2016 Cybersecurity Workshop. *Inside Medical Devices, Updates on Developments for Medical Devices*. Retrieved from: http://www.insidemedicaldevices.com.

5. National Institute of Standards and Technology. February 12, 2014. *Framework for Improving Critical Infrastructure Cybersecurity.*
6. US Department of Health and Human Services. *Office of Policy and Planning.* Retrieved from: http://www.phe.gov.
7. US DHS. 2010. *Transportation Systems Sector-Specific Plan,* p. 32, p. 35, p. 36, p. 37.
8. US DHS. 2015. *Emergency Services, Sector-Specific Plan.*
9. US DHS. 2012. *Emergency Services Sector, Cyber Risk Assessment.*

12

Sector-Specific Agencies' Approaches to Risk
Communications Sector, Information Technology Sector, and Financial Sector

INTRODUCTION

In late 2015, a security researcher discovered multiple vulnerabilities in various name-brand wireless routers. Discovered flaws included path traversals, used to access potentially sensitive application programming interface (APIs), and weaknesses that allow unauthenticated attackers to alter the setting of a device, bypass authentication, and remote code executions.[1] In another scenario, Google's Android OS was found to be prone to numerous vulnerabilities which could be exploited through e-mail, web browsing, and MMS when processing media files.

Both instances demonstrate potential risk to the Communications Sector via smartphones and the Internet. The Internet has evolved as a critical infrastructure and the protection of it is shared with the Information Technology (IT) Sector. In this chapter, we examine both the Communications Sector and IT sectors. Closely interdependent, these two sectors provide essential operations supporting the US economy, businesses, public safety, and government. This chapter follows with an examination of the Financial Services Sector (FSS), which shares some of the same challenges as the Communications and IT Sectors. Mobile commerce, social media, and the safeguarding of client and employee information present unique challenges to the FSS as it does to the Communications and IT Sectors. This chapter concludes with a summary of the remaining seven Critical Infrastructure Sectors not previously discussed.

COMMUNICATIONS SECTOR PROFILE

America's reliance on a digital infrastructure makes the Communications Sector critical. The nation's communications infrastructure is composed of wireline, wireless, satellite, cable, and broadcasting capabilities, as well as those transport networks that support the Internet and other key information systems. This complex system incorporates multiple technologies and services with diverse ownership, much of which comes from the private sector.[2] Many of these companies are interdependent upon each other and as such, have had a long-standing tradition of cooperation and trust among them. Over time, these companies have included disasters and accidental disruptions into their network resilience designs, business continuity plans, and disaster recovery policies (see Note 2, p. 2).

The Office of Cybersecurity and Communications (CS&C) is the Sector-Specific Agency for both the Communications and Information Technology Sectors. The CS&C coordinates national-level reporting that is consistent with the National Response Framework and works to prevent or minimize disruptions to critical information infrastructure in order to protect the public, the economy, and government services.[3]

GOALS AND PRIORITIES OF THE COMMUNICATIONS SECTOR

The vision and goals for the Communications Sector combines a critical reliance on assured communications with the purpose to protect, enhance, and improve the sector's national security and emergency preparedness. Table 12.1 presents these statements.

COMMUNICATIONS SECTOR: ASSESSING RISK

Historically speaking, the Communications Sector has been an important infrastructure in need of protection. However, the compelling events of

Table 12.1 Communications Sector: Vision and Goals

Vison Statement for the Communications Sector

The US has a critical reliance on assured communications. The Communications Sector strives to ensure that the nation's communications networks and systems are secure, resilient, and rapidly restored in the event of disruption.

Goals for the Communications Sector

Goal 1: Protect and enhance the overall physical and logical health of communications.

Goal 2: Rapidly reconstitute critical communications services in the event of disruption and mitigate cascading effects.

Goal 3: Improve the sector's national security and emergency preparedness (NS/EP) posture with federal, state, local, tribal, international, and private sector entities to reduce risk.

Source: DHS. 2010. *Communications Sector-Specific Plan*, p. 5.

9/11, Hurricane Katrina, and Hurricane Sandy in 2012, have shown how dramatically the communications infrastructure can be impacted and how significant the sector is in an all-hazards environment. The terrorist attacks on September 11, 2001, severely disrupted communications networks. Moreover, a major telecommunications hub was severely damaged in the collapse of the World Trade Center buildings, affecting more than 4 million data circuits. Hurricane Katrina impacted a three-state telecommunications infrastructure, leaving 3 million users without a dial tone and taking thirty-eight 911 emergency services centers and 1000 cell phone towers out of operation (see Note 2, p. 6). Hurricane Sandy disrupted telecommunications services in several Northeastern states, impacting 911 calls and wireless cell towers.

It is clear that the Communications Sector faces both natural and man-made threats and that these infrastructure failures can be wide-reaching. When this occurs, it does so in three specific ways: (a) physical destruction of network components, (b) disruption in supporting network infrastructure, and (c) network congestion.[4] To assess the risk of these elements requires ongoing activity aimed at new asset and network configurations, and the analysis of existing assets in light of new threats (see Note 2, p. 27).

The Communications Sector approaches risk using a strategic framework based on the formula of consequence, vulnerability, and threat. As mentioned previously, the Communications Sector is integrally linked with the IT Sector (discussed later in this chapter).

The Communications Sector-Specific Plan (CSSP) Risk Assessment Framework is built on the goals of the CSSP and aims to increase the resilience of the Communications Sector. These basic risk assessment goals are as follows:

- **Resilient Infrastructure:** Critical infrastructure and their communications capabilities should be able to withstand natural or man-made hazards with minimal interruption or failure.
- **Diversity:** Facilities should have diverse primary and backup communications capabilities that do not share common points of failure.
- **Redundancy:** Facilities should use multiple communications capabilities to sustain business operations and eliminate single points of failure that could disrupt primary services.
- **Recoverability:** Plans and processes should be in place to restore operations quickly if an interruption or failure occurs (see Note 2, p. 28).

Table 12.2 summarizes the CSSP risk framework. Note that sector assessments are ongoing and continually updated.

Table 12.2   Communications Sector-Specific Plan (CSSP) Risk Framework Summary

Industry Self-Assessments	Government Sponsored Assessments		Government-Sponsored Cross Sector Dependency Analysis
Internal Industry Assessments	National Sector Risk Assessment (NSRA)	Detailed Risk Assessments	Sector Dependency Assessments
Recognition: industry routinely conducts self-assessments as a part of its business operations.	Goal: examine Communications Sector architecture to identify national risks.	Goal: conduct detailed risk assessments on architecture elements that have been identified as being high risk by NSRA.	Goal: assist other sectors in the assessment of communications dependency for high-risk assets.

(Continued)

Table 12.2 (*Continued*)   Communications Sector-Specific Plan (CSSP) Risk Framework Summary

Industry Self-Assessments	Government Sponsored Assessments		Government Sponsored Cross Sector Dependency Analysis
Approach: owners and operators conduct self-assessments of their networks voluntarily.	Approach: industry and government conduct a high-level qualitative risk analysis of the entire Communications Sector.	Approach: government works in conjunction with industry to conduct detailed quantitative assessments with respect to mission impact.	Approach: identify high-level critical sector communications dependencies and leverage NCS risk assessment methodologies to identify communications dependencies specific to a facility or function.

Source: DHS. 2010. *Communications Sector-Specific Plan*, p. 29.

COMMUNICATIONS SECTOR: INFORMATION SHARING POLICIES

Homeland Security Presidential Directive 7 (HSPD-7) assigns the DHS lead responsibility for coordinating the protection of national infrastructure, including the Communications Sector. Initially, DHS delegated this responsibility to the National Communications System (NCS), an office created in 1962 for crisis communications which was then moved to the DHS when it was created in 2003. In 2012, the NCS was disbanded by Presidential Executive Order (EO) 13618, Assignment of National Security and Emergency Preparedness Communications Functions.

As mentioned previously, the Office of Cybersecurity and Communications (CS&C) and since become the sector-specific agency (SSA) for the Communications and IT Sectors. Information sharing is the key part of DHS mission and the Communications Sector. In this capacity, the Communications Sector works closely with the DHS's National Cybersecurity and Communications Integration Center (NCCIC) to reduce the likelihood and severity of incidents that could potentially affect the infrastructure.[3] The NCCIC supports cyber situational awareness, incident response, and management 24/7. It is a national center that supports cyber and communications integration for the federal government, intelligence community, and law enforcement. The NCCIC shares information among public and private sector partners to build awareness of vulnerabilities, incidents, and mitigations (see Note 3).

IT SECTOR PROFILE

The IT Sector is central to the nation's security, economy, and public health and safety.[5] As a functions-based sector, it comprises not only physical assets but also virtual systems and networks that enable key capabilities and services in both the public and private sectors (see Note 5, p. 1). The functions of the IT Sector are vital to nearly every segment of modern society with businesses, governments, academia, and private citizens increasingly dependent upon its functions. Both virtual and distributed, these functions produce and provide hardware, software, and IT systems and services, and—in collaboration with the communications sector—the Internet (see Note 5). IT Sector functions are operated by owners and operators and their respective associations. Together, they maintain and reconstitute networks (i.e., the Internet, local networks, and wide area networks) and their associated services (see Note 5). The following are six critical functions of the IT Sector:

- Provide IT products and services
- Provide incident management capabilities
- Provide domain name resolution services
- Provide identity management and associated trust support services
- Provide Internet-based content, information, and communications services
- Provide Internet routing, access, and connection services (see Note 5, p. 1)

GOALS AND PRIORITIES OF THE IT SECTOR

The IT Sector has a specific vision and goals to support risk management of its critical functions. These are noted in Table 12.3.

Table 12.3 Information Technology (IT) Sector Vision and Goals

IT Sector Vision

To achieve a sustained reduction in the impact of incidents to the sector's critical infrastructure

Goals for the IT Sector

Goal 1: Identify, assess, and manage risks to the IT sector's critical functions and international dependencies.

Goal 2: Improve situational awareness during normal operations, potential or realized threats and disruptions, intentional or unintentional incidents, crippling attacks (cyber or physical) against IT sector infrastructure, technological emergencies and failures, or presidentially declared disasters.

Goal 3: Enhance the capabilities of public and private sector partners to respond to and recover from realized threats and disruptions, intentional or unintentional incidents, crippling attacks (cyber or physical) against IT Sector Infrastructure, technological emergencies or failures, or presidentially declared disasters, and develop mechanisms for reconstitution.

Goal 4: Drive continuous improvement of the IT Sector's risk management, situational awareness, and response, recovery, and reconstitution capabilities.

Source: DHS. 2010. *Information Sector-Specific Plan*, p. 2.

IT SECTOR: ASSESSING RISK

The risk environment of the IT Sector consists of varied and complex threats. Aside from man-made unintentional and natural threats, the IT Sector also faces cyber and physical threats from criminals, hackers, terrorists, and nation-states, all of whom have demonstrated capabilities and intentions to attack IT critical functions (see Note 5, p. 17). These threats, coupled with a high degree of interdependency, makes assessing risk a difficult task. To more fully address this risk environment, the IT Sector approaches risk from a top-down and functions-based approach. The IT Sector is unique in that it evaluates risk across the sector by focusing on critical functions rather than specific organizations or assets. Specifically, there are two levels of risk management that the IT Sector focuses on:

- **The individual enterprise level:** This level involves cybersecurity initiatives and practices to maintain the health of information security programs and infrastructures. In the private sector, these enterprise approaches are based on business objectives, such as shareholder values, efficacy, and customer service. On the other hand, the private sector usually bases their enterprise approaches on mission effectiveness or providing a public service (see Note 5, p. 2).

- **The sector or national level:** At this level, the IT Sector manages risk to its six critical functions to promote the assurance and resilience of the IT infrastructure and to protect against cascading consequences based on the sector's interconnectedness and the critical functions' interdependencies (see Note 5, p. 2).

IT Sector Baseline Risk Assessment Method

The preferred method of risk in the IT Sector is the IT Sector Baseline Risk Assessment (ITSRA) approach. ITSRA serves as a foundation for the sector's national-level risk management activities and was developed in collaboration by public and private sector partners and subject matter experts. The intent of the ITSRA was not to conflict with individual company or organizational risk management activities, but rather, to provide a sector and national level all-hazards risk profile. Included in this profile is the ability to assess risk from man-made deliberate, man-made unintentional, and natural threats that could affect the ability of the sector to support both the economy and security of our nation (see Note 5). ITSRA leverages existing risk-related definitions, frameworks, and taxonomies from various entities, including public and private IT Sector partners and standards and guidance organizations. In doing so, ITSRA reflects current knowledge about risk and adapts them in a way that enables a functions-based risk assessment (see Note 5, p. 22). The ITSRA methodology consists of five steps:

1. Step 1: Scope Assessment
2. Step 2: Assess Threats
3. Step 3: Assess Vulnerabilities
4. Step 4: Assess Consequences
5. Step 5: Create Risk Profile (see Note 5, p. 18)

Inherent within these steps are the threat, vulnerability, and consequence frameworks in the sector's risk assessment methodology. These approaches are described as follows.

Assessing Threats
The IT Sector threat analysis approach considers the full spectrum of intentional and unintentional man-made and natural threats. It is interesting to note that traditional threat analysis is not sufficient here. Traditional threat

analysis identifies an actor and the actor's intentions, motives, and capabilities to compromise a given target. However, in an IT sector analysis, this approach is not enough because of the unique risk environment where actors are not always easily identifiable or traceable. Furthermore, the attacks can move from conception to exploitation in a matter of hours (see Note 5, p. 22).

This is where the ITSRA becomes a critical piece to the risk assessment process. Because of the difficulty with identifying threat actors, especially those in cyberspace, the IT sector focuses on a threat's capabilities to exploit vulnerabilities before identifying the specific actors (see Note 5, p. 22). The IT sector defines threat capability as the availability or ease of use of tools or methods that could be used to damage, disrupt, or destroy critical functions (see Note 5, p. 22). A capability assessment of a natural threat considers those that could have a nationally significant impact. When assessing an intentional man-made threat, the capabilities approach is applied differently using tools or methods that can be easily configured to exploit critical functions. This is challenging, especially since the IT sector is also vulnerable to unintentional man-made threats due to its high reliance on humans (see Note 5, p. 22).

Assessing Vulnerabilities

Assessing vulnerabilities in the IT sector considers the people, process, technology, and physical vulnerabilities that, if exploited by a threat, could affect the confidentiality, integrity, or availability of critical functions (see Note 5, p. 23). More specifically, these vulnerabilities are as follows:

- **People:** includes the factors that affect the workforce such as human resource practices (personnel security), demographics (citizenship, qualifications), training and education (quality and quantity of institutions that teach and train the workforce), and market environments (compensation and benefits).
- **Processes:** includes vulnerabilities associated with the sequence and management of operations or activities; for example, manufacturing, logistics, information flow, and efficiency and effectiveness.
- **Technologies:** includes factors like reliance on hardware and software, and system dependencies and interdependencies.
- **Physical:** consists of vulnerabilities associated with the physical characteristics of facilities or locations. Geographic locations, weather, and natural vulnerabilities such as earthquakes, floods, and other natural disasters are included (see Note 5, p. 24).

Assessing Consequences

The IT Sector's consequence framework is common to all threat types (deliberate, unintentional, and natural). The IT Sector uses HSPD-7 consequence categories and criteria for evaluating events of national significance and the impacts they could have on national security, economic security, public health and safety, and public confidence (if a critical function is disrupted or degraded) (see Note 5, p. 25). Some of the questions considered under the consequence assessment are the following:

- What is the potential for loss of life, injuries, or adverse impact on public health and safety?
- How many users could be severely affected?
- What are the economic impacts, including asset replacement, business interruption, and remediation costs?
- Will federal, state or local governments be adversely affected? (see Note 5, p. 25)

Once the threat, vulnerability, and consequence frameworks have been properly assessed, a comprehensive risk profile identifying the risks of concern for the sector can be developed. ITSRA results in a sector-wide risk profile that describes the sector-wide risks as well as the function-specific risks and their associated existing mitigations. Once the profile is in place, it can then be used to develop the risk management strategy for each of the functions and guide mitigation decisions. Table 12.4 shows the IT sector's risks of concern as developed by subject matter experts for the IT sector.

IT Sector and Policy Initiatives

Since the IT Sector is comprised of a substantial amount of private sector owners and operators, it operates by a slightly different paradigm than the other Critical Infrastructure and Key Resources (CIKR) Sectors. For example, when it comes to policies of research and development (R&D), the government invests a substantial amount of resources in cybersecurity, yet the private sector also makes substantial contributions. Innovation is highly competitive and an ongoing process in the private sector and as such it fuels new products and capabilities (see Note 5, p. 41). A collaborative public–private partnership is necessary to achieve cybersecurity as the IT Sector advances its R&D agenda. It becomes a balancing act for the IT Sector to leverage its private sector R&D investment while sharing information on government R&D initiatives and priorities.

Table 12.4 IT Sector's Risks of Concern, Using the Baseline IT Sector Baseline Risk Assessment (ITSRA)

IT Sector Critical Function	Risks of Concern
Produce and provide IT products and services.	Production or distribution of untrustworthy critical product or service through a successful man-made deliberate attack on a supply chain vulnerability.
Provide domain name resolution services.	Breakdown of a single interoperable Internet through a man-made attack, and resulting failure of governance policy; large-scale man-made Denial-of-Service attack on the domain name system (DNS) infrastructure.
Provide Internet-based content, information, and communications services.	Man-made unintentional incident caused in Internet content services results in a significant loss of e-commerce capabilities.
Provide Internet routing, access, and connection services.	Partial or complete loss of routing capabilities through a man-made deliberate attack on the Internet routing infrastructure.
Provide incident management capabilities.	Impact to detection capabilities because of a lack of data availability resulting from a natural threat.

Source: DHS. 2010. *Information Technology Sector-Specific Plan*, p. 26.

As mentioned previously, the IT Sector is interdependent and interconnected with other sectors. Therefore, information sharing becomes a critical activity. Currently, the IT Sector has means for sharing policy and operational information and information sharing is frequently accomplished on a voluntary basis. Private sector organizations typically are not required or mandated to share information and may even face federal or state government limits on disclosure of sensitive information (see Note 5, p. 56). Information sharing can be even further complicated with the public sector by government officials and specific mandates which govern such activities. On the other hand, government agencies might be required to disclose information under the Freedom of Information Act (FOIA) or comparable state disclosure laws (see Note 5, p. 56).

Because information sharing in the IT Sector is so vital to maintaining situational awareness and addressing threats, an enhanced IT Sector information-sharing framework has been established. Operational information is exchanged through the Information Technology Information Sharing and Analysis Center (IT-ISAC) which serves as a central repository for security-related information about threats, vulnerabilities, and best practices related to physical and cyber events. The IT-ISAC is the IT Sector's focal point for coordinating the sharing and analysis of operational and strategic private sector information between and among members, as well as with other public and private partners (see Note 5, pp. 55–58).

In addition to IT-ISAC, the IT Sector partners with the United States Computer Emergency Readiness Team (US-CERT), which is a partnership between DHS and the public and private sectors designed to facilitate the protection of cyber infrastructure through cyber analysis, warning, and information sharing; the Multi-state Information Sharing and Analysis Center (MS-ISAC) serves as a focal point for information sharing with and among State and local governments; and the National Infrastructure Coordinating Center (NICC) is a 24/7 watch operation that maintains operational and situational awareness of the nation's CIKR Sectors (see Note 5, p. 58). In addition to these partnerships, the IT Sector's vision for sharing and reporting incidents are as follows:

- Collect, disseminate, and share information along horizontal and vertical paths of an organization and among organization
- Communicate in a regular and predictable manner so that information is passed to all appropriate partners and entities are not inadvertently omitted
- Establish formal policies or procedures to prescribe the flow of information between and among public and private IT Sector partners at all levels
- Provide intelligence collection and other information requirements to DHS in accordance with the 2013 NIPP
- Establish and maintain feedback mechanisms to ensure shared information is useful
- Develop formal triggers or incident reporting thresholds to provide consistent guidance to owners and operators for determining when to elevate an event to a higher level or report it to the government (see Note 5, pp. 58–59)

FSS PROFILE

Recent natural disasters, large-scale power outages, and the increased number of sophisticated cyberattacks have demonstrated the vast array of potential risks facing the FSS.[6] DHS describes this vital sector as follows: "The Financial Services Sector includes thousands of depository institutions, providers of investment products, insurance companies, other credit and financing organizations, and the providers of the critical financial utilities and services that support these functions" (see Note 6). This complex sector comprises many different types of financial institutions from large global companies to community banks and credit unions. Components at risk in this sector include individual savings accounts, financial derivatives, credit extended to large organizations, or investments made to foreign countries (see Note 6). The Department of Treasury is designated as the SSA for the FSS.

The FSS is best understood by examining the services that it provides. They include the following:

1. Deposit, consumer credit, and payment systems products
2. Credit and liquidity products
3. Investment products
4. Risk transfer products (see Note 6)

Deposit, Consumer Credit, and Payment Systems Products

These products are provided by depository institutions who offer the bulk of wholesale and retail payment services, such as wire transfers, checking accounts, and credit and debit cards. Large volumes of transfer systems, automated clearinghouses (ACH), and automated teller machines (ATM) are the primary point of contact with the sector for many people. Other services such as mortgages, home equity loans, and various lines of credit, are also offered through these institutions. Technology has increased the ways in which customers can access these services. Aside from making deposits directly at banking institutions, they can use the Internet or ATMs. Mobile devices have also become a vehicle through which these services may be accessed, making the average consumer more susceptible to the risks facing this sector.

Credit and Liquidity Products

Individuals seeking a mortgage to purchase a home, or a business looking to expand their operations may need a line of credit directly from an institution or indirectly from the liquidity given to a financial service firm.

These products allow customers to make purchases that otherwise they might not be able to afford. Laws provide customer protections against fraud involving these products and include federal and state securities laws, banking laws, and laws that are tailored to the specifics of a particular class of lending activity (see Note 6).

Investment Products

Investments include debt securities (bonds and bond mutual funds), equities (stocks, or stock mutual funds), exchange-traded funds, and derivatives (such as options and futures). Individual customers and organizations use securities firms, depository institutions, pension funds, and the like for investing needs. There is a vast diversity of investment service providers offering these services in this portion of the financial sector, many competing on a global market (see Note 6).

Risk Transfer Products

There is a market need for services directed towards financial losses due to theft or the destruction of physical or electronic property. Loss events may come from a fire, cybersecurity incident, loss of income due to a death or disability, or other situations. Insurance companies and other organizations offer customers the ability to transfer various types of financial risks under a multitude of circumstances (see Note 6).

FSS MISSION AND GOALS

The FSS comprises closely interconnected private companies working together with the government to improve security and resilience. The mission and vision of the FSS combines security and reliance. Table 12.5 illustrates the FSS mission, vision, and goals.

The FSS promotes four primary goals to improve its security and resilience. These provide a framework for identifying and prioritizing collaborative programs and initiatives. These goals consist of (a) information sharing, (b) best practices, (c) incident responses and recovery, and (d) policy support. Table 12.6 details these goals and shared sector priorities which help to guide the daily operations of the FSS.

Table 12.5 Mission, Vision Statement, and Goals of the Financial Services Sector (FSS)

Mission Statement for the FSS

Continuously enhance security and resilience within the FSS through a strong community of private companies, government agencies, and international partners that establishes shared awareness of threats and vulnerabilities, continuously enhances baseline security levels, and coordinates rapid response to and recovery from significant incidents as they occur.

Vision Statement for the FSS

A secure and stable financial system operating environment that maintains confidence in the integrity of global financial transactions, assets, and data.

Source: DHS. 2015. ⁶*Financial Services Sector-Specific Plan*, p. 13.

Table 12.6 FSS Goals and Priorities

Information Sharing

Goal 1	Implement and maintain structured routines for sharing timely and actionable information related to cybersecurity and physical threats and vulnerabilities among firms, across sectors of industry, and between the private sector and government.
Priority	1. Improve the timeliness, quality, and reach of threat and trend information shared within the sector, across sectors, and between the sector and government.
	2. Address interdependencies by expanding information sharing with other sectors of critical infrastructures and international partners.
	3. Accelerate the sharing of information through structured information sharing processes and routines.

Best Practices

Goal 2	Improve risk management capabilities and the security posture of firms across the FSS and the service providers they rely on by encouraging the development and use of common approaches and best practices.
Priority	1. Promote sector-wide usage of the NIST Cybersecurity Framework, including among smaller and medium-sized institutions.
	2. Encourage the development and use of best practices for managing third-party risk.

Incident Response And Recovery

Goal 3	Collaborate with the homeland security, law enforcement, and intelligence communities; financial regulatory authorities; other sectors of industry; and international partners to respond to and recover from significant incidents.

(Continued)

263

Table 12.6 (*Continued*)   FSS Goals and Priorities

Priority	1. Streamline, socialize, and enhance the mechanisms and processes for responding to incidents that require a coordinated response.
	2. Routinely exercise government and private sector incident response processes.

Policy Support

Goal 4	Discuss policy and regulatory initiatives that advance infrastructure security and resilience priorities through robust coordination between government and industry.
Priority	1. Identify, prioritize, and support government research and development funding for critical financial infrastructure protection.
	2. Identify and support policies that enhance critical financial infrastructure security and resilience, including a more secure and resilient Internet.
	3. Encourage close coordination among firms, financial regulators, and executive branch agencies to inform policy development efforts.

FSS: ASSESSING RISK

The US banking and financial system institutions faces an evolving and dynamic set of risks. As noted previously, these include operational, liquidity, credit, legal, and reputational risk (see Note 6). The organizations that support our nation's financial system are also a vital component of the global economy. Furthermore, these organizations are tied together through a network of electronic systems with countless points of entry (see Note 6). As technology has made sector services more accessible, the risk factors have increased. Cybersecurity has emerged as a key concern for this sector, and one in which ongoing risks are consistently being assessed. Incidents to the FSS, man-made or natural, can have a devastating impact to the US economy. Recent events have illustrated how physical disruptions can have significant outcomes to this sector. The following are some of the examples:

- Securities markets and several futures exchanges were closed in lower Manhattan after the September 11, 2001, terrorist attacks until communications and other services were either transferred to other sites or restored.
- A series of coordinated distributed denial-of-service (DDoS) attacks against financial institutions began in the summer of 2012.

These attacks impacted customers access to banking information, but avoided the core systems and processes.

- Superstorm Sandy hit the east coast on October 29, 2012, causing a 2-day closure of major equities exchanges while fixed income markets were closed for 1 day.
- Major data breaches to retailers and other networks by cyber-criminals have resulted in stolen credit card information and other financial data (see Note 6).

Risk assessment is a long-standing activity in the FSS. There is both a regulatory and individual institution component. The US Department of the Treasury, financial regulators, the US Department of Homeland Security (DHS), law enforcement, and other government partners coordinate with financial institutions to share information about current and emerging threats to the sector (see Note 6). These entities work together by exchanging data, developing threat mitigation information, and meeting to collaborate on specific actions and regulatory processes.

As discussed previously, the sector's cybersecurity and physical risks are critical components which must be assessed. This is accomplished by identifying critical processes and their dependence on IT and supporting operations for the delivery of financial products and services. As technology improves the sector's services, newer risks may emerge. This is one of the major challenges to the FSS—staying ahead of the next cyber intrusion or attack. Furthermore, financial institutions and technology service providers are tightly interconnected—an incident impacting one firm has the potential to have cascading impacts on other firms, or even sectors (see Note 6).

Intensifying the risk are the interdependencies the FSS has with other sectors for critical services such as electricity, communications, and transportation. Managing risk requires the cooperation of many sector partners and other levels of government. A good example of this can be found in Section 9 of EO 13636, *Improving Critical Infrastructure Cybersecurity*, which requires that DHS identify critical infrastructure against which a cybersecurity incident could result in a catastrophic regional or national effects on public health or safety, economic security or national security. EO 1336 allows owners and operators of identified critical infrastructure whose business and operations are cyber dependent (rely extensively on network and communications technology) to be eligible for expedited processing of clearance through the DHS Private Sector Clearance Program. This program provides access to classified government cybersecurity threat information that may be crucial for these organizations (see Note 6).

FSS: POLICY INITIATIVES

Risk in the FSS Sector is evolving and as mentioned above, cybersecurity has become increasingly significant. Sector partners continue to make progress building private–public partnerships in a numerous ways such as the following:

- Creating a public–private cybersecurity exercise program to test and improve incident response processes
- Significantly expanding the sector's cybersecurity information sharing capabilities, including through the rapid growth of the Financial Services Information Sharing and Analysis Center (FSISAC) and the establishment of the Treasury's Financial Sector Cyber Intelligence Group (CIG)
- Establishing a formalized structure of joint working groups to advance specific tasks
- Formalizing processes for coordinating technical assistance activities
- Expanding collaboration with cross-sector international partners (see Note 6)

A key component of the FSS Sector's efforts toward security and resilience is the effective public policy framework it embraces. Partnerships with public and private sector organizations allow for the development and implementation of public policy proposals in support of keeping our financial systems secure. One example is the resources government provides for R&D of new technologies. This, along with the expertise from private sector owners and operators, has resulted in R&D resource allocation decision making by government agencies such as the DHS Office of Science and Technology Policy and the National Science Foundation (see Note 6). Finally, these collaborative efforts not only inform public policy decisions, but also provide a way for continued progress in securing this vital sector.

SUMMARY OF REMAINING SECTORS

We have covered in some detail the sector profiles and risk assessment methods for 9 of the 16 critical sectors. Those discussed were not deemed as more critical than others, but rather were selected because they illustrate substantial differences in their approaches to managing risk. Table 12.7 offers a snapshot of the remaining seven sectors, brief profile and their stated approach to risk. These sectors are summarized

Table 12.7   Summary Remaining Critical Infrastructure (CI) Sectors Approach to Risk Management

Sector	Profile	Approach to Risk Management
Commercial facilities sector	Facilities in this sector operate on the principle of open public access. Includes a diverse range of sites that draw large crowds of people for shopping, business, and entertainment, or lodging. Majority are privately owned. Consists of eight subsectors: • Entertainment and media • Gaming • Lodging • Outdoor events • Public assembly • Real estate • Retail • Sports leagues	Uses the basic Department of Homeland Security (DHS) framework for risk = threat, vulnerability, and consequences. DHS has provided strategic coordination and field operations support to assist owners and operators with risk assessments, such as the Computer-Based Assessment Tool (CBAT). Uses information sharing programs such as the Classified Intelligence Forum. Manages cyber risks through the Real Estate Information Sharing and Analysis Center (RE-ISAC), fusion centers, and the Industrial Control Systems Cyber Emergency Response Team (ICS-CERT).
Critical manufacturing sector	The critical manufacturing sector is crucial to the economic prosperity of the US. The core of the sector includes the following four industries: 1. Primary metal manufacturing 2. Machinery manufacturing 3. Electrical equipment, appliance, and component manufacturing	Uses the DHS framework for threat, vulnerability, and consequences. Assesses consequences based on four general categories as set forth in the National Infrastructure Protection Plan (NIPP): • Public health and safety impact • Economic impact

(Continued)

Table 12.7 Summary Remaining Critical Infrastructure (CI) Sectors Approach to Risk Management (*Continued*)

Sector	Profile	Approach to Risk Management
4. Transportation equipment manufacturing		• Psychological impact • Impact on government. Historically the critical manufacturing sector has utilized assessment methodologies such as fault tree analyses, process hazard analyses and others to identify vulnerabilities. Works closely with the DHS Homeland Infrastructure Threat and Risk Analysis Center (HITRAC) for sharing information.
Dams sector	There are more than 87,000 dams throughout the US, about 60% are privately owned. This sector delivers critical water retention and control services in the US including hydroelectric power generation, municipal and industrial water supplies, agricultural irrigation, sediment and flood control, river navigation for inland bulk shipping, industrial waste management, and recreation. The dams sector irrigates at least 10% of US cropland, helps protect more than 43% of the population from flooding, and generates about 60% of electricity in the Pacific Northwest.	Uses the basic DHS framework for risk = threat, vulnerability, and consequences at the facility and sector level. United States Army Corps of Engineers (USACE), the Bureau of Reclamation, and Tennessee Valley Authority (TVA) conduct comprehensive risk assessments at federally owned dams and levees under their self-regulating authorities. Private and municipal hydroelectric utilities under the jurisdiction of Federal Energy Regulatory Commission (FERC) also complete mandatory vulnerability and security assessments. Aside from regulatory aspects, DHS has conducted voluntary security assessments of 70% of critical dams sector assets. Conducts information sharing through the Homeland Security Information Network-Critical Infrastructure (HSIN-CI) Dams Portal and USACE.

| Chemical sector | The chemical sector is an integral part of the US economy. It relies on and supports a wide range of other critical infrastructure sectors. The majority of the facilities are privately owned, thus requiring DHS to work closely with private sector companies and associations. The sector is divided into five main segments:

• Basic chemicals
• Specialty chemicals
• Agricultural chemicals
• Pharmaceuticals
• Consumer products | Uses the basic DHS framework for risk = threat, vulnerability, and consequences.
Conducts information sharing through the Homeland Security Information Network–Critical Infrastructure (HSIN-CI).
Manages cyber risks through the following:

• Cyber-Dependent Infrastructure Identification
• Critical Infrastructure Cyber Community Voluntary Program
• Partnership-Developed Cybersecurity Resources (where owners and operators have worked with DHS and other partners to develop a DVD containing sector-specific tools and resources) |
| Nuclear reactors, materials, and waste sector | There are 99 commercial nuclear power plants in the US which provide about 20% of the nation's electrical generated power. The sector includes the following:

• Nuclear power plants
• Nonpower nuclear reactors used for research, testing, and training
• Manufacturers of nuclear reactors or components | Uses the basic DHS framework for risk = threat, vulnerability, and consequences at the facility and sector level.
Has used Probabilistic Risk Assessments (PRAs) for more than 30 years to analyze risk. PRA is a process for examining how engineered systems, such as nuclear power plants and human interactions with these systems work together to ensure safety and security. |

(Continued)

Table 12.7 Summary Remaining Critical Infrastructure (CI) Sectors Approach to Risk Management (*Continued*)

Sector	Profile	Approach to Risk Management
	• Radioactive materials used primarily in medical, industrial, and academic settings • Nuclear fuel cycle facilities • Decommissioned nuclear power reactors • Transportation, storage, and disposal of nuclear and radioactive waste	Uses DHS Radiological/Nuclear Terrorism Risk Assessment (RNTRA) to analyze information from the intelligence, law enforcement, scientific, medical, and public health communities to estimate human casualty and economic consequences of radiological and nuclear terrorism. The sector also employs force-on force exercises, continuous security enhancements, and integrated planning, training and exercises to address specific risks.
Defense Industrial Base (DIB)	This sector is the worldwide industrial complex that enables research and development, as well as design, production, delivery, and maintenance of military weapons systems, subsystems, and components, or parts to meet US military requirements. Included are more than 100,000 Defense Industrial Base (DIB) companies and their subcontractors—both domestic and foreign entities. This sector provides products and services that are essential to mobilize, deploy, and sustain military operations.	There are currently no regulatory requirements for the DIB companies to conduct risk assessments. The Department of Defense (DOD) works with DIB partners to assess those risks to DOD missions resulting from disruption or degradation of DIB critical infrastructure and key resources. Uses CIP-MAA to evaluate plausible threats or hazards. Manages cyber threats by working with HITRAC on information sharing. Also uses the DIB-DOD Collaborative Information Sharing Environment (DCISE).

| Government facilities | Includes a wide variety of government buildings, located in the US and overseas, that are owned or leased by federal, state, local, and tribal governments. These include general use office buildings and special-use military installations, embassies, courthouses, national laboratories, and structures that may house critical equipment, systems, networks, and functions. Cyber elements are also included. | Uses the basic DHS framework for risk = threat, vulnerability, and consequences. Sector includes the following two subsectors:
• Education facilities
• National monuments and icons |

Source: US DHS. Critical Infrastructure sector profiles and sector-specific plans. Retrieved from: www.dhs.gov.

here because they represent methods previously discussed in other sectors. For a deeper explanation of these sectors and their individual approaches to risk management, you can access the sector-specific plans (SSPs) at the official website for the DHS at https://www.dhs.gov/critical-infrastructure-sectors.

CONCLUSION

The Communications Sector, IT Sector, and FSS not only illustrate the complexities of critical infrastructure, but also show the interconnectedness of risks. Each of these three sectors relies on digital technologies, and support critical services that depend upon each other in some significant way. The remaining seven sectors were presented in a brief overview which shows the sector profile and individual approach to risk management. We conclude that while individual sectors offer unique methods and tools of risk assessment, all are continually working through the SSAs to improve upon SSPs. These SSPs direct and combine not only the sectors' efforts to secure and strengthen the resilience of the respective sector, but also the sectors' contributions to national infrastructure security and resilience as set forth in Presidential Policy Directive 21 (PPD-21). Collectively, these 16 critical infrastructure sectors and their individual approaches to managing risk offer a unique policy perspective. Understanding critical infrastructure protection as an emergent process that is continuously evolving is vital to the goal of a secure and resilient nation.

REVIEW QUESTIONS

1. Discuss the Communications Sector and IT sector. What is the function of each, and how are they different?
2. What are the interdependencies that all three sectors presented in this chapter share?
3. Explain the emerging issue of cybersecurity and the impact it has on the Communications sector, IT sector, and FSS.
4. Discuss the various approaches to managing risk that each sector uses. Is there an overlap in methods? Why or why not?

NOTES

1. Kovacs, E. December 14, 2015. Wireless Routers Plagued by Unpatched Flaws. *Security Week.*
2. US DHS. 2010. *Communications Sector-Specific Plan*, p. 2, p. 6, p. 27, p. 28.
3. DHS. *National Cybersecurity and Communications Integration Center.* Retrieved from: https://www.dhs.gov/national-cybersecurity-and-communications -integration-center.
4. Townsend, A.M., and Moss, M.L. 2005. *Telecommunications Infrastructure in Disasters: Preparing Cities for Crisis Communications, Center for Catastrophe and Preparedness Response.* New York, NY: NY University Press.
5. US DHS. 2010. *Information Technology Sector-Specific Plan.*
6. US DHS. 2015. *Financial Services Sector-Specific Plan.*

13

The Future of Critical Infrastructure Protection
Risk, Resilience, and Policy

INTRODUCTION

Studying critical infrastructures from a policy perspective provides a comprehensive examination of the executive orders (EOs), national strategies, presidential policy directives, and methods have evolved in the homeland security enterprise over the past 15 years. Sector-specific agencies (SSAs), along with the individual approaches each sector takes toward managing risk, are also important to consider as the protection of these 16 critical infrastructures continues to evolve. As we look to the future of protecting our critical infrastructures, several key issues emerge. This chapter examines those issues that continue to challenge and shape our responses to critical infrastructure protection, risk management, and resilience efforts.

INCREASED NEXUS BETWEEN CYBER AND PHYSICAL SECURITY

The March 2016 cyberattack on MedStar Health, one of the largest healthcare systems in the Baltimore to Washington, DC, area, shows how rapidly the digitization of the Healthcare and Public Health Sector is creating new threats. Pressure to put patient healthcare records, test results, and other medical systems online have made the healthcare industry an easy target, and its security systems tend to be less mature than those in other sectors. As discussed in Chapter 11, this reliance on technology for medical purposes has opened a new set of vulnerabilities where devices can malfunction, treatments can be interrupted, and breaches to patient information can occur. The MedStar data breach began with a virus that infiltrated its computer systems and forced the shutdown of its entire network. As a result, e-mail, patient records, and other medical systems were shut down. Patients were turned away, surgeries were postponed, and paper records of visits became the norm. Some employees reported seeing pop-up messages indicating the attack was "ransomware"—a kind of software that can lock people out of systems until they make a bitcoin payment.[1] Clearly the push for digitizing the healthcare industry is rapidly making it a target for hackers.

An emerging issue for critical infrastructure protection is the increased nexus between cyber and physical security. EO 1336 Improving Critical Infrastructure Cybersecurity and Presidential Policy Directive 21—Critical Infrastructure Security and Resilience are two of the first official acknowledgments of the complex connection between physical and cybersecurity.[2] These federal policies, along with public–private plans, establish the roles and responsibilities for federal agencies working with the private sector and other entities to enhance the cyber and physical security of public and private critical infrastructures.[3] With increased technologies, there is a new linkage between physical and cyber infrastructures.

We now rely on cyber systems to run just about everything from mass transit to pipelines, electricity, and as the MedStar example illustrates, hospital networks.[4] This connection now means that both cyber and physical security measures are needed to protect critical infrastructures against potential threats. Physical security measures prevent the unauthorized access to servers, and other technologies which carry sensitive information. Cybersecurity measures can thwart an attack which may have physical consequences. For example, an attack on a water treatment control system could have damaging effects on human lives as well as the environment and the economy (see Note 4). For these reasons, the federal government and Department of Homeland Security (DHS) have taken an integrated approach to critical infrastructure protection by including the evolving risk and increased role of cybersecurity in securing physical assets.

In the November 2015 Government Accountability Office (GAO) Report, it was concluded that SSAs need to better measure cybersecurity progress (see Note 3). In the study, the GAO's objectives were to determine the extent to which SSAs have (a) identified the significance of cyber risks to their respective sectors' networks and industrial control systems, (b) taken actions to mitigate cyber risks within their respective sectors, (c) collaborated across sectors to improve cybersecurity, and (d) established performance metrics to monitor improvements in their respective sectors (see Note 3). The GAO analyzed policy, plans, and other documentation and interviewed public and private sector officials for eight of the nine SSAs who have responsibility for 15 of the 16 sectors. It was found that the Departments of Defense, Energy, and Health and Human Services established these performance metrics for their three sectors, but that the SSAs for the other 12 sectors had not yet developed them and were unable to report on the effectiveness of cyber risk mitigation activities in their sectors. One of the reasons reported was the SSA reliance on private sector partners to voluntarily share information needed to measure these efforts. In response, the GAO recommended that collaboration with sector partners needs to be more prevalent in certain SSAs and that performance metrics need to be established (see Note 3).

INTERDEPENDENCE BETWEEN SECTORS

As we have learned, critical infrastructures do not operate alone. They interact with other sectors and help them function by providing essential resources and services. While each has unique functions, they are also dependent upon and interdependent with other critical infrastructures. Dependency may be defined as a relationship between two infrastructures in a single direction, or one infrastructure influencing the state of another. For example, the reliance on electric power and fuels by a multitude of industries means that all Critical Infrastructure Sectors are dependent upon the energy sector. The Food and Agriculture Sector is dependent upon the Water and Wastewater Systems Sector for clean irrigation and processed water, the transportation system for movement of products and livestock, and the Chemical Sector for fertilizers and pesticides used in the production of crops. Interdependency is bidirectional and multidirectional, with two or more infrastructures influencing each other. The Water and Wastewater Systems Sector is a good example of a critical infrastructure which contains numerous interdependencies with other critical sectors. A disruption in water service, posed by a natural hazard, terrorism, or accident, threatens other sectors such as emergency services, healthcare, and transportation. Furthermore, interdependencies are the centerpiece of the National Infrastructure Protection Plan (NIPP).[5]

Consideration of dependencies and interdependencies of critical infrastructures is vital in assessing risk and resiliency. A case study of the interconnectedness of risks posed by Hurricane Sandy for New York shows how a single disaster can cause enormous economic damages because of the interdependent infrastructure systems. Hurricane Sandy had a significant impact on the Energy Sector with the most damage found in power outages. More than 2 million people were impacted with loss of power. In the Energy Sector, regional refineries were shut down and more than 8 million customers lost power in 21 affected states. The Water and Wastewater Sector was affected with crippled treatment plants and raw sewage that flowed into the waterways of New York and New Jersey, continuing a month after the storm. The Healthcare Sector took a significant hit with five acute care hospitals and one psychiatric hospital closed. As a result, nearly 2000 patients had to be evacuated. The Transportation Sector was also impacted with tunnels, subways, and railroad tunnels shutdown due to flooding and damage to equipment. It has been estimated that approximately 8.6 million daily public transit riders, 4.2 million drivers, and 1 million airport passengers were impacted.[6]

One of the challenges for critical infrastructure protection and risk management is the potential for cascading failures. As illustrated by Hurricane Sandy, a wider network of risk must be considered. From a policy perspective, that means that risk assessment and plans for resilience must consider the interconnectedness of all critical infrastructures and their various functions. In addition, there have been efforts to develop models that accurately simulate critical infrastructure behavior and identify interdependencies and vulnerabilities.[7] Over the years, several taxonomies have been presented to describe the various types of dependencies between sectors. Rinaldi, Peerenboom, and Kelly (2001) describe the following four general categories:

- Physical—a physical reliance on material flow from one infrastructure to another.
- Cyber—a reliance on information transfer between infrastructures.
- Geographic—a local environmental event affects components across multiple infrastructures due to physical proximity.
- Logical—a dependency that exists between infrastructures that does not fall into one of the aforementioned categories.[8]

The complexity of these interdependencies calls for the use of modeling and simulation capabilities. Modeling and analysis of interdependencies between critical infrastructures may be used to understand infrastructure systems and may be used to support vulnerability and risk assessments, training exercises, and performance measurement. The challenges are similar to any modeling domain: data accessibility, model development, and model validation.[9] The National Infrastructure Simulation and Analysis Center (NISAC) is responsible for developing these modeling capabilities for our nation's infrastructures. Expert analysts study the details of all 16 critical infrastructures, from asset level to systems level; the interactions between sectors, and how various sectors respond to natural disasters, cyberthreats, or terrorist attacks.[10]

RISKS ASSOCIATED WITH CLIMATE CHANGE

Extreme weather events in 2015 marked the eighth consecutive year that severe weather caused undue damage to portions of the US. These weather and climate events, 10 in all, included the drought in southern California, wildfires in western states and Alaska, tornadoes in the southern plains and Midwest, major flooding in Texas and South Carolina, a winter storm in the central east that buried Boston, and five severe storm events in the Midwest/Ohio Valley. The National Oceanic Atmospheric Administration (NOAA) estimated that these damages exceeded $10 billion, roughly $1 billion per event.[11] In recent years, the impact of climate change on severe weather events has received a lot of attention. Although no specific weather event has been directly credited to climate change, there is awareness in the scientific community that it can worsen the impact, frequency, and intensity of such events.[12]

Typically, these events result in significant damages to infrastructures we rely upon every day such as water, energy, transportation, communications, and emergency services (see Note 12). Researchers maintain that in order to better assess risk from weather events it is important to determine how future climates might impact our critical infrastructure systems. Presently, there are areas in the US that are at risk from the impact of climate change, such as in the Gulf Coast where several of the largest sea ports in the US are located. The combination of relative sea level rise and more intense hurricanes and tropical storms in this area could lead to significant disruptions and damage. Another example of climate risk locations can be found in the Tri-State area of New York,

New Jersey, and Connecticut, where many transportation infrastructure facilities are located, all within the range of current and projected 50-year coastal storm surges (see Note 12).

As discussed earlier, the interdependent nature of our critical infrastructure also creates new vulnerabilities and opportunities for disruption across supply chains. Extreme weather events associated with climate change can also impact these interconnected systems. The Energy Sector is particularly vulnerable. For example, in September 2011 high temperatures and a high demand for electricity tripped a transformer in Yuma, Arizona. This triggered a chain of events that shut down the San Onofre nuclear power plant and resulted in a large-scale power outage across the entire San Diego distribution system. Approximately 2.7 million customers were without power with outages lasting as long as 12 hours (see Note 12). In another example, three Browns Ferry Reactors in Alabama automatically shut down when strong storms knocked out off-site power. Emergency diesel generators had to be used for 5 days.

The increased number of billion-dollar natural disasters has strained the federal government both in dollars and in resources. In response, DHS has developed a Climate Change Adaptation Roadmap and Climate Action Plan which aligns to the President's Climate Action Plan and EO 13653, *Preparing the United States for the Impacts of Climate Change* (see Note 12). This plan directs federal agencies to do the following:

- **Modernize federal programs to support climate-resilient investments**—the EO directs agencies to review their policies and programs to find better ways to create stronger standards for building infrastructure.
- **Manage lands and waters for climate preparedness and resilience**—the EO directs agencies to identify changes that must be made to land- and water-related policies, programs, and regulations to strengthen the climate resilience of our watersheds, natural resources, and ecosystems.
- **Provide information, data, and tools for climate change preparedness and resilience**—the EO directs agencies to work together and with information users to develop new climate preparedness tools.
- **Plan for climate change-related risk**—the EO directs federal agencies to develop and implement strategies to evaluate and address their most significant climate change–related risks.[13]

The challenges that climate change presents for critical infrastructure protection are not without controversy. On the one hand, creating stronger infrastructure to withstand the impacts of climate change and extreme weather events is an important undertaking. So much so that DHS and the White House have established a plan for this risk environment. Additionally, the DHS National Protection and Programs Directorate (NPPD) works to manage risk to critical infrastructure by supporting climate preparedness, adaptation, and resilience efforts locally (see Note 12). However, critics argue that money spent on improving structures, resilience technologies, and other target hardening efforts are unwise. These investments are costly and one extreme weather event could easily destroy an entire critical sector.

Mitigation efforts are costly. For example, the St. John's Regional Medical Center in Joplin, Missouri, was wiped out by a 2011 tornado. It has since been rebuilt with newer technologies that include windows that can resist up to 250 miles/hour at a cost of $170 per square foot—$70 dollars more than standard windows.[14] In Edna, Texas, a coastal city at risk for hurricanes, a $2.5 million dome shelter was built for the town's 5500 residents. The shelter doubles as a gymnasium and was built to withstand winds up to 300 miles/hour. FEMA provided 75% of the cost with plans to invest $683 million in similar shelters in 18 additional states (see Note 14).

At the local level, many city leaders are developing innovative ideas to address extreme weather due to climate change. There is a recognition that increasing a cities' resilience to climate change keeps people and businesses safe—a key for economic growth and stability. Some of these initiatives include upgraded public transportation systems, providing cleaner and more reliable energy, and improving air quality.[15] In Cleveland, Ohio, outbreaks of winter cold are becoming more severe as are more heat waves. Located in the Great Lakes Region, the city of Cleveland, Ohio, is not subject to the most dramatic evidence of climate change that the coastal areas are experiencing. While there is not a concern for rising sea levels or hurricanes, there is plenty of evidence that climate change is impacting severe weather in this area. More severe weather equates to higher costs. It is estimated that between 2010 and 2015, 36% of US extreme weather events that caused more than $1 billion in damage occurred in the Great Lakes Region.[16] The Center for American Progress, a Washington-based think tank, recently published a report entitled, "Resilient Midwestern Cities: Improving Equity in a Changing Climate."[17] In it, the city of Cleveland was one of five cities praised for their climate resilience efforts. These include energy efficiency and stormwater management programs that target some of the city's most vulnerable neighborhoods. Poverty in Cleveland is rivaled only by Detroit, Michigan, with more than one-third of its total residents and half of its children living in poverty (see Note 16). As we saw with Hurricane Katrina, poor and low-income residents are impacted the most from a severe weather event because of existing economic and social hardships.

Addressing the issue of critical infrastructure protection and the stresses of climate change is an evolving issue. Efforts are being focused on programs and initiatives at both the local and regional levels. While climate change may be controversial, the intensity of storms and increase of weather events is clearly on the rise. Critical infrastructures are vulnerable to these weather and climate changes, and our policies should reflect a stronger effort to mitigate them.

AN AGING AND OUTDATED INFRASTRUCTURE

A serious issue facing the future of critical infrastructure protection in the US is the poor preservation and maintenance of our infrastructure systems. Old and deteriorating bridges, highways, transportation systems, and the power grid all pose significant risks to the economy and our ability to recover from natural or man-made disasters, the effects of climate change, and terrorist events. Of particular concern are the Energy and Transportation Systems Sectors. In April 2015, the first installment of the Energy Department's Quadrennial Energy Review was published offering a grim picture for the US electrical grid, power transmission lines, natural gas and oil, pipelines, ports, railways and other critical pieces of national infrastructure.[18]

The report concludes that the US energy landscape is changing and that policy discussions have shifted from concerns about rising oil imports and high gasoline prices, to debates about how much and what kinds of US energy should be exported.[19] Additional concerns include the transportation of large amounts of crude oil by rail, and how to meet the demands for future energy supplies. The report also found that threats to the Energy Sector are growing, especially with respect to the electrical grid which is badly in need of modernization. The risk of terrorist attacks and severe weather events caused by climate change are on the rise while the reliability and safety of the grid has remained stagnant or, in some cases gone backward (see Note 19, p. S-5).

Similarly, the oil and gas infrastructures have not kept pace with changes in the size and geography of oil and gas production. "Our ports, waterways, and rail systems are congested," the report concludes, "with the growing demands for handling energy commodities increasingly in competition with transport needs for food and other non-energy freight. Although improvements are being made, much of the relevant infrastructure—pipelines, rail systems, ports, and waterways alike— is long overdue for repairs and modernization" (see Note 19, p. S-6). The report describes our pipeline system as one compelling example. Approximately 50% of the nation's gas transmission and gathering pipelines were constructed in the 1950s and 1960s. These were built out of the interstate pipeline network in response to the booming post-World War II economy. The cost to modernize this network has been estimated between $2.6 billion and $3.5 billion per year between 2015 and 2030, depending upon the demand for natural gas. Additionally, the total cost of replacing cast iron and bare steel pipes in gas distribution systems has been estimated at $270 billion (see Note 19, p. S-7).

Aligning with the previous discussion on climate change, the report found the most important environmental factor affecting the Energy Sector now and going forward is global climate change. Rising sea levels, thawing permafrost, and frequency of extreme storms are already impacting our aging infrastructures (see Note 19, p. S-6). In response to these issues the Obama Administration announced a Climate Action Plan in June 2013. This plan included the following three pillars:

1. Reducing US emissions of greenhouse gases (GHGs)
2. Increasing domestic preparedness for and resilience against the changes in climate that no longer can be avoided
3. Engaging internationally to encourage and assist other countries in taking similar steps (see Note 19, p. S-7)

Specific infrastructure projects that must be addressed in the Energy Sector are also outlined in the report, some require Congressional appropriations. These include a $2.5 billion energy department initiative to improve natural-gas distribution; a $3.5 billion plan to modernize the US electric grid; and at least $1.5 billion to improve and extend the life of the crucial Strategic Petroleum Reserve (see Note 18).

The US Transportation System Sector is also vulnerable as an aging and deteriorating infrastructure. For instance, more than 63,000 highway bridges have been classified as structurally deficient due to age, erosion, and other structural problems. As conditions on these bridges worsen, restrictions are put in place or they are taken out of service. Extreme weather and natural disasters also contribute to deterioration and risk. The impact on other critical sectors is undeniable. Most sectors are dependent upon highway bridges to conduct daily operations such as the delivery of products and goods.[20] Furthermore, the failure of a bridge can directly impact the Energy and Communications Sectors as power lines, fiber optic cables and other utility lines can be collocated underneath a bridge (see Note 20). The implications of an aging critical infrastructure are particularly important for the Emergency Services Sector. The ability to quickly and efficiently respond to a disaster can become less reliable if a bridge collapses or the ability to communicate is compromised by a failure in the power grid. Some of these aging infrastructures can also become the hazard just like the I-35 bridge collapse in Minnesota in 2007.[21]

The American Society of Civil Engineers (ASCE) depicts the condition and performance of the nation's infrastructure in the form of a report card every 4 years. The 2013 Report Card for America's Infrastructure gave the US a D+ grade, estimating more than $3.6 trillion in investments are needed by 2020 to counteract declining conditions.[22] An advisory council for the ASCE bases its grades on the following nine criteria: capacity, condition, funding, future need, operation, maintenance, public safety, resilience, and innovation (see Note 22). According to ASCE, since 1998 these grades have been near failing due to delayed maintenance and underinvestment in most categories. Table 13.1 illustrates the various categories and grades given by the ASCE for the 2103 Report Card.

The consequences of a decaying urban infrastructure can be devastating, as found with the Flint, Michigan, Water Crisis which began in April 2014. Flint, Michigan, is a city 70 miles north of Detroit with over 40% of

Table 13.1 2013 Report Card for America's Infrastructure

Energy	D+	Schools	D
Public parks and recreation	C−	Transit	D
Roads	D	Rail	C+
Ports	C	Inland waterways	D−
Bridges	C+	Aviation	D
Wastewater	D	Solid waste	B−
Levees	D−	Hazardous waste	D
Drinking water	D	Dams	D

Source: ASCE. 2013 Report Card for America's Infrastructure. Retrieved from: http://www.infrastructurereportcard.org/executive-summary/.

its residents living below the poverty level. The state of Michigan took over the finances of the city in 2011 after an audit projected a $25 million deficit.[23] A shortfall in the funding for the water supply prompted a change from the treated Detroit water system to the Flint River, a system in which officials had failed to apply corrosion inhibitors. Beginning in April 2014, the drinking water in Flint had a series of problems that culminated with lead contamination. The corrosive Flint River water caused lead from aging pipes to leak into the water supply, resulting in extremely high levels of lead in the drinking water.

It has been estimated that between 6000 and 12,000 children in the city of Flint have been exposed to the toxic levels and as a result may suffer from serious health issues. Research shows that a percentage of children under 5 with elevated blood lead levels had more than doubled since the change in the water supply (see Note 23). In addition, cases of Legionnaire's Disease spiked in the county and numerous residents were complaining of hair loss and rashes, as well as vision and memory problems. On January 5, 2016, Governor Snyder declared a state of emergency for Genesee County, home to Flint. This was followed by a state of emergency declaration by President Barack Obama. National Guard Troops and the Red Cross responded to Flint, distributing bottled water and water filters to homes. Criminal charges were filed against two state and one city employee in April 2016. The accusations include misleading federal regulatory officials, manipulating water sampling, and tampering with reports.[24]

The Flint Water Crisis not only sheds a light on poor decision making and critical infrastructure problems in Michigan, but also throws a harsh spotlight on urban infrastructure issues across the country (see Note 24). The infrastructure crisis has been long unfolding inside city halls. The Mayors are often the last to receive money for infrastructure projects such as water quality, pipe stability, buses, transit systems, and crumbling bridges. Local governments are struggling to find dollars from both their governors and their states to support these projects that seem to take a backseat to other policy priorities.

INFORMATION SHARING

The National Strategy for Infrastructure Protection (NIPP) 2013 emphasizes the importance of integrating information sharing as an essential component of the risk management framework. Specifically, the NIPP directs the sharing of actionable and relevant information across the critical infrastructure community to build awareness and build risk-informed decision making.[25] The NIPP also directs that this information sharing be of a voluntary nature. "Voluntary collaboration between private sector owners and operators (including their partner associations, vendors, and others) and their government counterparts has been and will remain the primary mechanism for advancing collective action toward national critical infrastructure security and resilience" (see Note 25, p. 10).

The key word here is "voluntary". While most would agree that information sharing is crucial for homeland security and critical infrastructure protection, the execution of shared information is not seamless. Getting sector organizations out of their functional, jurisdictional, and competitive silos continues to be a major challenge. For example, a recent GAO report found that a lack of information sharing from the private sector was responsible for some SSAs' inability to implement proper cybersecurity metrics (see Note 3). These findings fueled a debate by some lawmakers that critical infrastructure industries should be required to report more cybersecurity data to the government. While an attempt to include such a mandate in the recently passed Cybersecurity Information Sharing Act (CISA) of 2015 failed, the controversy surrounding information sharing continues.

On December 18, 2015, President Barack Obama signed into law the CISA of 2015 which encourages the private sector and the federal government to share information on cyberthreats. Essentially, it allows private businesses to share cyber information with the federal government (specifically the Department of Defense) without the risk of being sued. Critics have argued that the provisions are too broad and that it opens the door to other, unrelated information being shared. This is but one example where neither the public nor private sector appears to be satisfied with the information it receives from the other. This "expectations gap" in information sharing comes from a mutually acknowledged reluctance to exchange sensitive information.[26] It has been argued that multiple variables conspire to hinder effective cross-sector information sharing, including an unsettled organizational landscape, questions of trust, and the fact that information sharing rarely provides an immediate payoff for businesses (see Note 26).

The benefits of sharing critical infrastructure information cannot be overstated, and the flow of it needs to be both horizontal and vertical. Various levels of government need to communicate with each other up and down while jurisdictions need to share information among all stakeholders—public and private. This two-way approach to information sharing is essential for critical infrastructure protection and risk management. Problems occur when information is held back or filtered before it is passed on. Because information is not mandated but rather encouraged, some critical sectors will have better success at it than others. Since 80% of the nation's critical infrastructure is owned by the private sector, collaboration between government and private business owners becomes vital. DHS has established several operations and tools such as the following to support information sharing within and among critical infrastructure sectors:

- Homeland Security Information Network—Critical Infrastructure (HSIN-CI)
- Infrastructure Protection Gateway (IP Gateway)
- National Infrastructure Coordinating Center (NCIC)
- Office of Cyber and Infrastructure Analysis (OCIA)
- Protected Critical Infrastructure Information (PCII) program.
- Protective Security Advisors (PSAs)
- Technical Resource for Incident Prevention (TRIP*wire*)
- DHS Daily Open Source Infrastructure Report[27]

DHS also partners with other organizations to provide additional information-sharing support to its security partners. These include the following:

- SSAs
- Information Sharing Environment
- National Explosives Task Force
- Fusion Centers (see Note 27)

Public–Private Partnerships

There is an underlying tension between public and private sector views when it comes to critical infrastructure protection. With over 80% of our nation's critical infrastructure under private sector control, public–private sector collaboration is essential. While DHS and its Office of Infrastructure Protection (OIP) provide structure for these coordination efforts, obstacles to these partnerships still exist. In *Realizing the Promise of Public–Private Partnerships in US Critical Infrastructure Protection*, Austen D. Givens and Nathan E. Busch (2013) argue, "Challenges result from imprecise contracts that create a mismatch in expectations, a lack of centralized mechanisms for coordinating integrated actions, a tendency on the part of actors in a partnership to act out of self-interest, and the prospect of public and private sector actors relying on the other to bear the costs of the partnership" (see Note 26).

An example of unmet expectations and cost overruns can be found in the DHS Secure Border Initiative known as "Virtual Fence."[28] Virtual Fence was a program designed to monitor the US–Mexico border through a series of surveillance radars, cameras, and sensors. The initiative failed because the harsh terrain caused malfunctions and different technologies that made up Virtual Fence were difficult to integrate. Additionally, the program became too expensive. The project, carried out by the Boeing Corporation under a contract initially signed by President George W. Bush in 2005, was plagued by delays and cost overruns. Originally, the Virtual Fence Project was estimated to cost $7 billion for the fence to cover the entire 2000-mile US southern border. However, a pilot test discovered the actual cost to be $1 billion to cover only 53 miles of the border—just 2% of the total project (see Note 28). DHS canceled the Virtual Fence project in January 2011, noting that it "did not meet the current standards for viability and cost effectiveness" (see Note 28). The failure of the Virtual Fence project illustrates the complexities of public–private partnerships and how unmet expectations, poor execution, and out of control costs can ruin an initiative (see Note 28).

When it comes to costs, businesses need incentives to spend on their own protection measures. There is a difference between the private sector spending money on protecting their own operations versus developing critical infrastructure technologies. DHS has instituted a number of initiatives to encourage businesses to participate in critical infrastructure protection measures, such as adopting the 2014 Cybersecurity Framework and the following:

- Cybersecurity insurance
- Grants
- Process preference
- Liability limitation
- Streamline regulations
- Public recognition
- Rate recovery for price regulated industries
- Cybersecurity research[29]

The private sector also has a built-in incentive to collaborate on critical infrastructure protection measures. The continuity of operations in the aftermath of a crisis is critical and not doing so could force a business into bankruptcy, as evident in the wake of Hurricane Katrina (see Note 26). Enhancing the effectiveness of public–private partnerships can be a challenge and it will take considerable efforts by both sides to improve these collaborations.

CONCLUSION

Critical infrastructure protection, risk, and resilience are dynamic and ever-changing components of the homeland security enterprise. It is clear that DHS and its partners must continue to support these efforts in an environment of increasing cyberthreats and diminished resources. Current challenges include the increased nexus between cyber and physical security, interdependencies between and across sectors, the effects of climate change, an aging infrastructure, and issues with information sharing. Addressing these challenges and the priorities and concerns of all critical infrastructure stakeholders is an essential step toward developing homeland security strategic plans that reflect the whole community and provide for a safe and secure nation.

REVIEW QUESTIONS

1. Describe the nexus between cyber and physical security. What is the importance of it for the current climate of critical infrastructure protection?
2. Why is information sharing an issue between public and private sector partners? What suggestions do you have to improve upon quality and frequency of information being shared?
3. How does climate change impact critical infrastructure protection? Cite two examples of how it is changing the way we perceive extreme weather events.
4. Discuss the key challenges facing critical infrastructure protection in the future. How do these challenges impact the concepts of risk and resilience? What suggestions do you have to address these challenges?

NOTES

1. Johnson, C., and Zapotosky, M. April 1, 2016. Under Pressure to Digitize Everything, Hospitals Are Hackers' Biggest New Target. *The Washington Post.*
2. Berger, V. December 19, 2013. Converging Physical and Cyber Security. *FCW Magazines.*
3. GAO Report to the Committee on Homeland Security, House of Representatives. December 2015. *Critical Infrastructure Protection Sector-Specific Agencies Need to Better Measure Cybersecurity Progress.*
4. US DHS. March 20, 2013. *Written Testimony of National Protection and Programs Directorate Under Secretary Rand Beers for a House Committee on Appropriations, Subcommittee on Homeland Security Oversight Hearing Titled, Cybersecurity and Critical Infrastructure.* www.dhs.gov.
5. Zimmerman, R. 2009. Understanding the Implications of Critical Infrastructure Interdependencies for Water. *Published Articles & Papers. Paper 7.*
6. Haragucki, M., and Soojun, K. 2015. Critical infrastructure systems: A case study of the interconnectedness of risk posed by hurricane sandy for New York City. Input Paper Prepared for the Global Assessment Report on Disaster Reduction.
7. Pederson, P., Dudenhoffer, D., Hartley, S., and Permann, M. 2006. *Critical Infrastructure Interdependency Modeling: A Survey of US and International Research.* Washington, DC: Technical Support Working Group, Idaho National Laboratory.
8. Rinaldi, S., Peerenboom, J., and Kelly, T. December 2001. Identifying, understanding, and analyzing critical infrastructure interdependencies. *IEEE Control Systems Magazine*, pp. 11–25.
9. Modeling and Simulation of Critical Infrastructure Systems for Homeland Security Applications. June 14–15, 2011. *DRAFT for discussion at DHS/NIST Workshop on Homeland Security Modeling & Simulation.*
10. *National Infrastructure Simulation and Analysis Center.* Retrieved from: http://www.sandia.gov/nisac/overview/.
11. NOAA. *Billion-Dollar Weather and Climate Disasters: Overview.* Retrieved from: https://www.ncdc.noaa.gov/billions/.
12. Barr, L., and Nider, S. August 20, 2015. Critical Infrastructure & Climate Adaptation, George Mason University Center for Infrastructure Protection & Homeland Security. *CIP Report.*
13. *FACT SHEET: Executive Order on Climate Preparedness.* November 1, 2013. Retrieved from: https://www.whitehouse.gov/the-press-office/2013/11/01/fact-sheet-executive-order-climate-preparedness.
14. *Pound Foolish: Federal Community-Resilience Investments Swamped by Disaster Damages,* Center for American Progress. Retrieved from: https://www.americanprogress.org/issues/green/report/2013/06/19/67045/pound-foolish/.

15. *Storm Ready Cities: How Climate Resilience Boosts Metro Areas and the Economy, Center for American Progress.* Retrieved from: https://www.americanprogress .org/issues/green/report/2013/06/19/67045/pound-foolish/.
16. Litt, S. April 16, 2016. Cleveland praised for climate change resilience efforts by Center for American Progress, *The Cleveland Plain Dealer*.
17. Center for American Progress. April 2016. Report: Resilient Midwestern Cities: Improving Equity in Changing Climate.
18. Wolfgang, B. April 21, 2015. Billions of Dollars Needed to Fix Aging Vulnerable US Energy Infrastructure, Report. *The Washington Times*.
19. QER Report. April 2015. Energy Transmission, Storage, and Distribution Infrastructure.
20. DHS National Protection and Programs Directorate (OCIA). 2016. *Critical Infrastructure Security and Resilience Note: Aging and Failing Infrastructure Systems: Highway Bridges.* Retrieved from: http://www.dhs.gov.
21. FEMA. June 2011. *Strategic Foresight Initiative. Critical Infrastructure: Long-term Trends and Drivers and Their Implications for Emergency Management.*
22. American Society of Civil Engineers (ASCE). 2013. *Report Card for America's Infrastructure.* Retrieved from: http://www.infrastructurereportcard.org /grades/.
23. Flint Water Crisis Fast Facts. CNN. Retrieved from: http://www.cnn.com /2016/03/04/us/flint-water-crisis-fast-facts/.
24. McLaughlin, E., and Shoichet, C. April 20, 2016. Charges against 3 in Flint water crisis, only the beginning. CNN. Retrieved from: http://www.cnn.com /2016/04/20/health/flint-water-crisis-charges/.
25. DHS, NIPP 2013. *Partnering for Critical Infrastructure Security and Resilience.* www.dhs.gov.
26. Givens, A., and Busch, N. 2013. Realizing the promise of public-private partnerships in US critical infrastructure protection. *International Journal of Critical Infrastructure Protection*, 6, 1, 1–28.
27. DHS. 2016. Information Sharing: A Vital Resource for Critical Infrastructure Security. www.dhs.gov.
28. Busch, N., and Givens, A. 2012. Public-private partnerships in homeland security: opportunities and challenges, *Homeland Security Affairs*.
29. Daniel, M. 2013. *Incentives to Support Adoption of the Cybersecurity Framework*, DHS, WhiteHouse blog.

APPENDIX: PRESIDENTIAL POLICY DIRECTIVES AND OTHER KEY DOCUMENTS

It is not required that the Presidential Policy Directives be published in the Federal Register or the Code of Federal Regulations. When a president issues an executive order or a presidential directive, they remain in effect even after a new president takes office, unless otherwise stated in the document or until the new president takes action on that issue. Presidential directives are signed by the president and then issued by the National Security Council (NSC), the agency that advises the president on national security and foreign policy matters.

After the terrorist attacks of September 11, 2001, on New York and Washington, DC, President George W. Bush established the Office of Homeland Security on October 8, 2001, in the Executive Order 13228. The new agency was to assist the president with planning and coordinating the federal responses to combat further terrorist acts and maintain the security of the US.

A few days later, on October 29, 2001, President Bush then issued the first of a series of directives referred to as the Homeland Security Presidential Directives (HSPDs). The first of these directives detailed the organization and operation of the Homeland Security Council (HSC). Since then, there have been 24 HSPDs. These are detailed here.

HSPD-1: Organization and Operation of the HSC: HSPD-1 created the HSC and defined its responsibilities. As defined under HSPD-1, the HSC is to coordinate efforts regarding homeland security by the federal government and other governments throughout the country, and to oversee 11 Policy Coordination Committees.

HSPD-2: Combating Terrorism Through Immigration Policies: The second HSPD established a task force to work to prevent aliens who are identified as engaging in or supporting terrorism from entering the US. Further, any aliens involved in this activity who are already in the US could be detained, prosecuted, or deported. HSPD-2 also established the Foreign Terrorist Tracking Task Force that would oversee the action of federal agencies that implemented this policy. HSPD-2 also expanded the enforcement capabilities of the Immigration and Naturalization Service (INS) and the Customs Service, and oversaw a program to combat abuse of the international student visa program. This HSPD also stressed coordination with the immigration efforts of both Canada and Mexico.

HSPD-3: Homeland Security Advisory System: In HSPD-3, the president established a more effective plan to disseminate information about terrorist threats to federal, state, and local officials and to the public. This included a new Homeland Security Advisory System that would provide details about any potential terrorist acts. The System revolved around a five-level, color-coded Threat Condition indicator that would correspond to the threat situation. This would allow agencies the flexibility to alter their responses as the level of risk changed.

HSPD-4: National Strategy to Combat Weapons of Mass Destruction: This HSPD supported the use of new technology in the fight against terrorism. It also increased the use of intelligence collection and analysis, strengthened relationships and alliances with other countries, and established new partnerships with former adversaries in an effort to counteract potential threats.

HSPD-5: Management of Domestic Incidents: This directive created a comprehensive national incident management system that would encompass prevention, preparation, response, and recovery from terrorist attacks, natural disasters, and other emergencies. With increased communication, this system would ensure that officials in all levels of government work efficiently and effectively together to protect citizens and property. The directive also organized response and outlined specific roles for different government officials.

HSPD-6: Integration and Use of Screening Information: In HSPD-6, the Terrorist Threat Integration Center was established. There was also more attention given to the use of information about individuals who are either known or suspected to have engaged in terrorist activities. Intelligence on these individuals will be used to support screening processes, diplomatic, military, law enforcement, immigration, and visa programs.

HSPD-7: Critical Infrastructure Identification, Prioritization, and Protection: The purpose of HSPD-7 was to create a national policy to assist agencies to identify and prioritize critical infrastructure and key resources within the US and then to develop plans to protect them from terrorist attacks and natural disasters. In the directive, relevant terms were more clearly defined and the roles of various federal, state, and local agencies were outlined.

HSPD-8: National Preparedness: The content of HSPD-8 included new processes to improve response coordination. The response methods for federal departments and agencies were described, as well as preparation and prevention activities. These included new policies to strengthen preparedness by different agencies. A national domestic all-hazards preparedness goal was created, including new ways to improve the delivery of federal preparedness and assistance to state and local government offices. HSPD-8 was a companion to HSPD-5.

HSPD-8 Annex 1: National Planning: Annex 1 to HSPD-8 provided more detail about ways to further strengthen the preparedness of the US. Here, a standard and comprehensive approach to national planning was described. This information was intended to provide additional guidance to those who conduct planning policies in accordance with the National Incident Management System (2004) in the National Strategy for Homeland Security (2007).

HSPD-9: Defense of United States Agriculture and Food: The president described a national policy to protect the agriculture and food system in the US against a terrorist attack or other major disasters. This is essential because the agriculture and food system in the US is an extensive, open, interconnected, and complex structure that is a possible target for terrorist attacks. Moreover, the system is vulnerable to disease, pest, or poisonous agents that can be either intentionally or unintentionally introduced. HSPD-9 helps to provide a high level of protection against a possible attack on the nation's food system.

HSPD-10: Biodefense for the 21st Century: A comprehensive framework for our Nation's Biodefense is outlined in this HSPD-10. The plan is based on a comprehensive study of the country's current capabilities. The plan integrates efforts of national and homeland security, medical, public health, intelligence, diplomatic, and law enforcement communities. The primary components of the national biodefense program are Threat Awareness, Prevention and Protection, Surveillance and Detection, and Response and Recovery. A classified version of this document contains more detailed information for federal departments and agencies.

HSPD-11: Comprehensive Terrorist-Related Screening Procedures: In this Presidential Directive, a comprehensive approach to terrorist-related screening procedures was developed. This Directive builds upon what was announced in HSPD-6 to create screening procedures that would be more effective in detecting those individuals who are either known or suspected of engaging in terrorist activities against the US. In addition, this document requires that the Secretary of Homeland Security submit a report detailing plans to implement the new policies and any progress made toward the goals.

HSPD-12: Policy for a Common Identification Standard for Federal Employees and Contractors: Because there are such a wide disparity in both the quality and security of identification that is used by individuals seeking to gain access to secure facilities, this Directive seeks to enhance security of these facilities through better identification. At the same time, these policies will reduce identity fraud and protect personal privacy. A standard that will be used by all government agencies will be established.

HSPD-13: Maritime Security Policy: Policy guidelines were established in HSPD-13 to protect the country's maritime interests. In this document, a Maritime Security Policy Coordinating Committee was created that will coordinate efforts at maritime security. It also supports security in "all areas and things of, on, under, relating to, adjacent to, or bordering on a sea, ocean, or other navigatable waterway, including all maritime-related activities, infrastructure, people, cargo, and vessels and other conveyances."

HSPD-14: Domestic Nuclear Detection: In HSPD-14, the Domestic Nuclear Detection Office (DNDO) was established to protect the nation from radiological and nuclear threats. The DNDO was asked to develop the blueprints for a global nuclear detection system, and then acquire and support the deployment of the domestic detection system that will detect and report attempts to import or transport a nuclear device or radiological material.

HSPD-15: US Strategy and Policy in the War on Terror: This document is classified, but it has been described as limiting the bureaucratic hindrances that may limit federal agencies in their efforts to combat terrorism. It has also been noted that the directive attempts to coordinate all elements of the War on Terrorism, including diplomatic, legal, financial, and military components. This coordination works to meet six goals: (a) Deny terrorists the resources they need to operate and survive; (b) Enable partner nations to counter terrorism; (c) Deny proliferation of weapons of mass destruction, recover and eliminate uncontrolled materials, and maintain a capacity for consequence management; (d) Defeat terrorists and their organizations; (e) Counter state and nonstate support for terrorism in coordination with other US government agencies and partner nations; and (f) Contribute to the establishment of conditions that counter ideological support for terrorism.

HSPD-16: Aviation Strategy: In HSPD-16, the administration provided details for a national Aviation Security policy. The supporting plans address the following areas: aviation transportation system security, aviation operational threat response, aviation transportation system recovery, air domain surveillance and intelligence integration, domestic outreach, and international outreach. The Directive also described an Operational Threat Response Plan that will seek a comprehensive and coordinated response to air threats against the US or US interests. Other plans described in the Directive include the Aviation Transportation System Recovery Plan, the Air Domain Surveillance and Intelligence Integration Plan, the Domestic Outreach Plan, and the International Outreach Plan.

HSPD-17: Nuclear Materials Information Program: While the specifics of HSPD-17 are classified, this directive has been described as pursuing policies to consolidate information gathered from many sources regarding worldwide nuclear materials and their security status, which will then be continuously updated. This will help officials recognize any gaps in the location of nuclear materials. It was also required that a national registry for identifying and tracking nuclear material samples held throughout the US will be maintained.

HSPD-18: Medical Countermeasures Against Weapons of Mass Destruction: In HSPD-18, medical countermeasure needed related to chemical, biological, radiological and nuclear (CBRN) threats were identified. The document also addresses the need for the nation to prepare for an attack by terrorists who might use a weapon of mass destruction. It was noted in HSPD-18 that the ability to have sufficient resources on hand at all times and at all places is not realistic.

HSPD-19: Combating Terrorist Use of Explosives in the United States: In HSPD-19, the president sought to create a national policy regarding explosives, and called for a national policy on the prevention and detection of, protection against, and response to terrorist use of explosives in the US.

297

HSPD-20: National Continuity Policy: HSPD-20 established a comprehensive national policy on the continuity of federal government structures and operations. To help with this, a single National Continuity Coordinator would be appointed who would be responsible for coordinating the development and implementation of federal continuity policies. This document also established the National Essential Functions that outlined continuity requirements for all federal agencies.

HSPD-20 Annex A: Continuity Planning: Annex A of HSPD-20 assigned federal agencies with specific responsibilities should an emergency occur. According to the document, National Continuity Policy, all federal departments and agencies would be assigned to one of four categories depending on their defined responsibilities during an emergency. These categories are used for continuity planning, communications requirements, emergency operations capabilities, and other related requirements.

HSPD-21: Public Health and Medical Preparedness: HSPD-21 established a national strategy to allow for a level of public health and medical preparedness in case of a disaster. It is the policy under this document that the US plan for the public's health and medical needs in an emergency, as well as the continued flow of information to officials in a rapid and coordinated manner. This directive replaces HSPD-7.

HSPD-22: Domestic Chemical Defense: This directive is classified but for the title.

HSPD-23: National Cyber Security Initiative: The official content of HSPD-23 has not been released to the public, but officials in the Department of Homeland Security released a statement on April 8, 2008, that indicated that HSPD-23 "formalized a series of continuous efforts designed to further safeguard federal government systems and reduce potential vulnerabilities, protect against intrusion attempts, and better anticipate future threats." The release also defined that "while efforts to protect our federal network systems from cyber attacks remain a collaborative, government-wide effort, the DHS has lead responsibility for assuring the security, resiliency, and reliability of the Nation's Information Technology (IT) and communications infrastructure."

HSPD-24: Biometrics for Identification and Screening to Enhance National Security: HSPD-24 established a framework to ensure that federal agencies use compatible methods and procedures as they collect, store, use, analyze, and share biometric information to ensure it is done so lawfully and in a way that respects personal information and privacy rights.

EXECUTIVE ORDERS

Related Topics

- Security
- Cybercrime & Hacking
- Cyberattacks

Executive Order 13636—Improving Critical Infrastructure Cybersecurity *February 12, 2013*
By the authority vested in me as President by the Constitution and the laws of the United States of America, it is hereby ordered as follows:

Section 1. Policy. Repeated cyber intrusions into critical infrastructure demonstrate the need for improved cybersecurity. The cyber threat to critical infrastructure continues to grow and represents one of the most serious national security challenges we must confront. The national and economic security of the United States depends on the reliable functioning of the Nation's critical infrastructure in the face of such threats. It is the policy of the United States to enhance the security and resilience of the Nation's critical infrastructure and to maintain a cyber environment that encourages efficiency, innovation, and economic prosperity while promoting safety, security, business confidentiality, privacy, and civil liberties. We can achieve these goals through a partnership with the owners and operators of critical infrastructure to improve cybersecurity information sharing and collaboratively develop and implement risk-based standards.

Sec. 2. Critical Infrastructure. As used in this order, the term critical infrastructure means systems and assets, whether physical or virtual, so vital to the United States that the incapacity or destruction of such systems and assets would have a debilitating impact on security, national economic security, national public health or safety, or any combination of those matters.

299

Sec. 3. Policy Coordination. Policy coordination, guidance, dispute resolution, and periodic in-progress reviews for the functions and programs described and assigned herein shall be provided through the interagency process established in Presidential Policy Directive-1 of February 13, 2009 (Organization of the National Security Council System), or any successor.

Sec. 4. Cybersecurity Information Sharing.

(a) It is the policy of the United States Government to increase the volume, timeliness, and quality of cyber threat information shared with U.S. private sector entities so that these entities may better protect and defend themselves against cyber threats. Within 120 days of the date of this order, the Attorney General, the Secretary of Homeland Security (the "Secretary"), and the Director of National Intelligence shall each issue instructions consistent with their authorities and with the requirements of section 12(c) of this order to ensure the timely production of unclassified reports of cyber threats to the U.S. homeland that identify a specific targeted entity. The instructions shall address the need to protect intelligence and law enforcement sources, methods, operations, and investigations.

(b) The Secretary and the Attorney General, in coordination with the Director of National Intelligence, shall establish a process that rapidly disseminates the reports produced pursuant to section 4 (a) of this order to the targeted entity. Such process shall also, consistent with the need to protect national security information, include the dissemination of classified reports to critical infrastructure entities authorized to receive them. The Secretary and the Attorney General, in coordination with the Director of National Intelligence, shall establish a system for tracking the production, dissemination, and disposition of these reports.

(c) To assist the owners and operators of critical infrastructure in protecting their systems from unauthorized access, exploitation, or harm, the Secretary, consistent with 6 U.S.C. 143 and in collaboration with the Secretary of Defense, shall, within 120 days of the date of this order, establish procedures to expand the Enhanced Cybersecurity Services program to all critical infrastructure sectors. This voluntary information sharing program will provide classified cyber threat and technical information from the Government to eligible critical infrastructure companies or commercial service providers that offer security services to critical infrastructure.

(d) The Secretary, as the Executive Agent for the Classified National Security Information Program created under Executive Order 13549 of August 18, 2010 (Classified National Security Information Program for State, Local, Tribal, and Private Sector Entities), shall expedite the processing of security clearances to appropriate personnel employed by critical infrastructure owners and operators, prioritizing the critical infrastructure identified in section 9 of this order.

(e) In order to maximize the utility of cyber threat information sharing with the private sector, the Secretary shall expand the use of programs that bring private sector subject-matter experts into Federal service on a temporary basis. These subject matter experts should provide advice regarding the content, structure, and types of information most useful to critical infrastructure owners and operators in reducing and mitigating cyber risks.

Sec. 5. Privacy and Civil Liberties Protections.

(a) Agencies shall coordinate their activities under this order with their senior agency officials for privacy and civil liberties and ensure that privacy and civil liberties protections are incorporated into such activities. Such protections shall be based upon the Fair Information Practice Principles and other privacy and civil liberties policies, principles, and frameworks as they apply to each agency's activities.

(b) The Chief Privacy Officer and the Officer for Civil Rights and Civil Liberties of the Department of Homeland Security (DHS) shall assess the privacy and civil liberties risks of the functions and programs undertaken by DHS as called for in this order and shall recommend to the Secretary ways to minimize or mitigate such risks, in a publicly available report, to be released within 1 year of the date of this order. Senior agency privacy and civil liberties officials for other agencies engaged in activities under this order shall conduct assessments of their agency activities and provide those assessments to DHS for consideration and inclusion in the report. The report shall be reviewed on an annual basis and revised as necessary. The report may contain a classified annex if necessary. Assessments shall include evaluation of activities against the Fair Information Practice Principles and other applicable privacy and civil liberties policies, principles, and frameworks. Agencies shall consider the assessments and recommendations of the report in implementing privacy and civil liberties protections for agency activities.

(c) In producing the report required under subsection (b) of this section, the Chief Privacy Officer and the Officer for Civil Rights and Civil Liberties of DHS shall consult with the Privacy and Civil Liberties Oversight Board and coordinate with the Office of Management and Budget (OMB).

(d) Information submitted voluntarily in accordance with 6 U.S.C. 133 by private entities under this order shall be protected from disclosure to the fullest extent permitted by law.

Sec. 6. Consultative Process. The Secretary shall establish a consultative process to coordinate improvements to the cybersecurity of critical infrastructure. As part of the consultative process, the Secretary shall engage and consider the advice, on matters set forth in this order, of the Critical Infrastructure Partnership Advisory Council; Sector Coordinating Councils; critical infrastructure owners and operators; Sector-Specific Agencies; other relevant agencies; independent regulatory agencies; State, local, territorial, and tribal governments; universities; and outside experts.

Sec. 7. Baseline Framework to Reduce Cyber Risk to Critical Infrastructure.

(a) The Secretary of Commerce shall direct the Director of the National Institute of Standards and Technology (the "Director") to lead the development of a framework to reduce cyber risks to critical infrastructure (the "Cybersecurity Framework"). The Cybersecurity Framework shall include a set of standards, methodologies, procedures, and processes that align policy, business, and technological approaches to address cyber risks. The Cybersecurity Framework shall incorporate voluntary consensus standards and industry best practices to the fullest extent possible. The Cybersecurity Framework shall be consistent with voluntary international standards when such international standards will advance the objectives of this order, and shall meet the requirements of the National Institute of Standards and Technology Act, as amended (15 U.S.C. 271 *et seq.*), the National Technology Transfer and Advancement Act of 1995 (Public Law 104-113), and OMB Circular A-119, as revised.

(b) The Cybersecurity Framework shall provide a prioritized, flexible, repeatable, performance-based, and cost-effective approach, including information security measures and controls, to help owners and operators of critical infrastructure identify, assess, and manage cyber risk. The Cybersecurity Framework shall focus on identifying cross-sector security standards and guidelines applicable to critical infrastructure. The Cybersecurity Framework will also identify areas for improvement that should be addressed through future collaboration with particular sectors and standards-developing organizations. To enable technical innovation and account for organizational differences, the Cybersecurity Framework will provide guidance that is technology neutral and that enables Critical Infrastructure Sectors to benefit from a competitive market for products and services that meet the standards, methodologies, procedures, and processes developed to address cyber risks. The Cybersecurity Framework shall include guidance for measuring the performance of an entity in implementing the Cybersecurity Framework.

(c) The Cybersecurity Framework shall include methodologies to identify and mitigate impacts of the Cybersecurity Framework and associated information security measures or controls on business confidentiality, and to protect individual privacy and civil liberties.

(d) In developing the Cybersecurity Framework, the Director shall engage in an open public review and comment process. The Director shall also consult with the Secretary, the National Security Agency, Sector-Specific Agencies and other interested agencies including OMB, owners and operators of critical infrastructure, and other stakeholders through the consultative process established in section 6 of this order. The Secretary, the Director of National Intelligence, and the heads of other relevant agencies shall provide threat and vulnerability information and technical expertise to inform the development of the Cybersecurity Framework. The Secretary shall provide performance goals for the Cybersecurity Framework informed by work under section 9 of this order.

(e) Within 240 days of the date of this order, the Director shall publish a preliminary version of the Cybersecurity Framework (the "preliminary Framework"). Within 1 year of the date of this order, and after coordination with the Secretary to ensure suitability under section 8 of this order, the Director shall publish a final version of the Cybersecurity Framework (the "final Framework").

(f) Consistent with statutory responsibilities, the Director will ensure the Cybersecurity Framework and related guidance is reviewed and updated as necessary, taking into consideration technological changes, changes in cyber risks, operational feedback from owners and operators of critical infrastructure, experience from the implementation of section 8 of this order, and any other relevant factors.

Sec. 8. Voluntary Critical Infrastructure Cybersecurity Program.

(a) The Secretary, in coordination with Sector-Specific Agencies, shall establish a voluntary program to support the adoption of the Cybersecurity Framework by owners and operators of critical infrastructure and any other interested entities (the "Program").

(b) Sector-Specific Agencies, in consultation with the Secretary and other interested agencies, shall coordinate with the Sector Coordinating Councils to review the Cybersecurity Framework and, if necessary, develop implementation guidance or supplemental materials to address sector-specific risks and operating environments.

(c) Sector-Specific Agencies shall report annually to the President, through the Secretary, on the extent to which owners and operators notified under section 9 of this order are participating in the Program.

(d) The Secretary shall coordinate establishment of a set of incentives designed to promote participation in the Program. Within 120 days of the date of this order, the Secretary and the Secretaries of the Treasury and Commerce each shall make recommendations separately to the President, through the Assistant to the President for Homeland Security and Counterterrorism and the Assistant to the President for

Economic Affairs, that shall include analysis of the benefits and relative effectiveness of such incentives, and whether the incentives would require legislation or can be provided under existing law and authorities to participants in the Program.

(e) Within 120 days of the date of this order, the Secretary of Defense and the Administrator of General Services, in consultation with the Secretary and the Federal Acquisition Regulatory Council, shall make recommendations to the President, through the Assistant to the President for Homeland Security and Counterterrorism and the Assistant to the President for Economic Affairs, on the feasibility, security benefits, and relative merits of incorporating security standards into acquisition planning and contract administration. The report shall address what steps can be taken to harmonize and make consistent existing procurement requirements related to cybersecurity.

Sec. 9. Identification of Critical Infrastructure at Greatest Risk.

(a) Within 150 days of the date of this order, the Secretary shall use a risk-based approach to identify critical infrastructure where a cybersecurity incident could reasonably result in catastrophic regional or national effects on public health or safety, economic security, or national security. In identifying critical infrastructure for this purpose, the Secretary shall use the consultative process established in section 6 of this order and draw upon the expertise of Sector-Specific Agencies. The Secretary shall apply consistent, objective criteria in identifying such critical infrastructure. The Secretary shall not identify any commercial information technology products or consumer information technology services under this section. The Secretary shall review and update the list of identified critical infrastructure under this section on an annual basis, and provide such list to the President, through the Assistant to the President for Homeland Security and Counterterrorism and the Assistant to the President for Economic Affairs.

(b) Heads of Sector-Specific Agencies and other relevant agencies shall provide the Secretary with information necessary to carry out the responsibilities under this section. The Secretary shall develop a process for other relevant stakeholders to submit information to assist in making the identifications required in subsection (a) of this section.

(c) The Secretary, in coordination with Sector-Specific Agencies, shall confidentially notify owners and operators of critical infrastructure identified under subsection (a) of this section that they have been so identified, and ensure identified owners and operators are provided the basis for the determination. The Secretary shall establish a process through which owners and operators of critical infrastructure may submit relevant information and request reconsideration of identifications under subsection (a) of this section.

Sec. 10. Adoption of Framework.

(a) Agencies with responsibility for regulating the security of critical infrastructure shall engage in a consultative process with DHS, OMB, and the National Security Staff to review the preliminary Cybersecurity Framework and determine if current cybersecurity regulatory requirements are sufficient given current and projected risks. In making such determination, these agencies shall consider the identification of critical infrastructure required under section 9 of this order. Within 90 days of the publication of the preliminary Framework, these agencies shall submit a report to the President, through the Assistant to the President for Homeland Security and Counterterrorism, the Director of OMB, and the Assistant to the President for Economic Affairs, that states whether or not the agency has clear authority to establish requirements based upon the Cybersecurity Framework to sufficiently address current and projected cyber risks to critical infrastructure, the existing authorities identified, and any additional authority required.

(b) If current regulatory requirements are deemed to be insufficient, within 90 days of publication of the final Framework, agencies identified in subsection (a) of this section shall propose prioritized, risk-based, efficient, and coordinated actions, consistent with Executive Order 12866 of September 30, 1993 (Regulatory Planning and Review), Executive Order 13563 of January 18, 2011 (Improving Regulation and Regulatory Review), and Executive Order 13609 of May 1, 2012 (Promoting International Regulatory Cooperation), to mitigate cyber risk.

(c) Within 2 years after publication of the final Framework, consistent with Executive Order 13563 and Executive Order 13610 of May 10, 2012 (Identifying and Reducing Regulatory Burdens), agencies identified in subsection (a) of this section shall, in consultation with owners and operators of critical infrastructure, report to OMB on any critical infrastructure subject to ineffective, conflicting, or excessively burdensome cybersecurity requirements. This report shall describe efforts made by agencies, and make recommendations for further actions, to minimize or eliminate such requirements.

(d) The Secretary shall coordinate the provision of technical assistance to agencies identified in subsection (a) of this section on the development of their cybersecurity workforce and programs.

(e) Independent regulatory agencies with responsibility for regulating the security of critical infrastructure are encouraged to engage in a consultative process with the Secretary, relevant Sector-Specific Agencies, and other affected parties to consider prioritized actions to mitigate cyber risks for critical infrastructure consistent with their authorities.

Sec. 11. Definitions.

(a) "Agency" means any authority of the United States that is an "agency" under 44 U.S.C. 3502(1), other than those considered to be independent regulatory agencies, as defined in 44 U.S.C. 3502(5).

(b) "Critical Infrastructure Partnership Advisory Council" means the council established by DHS under 6 U.S.C. 451 to facilitate effective interaction and coordination of critical infrastructure protection activities among the Federal Government; the private sector; and State, local, territorial, and tribal governments.

(c) "Fair Information Practice Principles" means the eight principles set forth in Appendix A of the National Strategy for Trusted Identities in Cyberspace.

(d) "Independent regulatory agency" has the meaning given the term in 44 U.S.C. 3502(5).

(e) "Sector Coordinating Council" means a private sector coordinating council composed of representatives of owners and operators within a particular sector of critical infrastructure established by the National Infrastructure Protection Plan or any successor.

(f) "Sector-Specific Agency" has the meaning given the term in Presidential Policy Directive-21 of February 12, 2013 (Critical Infrastructure Security and Resilience), or any successor.

Sec. 12. General Provisions.

(a) This order shall be implemented consistent with applicable law and subject to the availability of appropriations. Nothing in this order shall be construed to provide an agency with authority for regulating the security of critical infrastructure in addition to or to a greater extent than the authority the agency has under existing law. Nothing in this order shall be construed to alter or limit any authority or responsibility of an agency under existing law.

(b) Nothing in this order shall be construed to impair or otherwise affect the functions of the Director of OMB relating to budgetary, administrative, or legislative proposals.

(c) All actions taken pursuant to this order shall be consistent with requirements and authorities to protect intelligence and law enforcement sources and methods. Nothing in this order shall be interpreted to supersede measures established under authority of law to protect the security and integrity of specific activities and associations that are in direct support of intelligence and law enforcement operations.

(d) This order shall be implemented consistent with U.S. international obligations.

(e) This order is not intended to, and does not, create any right or benefit, substantive or procedural, enforceable at law or in equity by any party against the United States, its departments, agencies, or entities, its officers, employees, or agents, or any other person.

BARACK OBAMA

88—Statement on the Release of the "Framework for Improving Critical Infrastructure Cybersecurity" by the National Institute of Standards and Technology
February 12, 2014
Cyber threats pose one [of]* the gravest national security dangers that the United States faces. To better defend our Nation against this systemic challenge, 1 year ago, I signed an Executive order directing the administration

to take steps to improve information-sharing with the private sector, raise the level of cybersecurity across our critical infrastructure, and enhance privacy and civil liberties.

Since then, the National Institute of Standards and Technology has worked with the private sector to develop a Cybersecurity Framework that highlights best practices and globally recognized standards so that companies across our economy can better manage cyber risk to our critical infrastructure. Today I was pleased to receive the Cybersecurity Framework, which reflects the good work of hundreds of companies, multiple Federal agencies, and contributors from around the world. This voluntary Framework is a great example of how the private sector and Government can and should work together to meet this shared challenge.

While I believe today's Framework marks a turning point, it's clear that much more work needs to be done to enhance our cybersecurity. America's economic prosperity, national security, and our individual liberties depend on our commitment to securing cyberspace and maintaining an open, interoperable, secure, and reliable Internet. Our critical infrastructure continues to be at risk from threats in cyberspace, and our economy is harmed by the theft of our intellectual property. Although the threats are serious and they constantly evolve, I believe that if we address them effectively, we can ensure that the Internet remains an engine for economic growth and a platform for the free exchange of ideas.

I again urge Congress to move forward on cybersecurity legislation that both protects our Nation and our privacy and civil liberties. Meanwhile, my administration will continue to take action, under existing authorities, to protect our Nation from this threat.

98—Executive Order 13691—Promoting Private Sector Cybersecurity Information Sharing
February 13, 2015
By the authority vested in me as President by the Constitution and the laws of the United States of America, it is hereby ordered as follows:

Section 1. Policy.

In order to address cyber threats to public health and safety, national security, and economic security of the United States, private companies, nonprofit organizations, executive departments and agencies (agencies), and other entities must be able to share information related to cybersecurity risks and incidents and collaborate to respond in as close to real time as possible.

Organizations engaged in the sharing of information related to cybersecurity risks and incidents play an invaluable role in the collective cybersecurity of the United States. The purpose of this order is to encourage the voluntary formation of such organizations, to establish mechanisms to continually improve the capabilities and functions of these organizations, and to better allow these organizations to partner with the Federal Government on a voluntary basis.

Such information sharing must be conducted in a manner that protects the privacy and civil liberties of individuals, that preserves business confidentiality, that safeguards the information being shared, and that protects the ability of the Government to detect, investigate, prevent, and respond to cyber threats to the public health and safety, national security, and economic security of the United States.

This order builds upon the foundation established by **Executive Order 13636** of February 12, 2013 (Improving Critical Infrastructure Cybersecurity), and Presidential Policy Directive-21 (PPD-21) of February 12, 2013 (Critical Infrastructure Security and Resilience).

Policy coordination, guidance, dispute resolution, and periodic in-progress reviews for the functions and programs described and assigned herein shall be provided through the interagency process established in Presidential Policy Directive-l (PPD-l) of February 13, 2009 (Organization of the National Security Council System), or any successor.

Sec. 2. Information Sharing and Analysis Organizations.
- (a) The Secretary of Homeland Security (Secretary) shall strongly encourage the development and formation of Information Sharing and Analysis Organizations (ISAOs).
- (b) ISAOs may be organized on the basis of sector, sub-sector, region, or any other affinity, including in response to particular emerging threats or vulnerabilities. ISAO membership may be drawn from the public or private sectors, or consist of a combination of public and private sector organizations. ISAOs may be formed as for-profit or nonprofit entities.
- (c) The National Cybersecurity and Communications Integration Center (NCCIC), established under section 226(b) of the Homeland Security Act of 2002 (the "Act"), shall engage in continuous, collaborative, and inclusive coordination with ISAOs on the sharing of information related to cybersecurity risks and incidents, addressing such risks and incidents, and strengthening information security systems consistent with

sections 212 and 226 of the Act. (d) In promoting the formation of ISAOs, the Secretary shall consult with other Federal
entities responsible for conducting cybersecurity activities,
including Sector-Specific Agencies, independent regulatory
agencies at their discretion, and national security and law
enforcement agencies.

Sec. 3. ISAO Standards Organization.

(a) The Secretary, in consultation with other Federal entities
responsible for conducting cybersecurity and related activities, shall, through an open and competitive process, enter
into an agreement with a nongovernmental organization to
serve as the ISAO Standards Organization (SO), which shall
identify a common set of voluntary standards or guidelines
for the creation and functioning of ISAOs under this order.
The standards shall further the goal of creating robust information sharing related to cybersecurity risks and incidents
with ISAOs and among ISAOs to create deeper and broader
networks of information sharing nationally, and to foster the
development and adoption of automated mechanisms for the
sharing of information. The standards will address the baseline capabilities that ISAOs under this order should possess
and be able to demonstrate. These standards shall address,
but not be limited to, contractual agreements, business processes, operating procedures, technical means, and privacy
protections, such as minimization, for ISAO operation and
ISAO member participation.

(b) To be selected, the SO must demonstrate the ability to engage
and work across the broad community of organizations
engaged in sharing information related to cybersecurity risks
and incidents, including ISAOs, and associations and private
companies engaged in information sharing in support of their
customers.

(c) The agreement referenced in section 3(a) shall require that the
SO engage in an open public review and comment process for
the development of the standards referenced above, soliciting
the viewpoints of existing entities engaged in sharing information related to cybersecurity risks and incidents, owners
and operators of critical infrastructure, relevant agencies, and
other public and private sector stakeholders.

(d) The Secretary shall support the development of these standards and, in carrying out the requirements set forth in this section, shall consult with the Office of Management and Budget, the National Institute of Standards and Technology in the Department of Commerce, Department of Justice, the Information Security Oversight Office in the National Archives and Records Administration, the Office of the Director of National Intelligence, Sector-Specific Agencies, and other interested Federal entities. All standards shall be consistent with voluntary international standards when such international standards will advance the objectives of this order, and shall meet the requirements of the National Technology Transfer and Advancement Act of 1995 (Public Law 104-113), and OMB Circular A-119, as revised.

Sec. 4. Critical Infrastructure Protection Program.

(a) Pursuant to sections 213 and 214(h) of the Critical Infrastructure Information Act of 2002, I hereby designate the NCCIC as a critical infrastructure protection program and delegate to it authority to enter into voluntary agreements with ISAOs in order to promote critical infrastructure security with respect to cybersecurity.

(b) Other Federal entities responsible for conducting cybersecurity and related activities to address threats to the public health and safety, national security, and economic security, consistent with the objectives of this order, may participate in activities under these agreements.

(c) The Secretary will determine the eligibility of ISAOs and their members for any necessary facility or personnel security clearances associated with voluntary agreements in accordance with Executive Order 13549 of August 18, 2010 (Classified National Security Information Programs for State, Local, Tribal, and Private Sector Entities), and Executive Order 12829 of January 6, 1993 (National Industrial Security Program), as amended, including as amended by this order.

Sec. 5. Privacy and Civil Liberties Protections.

(a) Agencies shall coordinate their activities under this order with their senior agency officials for privacy and civil liberties and ensure that appropriate protections for privacy and civil liberties are incorporated into such activities. Such protections shall be based upon the Fair Information Practice Principles and other privacy and civil liberties policies, principles, and frameworks as they apply to each agency's activities.

(b) Senior privacy and civil liberties officials for agencies engaged in activities under this order shall conduct assessments of their agency's activities and provide those assessments to the Department of Homeland Security (DHS) Chief Privacy Officer and the DHS Office for Civil Rights and Civil Liberties for consideration and inclusion in the Privacy and Civil Liberties Assessment report required under **Executive Order 13636**.

Sec. 6. National Industrial Security Program. Executive Order 12829, as amended, is hereby further amended as follows:

(a) the second paragraph is amended by inserting "the Intelligence Reform and Terrorism Prevention Act of 2004," after "the National Security Act of 1947, as amended,";

(b) Sec. 101(b) is amended to read as follows: "The National Industrial Security Program shall provide for the protection of information classified pursuant to Executive Order 13526 of December 29, 2009, or any predecessor or successor order, and the Atomic Energy Act of 1954, as amended (42 U.S.C. 2011 *et seq.*).";

(c) Sec. 102(b) is amended by replacing the first paragraph with: "In consultation with the National Security Advisor, the Director of the Information Security Oversight Office, in accordance with Executive Order 13526 of December 29, 2009, shall be responsible for implementing and monitoring the National Industrial Security Program and shall:";

(d) Sec. 102(c) is amended to read as follows: "Nothing in this order shall be construed to supersede the authority of the Secretary of Energy or the Nuclear Regulatory Commission under the Atomic Energy Act of 1954, as amended (42 U.S.C. 2011 *et seq.*), or the authority of the Director of National Intelligence (or any Intelligence Community element) under the Intelligence Reform and Terrorism Prevention Act of 2004, the National Security Act of 1947, as amended, or Executive Order 12333 of December 8, 1981, as amended, or the authority of the Secretary of Homeland Security, as the Executive Agent for the Classified National Security Information Program established under Executive Order 13549 of August 18, 2010 (Classified National Security Information Program for State, Local, Tribal, and Private Sector Entities).";

(e) Sec. 201(a) is amended to read as follows: "The Secretary of Defense, in consultation with all affected agencies and with the concurrence of the Secretary of Energy, the Nuclear Regulatory Commission, the Director of National Intelligence, and the Secretary of Homeland Security, shall issue and maintain a National Industrial Security Program Operating Manual (Manual). The Secretary of Energy and the Nuclear Regulatory Commission shall prescribe and issue that portion of the Manual that pertains to information classified under the Atomic Energy Act of 1954, as amended (42 U.S.C. 2011 *et seq.*). The Director of National Intelligence shall prescribe and issue that portion of the Manual that pertains to intelligence sources and methods, including Sensitive Compartmented Information. The Secretary of Homeland Security shall prescribe and issue that portion of the Manual that pertains to classified information shared under a designated critical infrastructure protection program.";

(f) Sec. 201(f) is deleted in its entirety;

(g) Sec. 201(e) is redesignated Sec. 201(f) and revised by substituting "Executive Order 13526 of December 29, 2009, or any successor order," for "Executive Order No. 12356 of April 2, 1982.";

(h) Sec. 201(d) is redesignated Sec. 201(e) and revised by substituting "the Director of National Intelligence, and the Secretary of Homeland Security" for "and the Director of Central Intelligence.";

(i) a new Sec. 201(d) is inserted after Sec. 201(c) to read as follows: "The Manual shall also prescribe arrangements necessary to permit and enable secure sharing of classified information under a designated critical infrastructure protection program to such authorized individuals and organizations as determined by the Secretary of Homeland Security.";

(j) Sec. 202(b) is amended to read as follows: "The Director of National Intelligence retains authority over access to intelligence sources and methods, including Sensitive Compartmented Information. The Director of National Intelligence may inspect and monitor contractor, licensee, and grantee programs and facilities that involve access to such information or may enter into written agreements with the

Secretary of Defense, as Executive Agent, or with the Director of the Central Intelligence Agency to inspect and monitor these programs or facilities, in whole or in part, on the Director's behalf.";

(k) Sec. 202(d) is redesignated as Sec. 202(e); and

(l) in Sec. 202 a new subsection (d) is inserted after subsection (c) to read as follows: "The Secretary of Homeland Security may determine the eligibility for access to Classified National Security Information of contractors, licensees, and grantees and their respective employees under a designated critical infrastructure protection program, including parties to agreements with such program; the Secretary of Homeland Security may inspect and monitor contractor, licensee, and grantee programs and facilities or may enter into written agreements with the Secretary of Defense, as Executive Agent, or with the Director of the Central Intelligence Agency, to inspect and monitor these programs or facilities in whole or in part, on behalf of the Secretary of Homeland Security."

Sec. 7. Definitions.

(a) "Critical infrastructure information" has the meaning given the term in section 212(3) of the Critical Infrastructure Information Act of 2002.

(b) "Critical infrastructure protection program" has the meaning given the term in section 212(4) of the Critical Infrastructure Information Act of 2002.

(c) "Cybersecurity risk" has the meaning given the term in section 226(a)(1) of the Homeland Security Act of 2002 (as amended by the National Cybersecurity Protection Act of 2014).

(d) "Fair Information Practice Principles" means the eight principles set forth in Appendix A of the National Strategy for Trusted Identities in Cyberspace.

(e) "Incident" has the meaning given the term in section 226(a) (2) of the Homeland Security Act of 2002 (as amended by the National Cybersecurity Protection Act of 2014).

(f) "Information Sharing and Analysis Organization" has the meaning given the term in section 212(5) of the Critical Infrastructure Information Act of 2002.

(g) "Sector-Specific Agency" has the meaning given the term in PPD-21, or any successor.

Sec. 8. General Provisions

(a) Nothing in this order shall be construed to impair or otherwise affect:
  (i) the authority granted by law or Executive Order to an agency, or the head thereof; or
  (ii) the functions of the Director of the Office of Management and Budget relating to budgetary, administrative, or legislative proposals.

(b) This order shall be implemented consistent with applicable law and subject to the availability of appropriations. Nothing in this order shall be construed to alter or limit any authority or responsibility of an agency under existing law including those activities conducted with the private sector relating to criminal and national security threats. Nothing in this order shall be construed to provide an agency with authority for regulating the security of critical infrastructure in addition to or to a greater extent than the authority the agency has under existing law.

(c) All actions taken pursuant to this order shall be consistent with requirements and authorities to protect intelligence and law enforcement sources and methods.

(d) This order is not intended to, and does not, create any right or benefit, substantive or procedural, enforceable at law or in equity by any party against the United States, its departments, agencies, or entities, its officers, employees, or agents, or any other person.

BARACK OBAMA

126—Memorandum on Establishment of the Cyber Threat Intelligence Integration Center

February 25, 2015

Memorandum for the Secretary of State, the Secretary Of Defense, the Secretary of the Treasury, the Secretary of Commerce, the Attorney General, the Secretary of Homeland Security, the Director of National Intelligence, the Chairman of the Joint Chiefs of Staff, the Director of the Central Intelligence Agency, the Director of the Federal Bureau of, Investigation, and the Director of the National Security Agency

Subject: Establishment of the Cyber Threat Intelligence Integration Center

By the authority vested in me as President by the Constitution and the laws of the United States of America, I hereby direct as follows:

Section 1. Establishment of the Cyber Threat Intelligence Integration Center.

The Director of National Intelligence (DNI) shall establish a Cyber Threat Intelligence Integration Center (CTIIC). Executive departments and agencies (agencies) shall support the DNI's efforts to establish the CTIIC, including by providing, as appropriate, personnel and resources needed for the CTIIC to reach full operating capability by the end of fiscal year 2016.

Sec. 2. Responsibilities of the Cyber Threat Intelligence Integration Center. The CTIIC shall:

(a) provide integrated all-source analysis of intelligence related to foreign cyber threats or related to cyber incidents affecting U.S. national interests;

(b) support the National Cybersecurity and Communications Integration Center, the National Cyber Investigative Joint Task Force, U.S. Cyber Command, and other relevant United States Government entities by providing access to intelligence necessary to carry out their respective missions;

(c) oversee the development and implementation of intelligence sharing capabilities (including systems, programs, policies, and standards) to enhance shared situational awareness of intelligence related to foreign cyber threats or related to cyber incidents affecting U.S. national interests among the organizations referenced in subsection (b) of this section;

(d) ensure that indicators of malicious cyber activity and, as appropriate, related threat reporting contained in intelligence channels are downgraded to the lowest classification possible for distribution to both United States Government and U.S. private sector entities through the mechanism described in section 4 of **Executive Order 13636** of February 12, 2013 (Improving Critical Infrastructure Cybersecurity); and

(e) facilitate and support interagency efforts to develop and implement coordinated plans to counter foreign cyber threats to U.S. national interests using all instruments of national power, including diplomatic, economic, military, intelligence, homeland security, and law enforcement activities.

317

Sec. 3. Implementation.

(a) Agencies shall provide the CTIIC with all intelligence related to foreign cyber threats or related to cyber incidents affecting U.S. national interests, subject to applicable law and policy. The CTIIC shall access, assess, use, retain, and disseminate such information, in a manner that protects privacy and civil liberties and is consistent with applicable law, Executive Orders, Presidential directives, and guidelines, such as guidelines established under section 102A(b) of the National Security Act of 1947, as amended, Executive Order 12333 of December 4, 1981 (United States Intelligence Activities), as amended, and Presidential Policy Directive-28; and that is consistent with the need to protect sources and methods.

(b) Within 90 days of the date of this memorandum, the DNI, in consultation with the Secretary of State, the Secretary of Defense, the Attorney General, the Secretary of Homeland Security, the Director of the Central Intelligence Agency, the Director of the Federal Bureau of Investigation, and the Director of the National Security Agency shall provide a status report to the Director of the Office of Management and Budget and the Assistant to the President for Homeland Security and Counterterrorism on the establishment of the CTIIC. This report shall further refine the CTIIC's mission, roles, and responsibilities, consistent with this memorandum, ensuring that those roles and responsibilities are appropriately aligned with other Presidential policies as well as existing policy coordination mechanisms.

Sec. 4. Privacy and Civil Liberties Protections.

Agencies providing information to the CTIIC shall ensure that privacy and civil liberties protections are provided in the course of implementing this memorandum. Such protections shall be based upon the Fair Information Practice Principles or other privacy and civil liberties policies, principles, and frameworks as they apply to each agency's activities.

Sec. 5. General Provisions.

(a) Nothing in this memorandum shall be construed to impair or otherwise affect:

(i) the authority granted by law to an executive department, agency, or the head thereof; or

     (ii) the functions of the Director of the Office of Management and Budget relating to budgetary, administrative, or legislative proposals.

(b) This memorandum shall be implemented consistent with applicable law and subject to the availability of appropriations.

(c) This memorandum is not intended to, and does not, create any right or benefit, substantive or procedural, enforceable at law or in equity by any party against the United States, its departments, agencies, or entities, its officers, employees, or agents, or any other person.

(d) The DNI is hereby authorized and directed to publish this memorandum in the *Federal Register*.

BARACK OBAMA

THE WHITE HOUSE

Office of the Press Secretary
February 12, 2013
PRESIDENTIAL POLICY DIRECTIVE/PPD-21
SUBJECT: Critical Infrastructure Security and Resilience
The Presidential Policy Directive (PPD) on Critical Infrastructure Security and Resilience advances a national unity of effort to strengthen and maintain secure, functioning, and resilient critical infrastructure

INTRODUCTION

The Nation's critical infrastructure provides the essential services that underpin American society. Proactive and coordinated efforts are necessary to strengthen and maintain secure, functioning, and resilient critical infrastructure—including assets, networks, and systems—that are vital to public confidence and the Nation's safety, prosperity, and well-being. The Nation's critical infrastructure is diverse and complex. It includes distributed networks, varied organizational structures and operating models (including multinational ownership), interdependent functions and systems in both the physical space and cyberspace, and governance constructs that involve multilevel authorities, responsibilities, and regulations. Critical infrastructure owners and operators are uniquely positioned to manage risks to their individual operations and assets, and to determine effective strategies to make them more secure and resilient. Critical infrastructure must be secure and able to withstand and rapidly recover from all hazards. Achieving this will require integration with the national preparedness system across prevention, protection, mitigation, response, and recovery. This directive establishes national policy on critical infrastructure security and resilience. This endeavor is a shared responsibility among the Federal, state, local, tribal, and territorial (SLTT) entities, and public and private owners and operators of critical infrastructure (herein referred to as "critical infrastructure owners and operators"). This directive also refines and clarifies the critical infrastructure-related functions, roles, and responsibilities across the Federal Government, as well as enhances overall coordination and collaboration. The Federal Government also has a responsibility to strengthen the security and resilience of its own critical infrastructure, for the continuity of national essential functions, and to organize itself to partner effectively with and add value to the security and resilience efforts of critical infrastructure owners and operators.

POLICY

It is the policy of the United States to strengthen the security and resilience of its critical infrastructure against both physical and cyber threats. The Federal Government shall work with critical infrastructure owners and operators and SLTT entities to take proactive steps to manage risk and strengthen the security and resilience of the Nation's critical infrastructure, considering all hazards that could have a debilitating impact on national security, economic stability, public health and safety, or any combination thereof. These efforts shall seek to reduce vulnerabilities, minimize consequences, identify and disrupt threats, and hasten response and recovery efforts related to critical infrastructure. The Federal Government shall also engage with international partners to strengthen the security and resilience of domestic critical infrastructure and critical infrastructure located outside of the United States on which the Nation depends. The US efforts shall address the security and resilience of critical infrastructure in an integrated, holistic manner to reflect this infrastructure's interconnectedness and interdependency. This directive also identifies energy and communications systems as uniquely critical due to the enabling functions they provide across all Critical Infrastructure Sectors.

Three strategic imperatives shall drive the Federal approach to strengthen critical infrastructure security and resilience:

1. Refine and clarify functional relationships across the Federal Government to advance the national unity of effort to strengthen critical infrastructure security and resilience;
2. Enable effective information exchange by identifying baseline data and systems requirements for the Federal Government; and
3. Implement an integration and analysis function to inform planning and operations decisions regarding critical infrastructure.

All Federal department and agency heads are responsible for the identification, prioritization, assessment, remediation, and security of their respective internal critical infrastructure that supports primary mission essential functions. Such infrastructure shall be addressed in the plans and execution of the requirements in the National Continuity Policy. Federal departments and agencies shall implement this directive in a manner consistent with applicable law, Presidential directives, and Federal regulations, including those protecting privacy, civil rights, and civil liberties. In addition, Federal departments and agencies shall protect all information associated with carrying out this directive consistent with applicable legal authorities and policies.

ROLES AND RESPONSIBILITIES

Effective implementation of this directive requires a national unity of effort pursuant to strategic guidance from the Secretary of Homeland Security. That national effort must include expertise and day-to-day engagement from the Sector- Specific Agencies (SSAs) as well as the specialized or support capabilities from other Federal departments and agencies, and strong collaboration with critical infrastructure owners and operators and SLTT entities. Although the roles and responsibilities identified in this directive are directed at Federal departments and agencies, effective partnerships with critical infrastructure owners and operators and SLTT entities are imperative to strengthen the security and resilience of the Nation's critical infrastructure.

Secretary of Homeland Security

The Secretary of Homeland Security shall provide strategic guidance, promote a national unity of effort, and coordinate the overall Federal effort to

321

promote the security and resilience of the Nation's critical infrastructure. In carrying out the responsibilities assigned in the Homeland Security Act of 2002, as amended, the Secretary of Homeland Security evaluates national capabilities, opportunities, and challenges in protecting critical infrastructure; analyzes threats to, vulnerabilities of, and potential consequences from all hazards on critical infrastructure; identifies security and resilience functions that are necessary for effective public-private engagement with all Critical Infrastructure Sectors; develops a national plan and metrics, in coordination with SSAs and other critical infrastructure partners; integrates and coordinates Federal cross-sector security and resilience activities; identifies and analyzes key interdependencies among critical infrastructure sectors; and reports on the effectiveness of national efforts to strengthen the Nation's security and resilience posture for critical infrastructure.

Additional roles and responsibilities for the Secretary of Homeland Security include:

1. Identify and prioritize critical infrastructure, considering physical and cyber threats, vulnerabilities, and consequences, in coordination with SSAs and other Federal departments and agencies.
2. Maintain national critical infrastructure centers that shall provide a situational awareness capability that includes integrated, actionable information about emerging trends, imminent threats, and the status of incidents that may impact critical infrastructure.
3. In coordination with SSAs and other Federal departments and agencies, provide analysis, expertise, and other technical assistance to critical infrastructure owners and operators and facilitate access to and exchange of information and intelligence necessary to strengthen the security and resilience of critical infrastructure.
4. Conduct comprehensive assessments of the vulnerabilities of the Nation's critical infrastructure in coordination with the SSAs and in collaboration with SLTT entities and critical infrastructure owners and operators.
5. Coordinate Federal Government responses to significant cyber or physical incidents affecting critical infrastructure consistent with statutory authorities.
6. Support the Attorney General and law enforcement agencies with their responsibilities to investigate and prosecute threats to and attacks against critical infrastructure.
7. Coordinate with and utilize the expertise of SSAs and other appropriate Federal departments and agencies to map geospatially,

image, analyze, and sort critical infrastructure by employing commercial satellite and airborne systems, as well as existing capabilities within other departments and agencies; and

8. Report annually on the status of national critical infrastructure efforts as required by statute.

Sector-Specific Agencies

Each Critical Infrastructure Sector has unique characteristics, operating models, and risk profiles that benefit from an identified Sector-Specific Agency that has institutional knowledge and specialized expertise about the sector. Recognizing existing statutory or regulatory authorities of specific Federal departments and agencies, and leveraging existing sector familiarity and relationships, SSAs shall carry out the following roles and responsibilities for their respective sectors:

1. As part of the broader national effort to strengthen the security and resilience of critical infrastructure, coordinate with the Department of Homeland Security (DHS) and other relevant Federal departments and agencies and collaborate with critical infrastructure owners and operators, where appropriate with independent regulatory agencies, and with SLTT entities, as appropriate, to implement this directive.
2. Serve as a day-to-day Federal interface for the dynamic prioritization and coordination of sector-specific activities.
3. Carry out incident management responsibilities consistent with statutory authority and other appropriate policies, directives, or regulations.
4. Provide, support, or facilitate technical assistance and consultations for that sector to identify vulnerabilities and help mitigate incidents, as appropriate; and
5. Support the Secretary of Homeland Security's statutorily required reporting requirements by providing on an annual basis sector-specific critical infrastructure information.

Additional Federal Responsibilities

The following departments and agencies have specialized or support functions related to critical infrastructure security and resilience that shall be carried out by, or along with, other Federal departments and agencies and independent regulatory agencies, as appropriate.

1. The Department of State, in coordination with DHS, SSAs, and other Federal departments and agencies, shall engage foreign governments and international organizations to strengthen the security and resilience of critical infrastructure located outside the United States and to facilitate the overall exchange of best practices and lessons learned for promoting the security and resilience of critical infrastructure on which the Nation depends.

2. The Department of Justice (DOJ), including the Federal Bureau of Investigation (FBI), shall lead counterterrorism and counterintelligence investigations and related law enforcement activities across the Critical Infrastructure Sectors. DOJ shall investigate, disrupt, prosecute, and otherwise reduce foreign intelligence, terrorist, and other threats to, and actual or attempted attacks on, or sabotage of, the Nation's critical infrastructure. The FBI also conducts domestic collection, analysis, and dissemination of cyber threat information, and shall be responsible for the operation of the National Cyber Investigative Joint Task Force (NCIJTF). The NCIJTF serves as a multi-agency national focal point for coordinating, integrating, and sharing pertinent information related to cyber threat investigations, with representation from DHS, the Intelligence Community (IC), the Department of Defense (DOD), and other agencies as appropriate. The Attorney General and the Secretary of Homeland Security shall collaborate to carry out their respective critical infrastructure missions.

3. The Department of the Interior, in collaboration with the SSA for the Government Facilities Sector, shall identify, prioritize, and coordinate the security and resilience efforts for national monuments and icons and incorporate measures to reduce risk to these critical assets, while also promoting their use and enjoyment.

4. The Department of Commerce (DOC), in collaboration with DHS and other relevant Federal departments and agencies, shall engage private sector, research, academic, and government organizations to improve security for technology and tools related to cyber-based systems, and promote the development of other efforts related to critical infrastructure to enable the timely availability of industrial products, materials, and services to meet homeland security requirements.

5. The IC, led by the Director of National Intelligence (DNI), shall use applicable authorities and coordination mechanisms to provide, as appropriate, intelligence assessments regarding threats to critical infrastructure and coordinate on intelligence and other sensitive or proprietary information related to critical infrastructure. In addition, information security policies, directives, standards, and guidelines for safeguarding national security systems shall be overseen as directed by the President, applicable law, and in accordance with that direction, carried out under the authority of the heads of agencies that operate or exercise authority over such national security systems.

6. The General Services Administration, in consultation with DOD, DHS, and other departments and agencies as appropriate, shall provide or support government-wide contracts for critical infrastructure systems and ensure that such contracts include audit rights for the security and resilience of critical infrastructure.

7. The Nuclear Regulatory Commission (NRC) is to oversee its licensees' protection of commercial nuclear power reactors and non-power nuclear reactors used for research, testing, and training; nuclear materials in medical, industrial, and academic settings, and facilities that fabricate nuclear fuel; and the transportation, storage, and disposal of nuclear materials and waste. The NRC is to collaborate, to the extent possible, with DHS, DOJ, the Department of Energy, the Environmental Protection Agency, and other Federal departments and agencies, as appropriate, on strengthening critical infrastructure security and resilience.

8. The Federal Communications Commission, to the extent permitted by law, is to exercise its authority and expertise to partner with DHS and the Department of State, as well as other Federal departments and agencies and SSAs as appropriate, on:
   a. identifying and prioritizing communications infrastructure;
   b. identifying communications sector vulnerabilities and working with industry and other stakeholders to address those vulnerabilities; and
   c. working with stakeholders, including industry, and engaging foreign governments and international organizations to increase the security and resilience of critical infrastructure

within the communications sector and facilitating the development and implementation of best practices promoting the security and resilience of critical communications infrastructure on which the Nation depends.

9. Federal departments and agencies shall provide timely information to the Secretary of Homeland Security and the national critical infrastructure centers necessary to support cross-sector analysis and inform the situational awareness capability for critical infrastructure.

THREE STRATEGIC IMPERATIVES

1. Refine and Clarify Functional Relationships across the Federal Government to Advance the National Unity of Effort to Strengthen Critical Infrastructure Security and Resilience An effective national effort to strengthen critical infrastructure security and resilience must be guided by a national plan that identifies roles and responsibilities and is informed by the expertise, experience, capabilities, and responsibilities of the SSAs, other Federal departments and agencies with critical infrastructure roles, SLTT entities, and critical infrastructure owners and operators. During the past decade, new programs and initiatives have been established to address specific infrastructure issues, and priorities have shifted and expanded. As a result, Federal functions related to critical infrastructure security and resilience shall be clarified and refined to establish baseline capabilities that will reflect this evolution of knowledge, to define relevant Federal program functions, and to facilitate collaboration and information exchange between and among the Federal Government, critical infrastructure owners and operators, and SLTT entities. As part of this refined structure, there shall be two national critical infrastructure centers operated by DHS—one for physical infrastructure and another for cyber infrastructure. They shall function in an integrated manner and serve as focal points for critical infrastructure partners to obtain situational awareness and integrated, actionable information to protect the physical and cyber aspects of critical infrastructure. Just as the physical and cyber elements of critical infrastructure are inextricably linked, so are the vulnerabilities. Accordingly, an

integration and analysis function (further developed in Strategic Imperative 3) shall be implemented between these two national centers. The success of these national centers, including the integration and analysis function, is dependent on the quality and timeliness of the information and intelligence they receive from the SSAs and other Federal departments and agencies, as well as from critical infrastructure owners and operators and SLTT entities. These national centers shall not impede the ability of the heads of Federal departments and agencies to carry out or perform their responsibilities for national defense, criminal, counterintelligence, counterterrorism, or investigative activities.

2. Enable Efficient Information Exchange by Identifying Baseline Data and Systems Requirements for the Federal Government A secure, functioning, and resilient critical infrastructure requires the efficient exchange of information, including intelligence, between all levels of governments and critical infrastructure owners and operators. This must facilitate the timely exchange of threat and vulnerability information as well as information that allows for the development of a situational awareness capability during incidents. The goal is to enable efficient information exchange through the identification of requirements for data and information formats and accessibility, system interoperability, and redundant systems and alternate capabilities should there be a disruption in the primary systems. Greater information sharing within the government and with the private sector can and must be done while respecting privacy and civil liberties. Federal departments and agencies shall ensure that all existing privacy principles, policies, and procedures are implemented consistent with applicable law and policy and shall include senior agency officials for privacy in their efforts to govern and oversee information sharing properly.

3. Implement an Integration and Analysis Function to Inform Planning and Operational Decisions Regarding Critical Infrastructure. The third strategic imperative builds on the first two and calls for the implementation of an integration and analysis function for critical infrastructure that includes operational and strategic analysis on incidents, threats, and emerging risks. It shall reside at the intersection of the two national centers as identified in Strategic Imperative 1, and it shall include the capability to collate, assess,

327

and integrate vulnerability and consequence information with threat streams and hazard information to:

a. Aid in prioritizing assets and managing risks to critical infrastructure
b. Anticipate interdependencies and cascading impacts;
c. Recommend security and resilience measures for critical infrastructure prior to, during, and after an event or incident; and
d. Support incident management and restoration efforts related to critical infrastructure.

This function shall not replicate the analysis function of the IC or the National Counterterrorism Center, nor shall it involve intelligence collection activities. The IC, DOD, DOJ, DHS, and other Federal departments and agencies with relevant intelligence or information shall, however, inform this integration and analysis capability regarding the Nation's critical infrastructure by providing relevant, timely, and appropriate information to the national centers. This function shall also use information and intelligence provided by other critical infrastructure partners, including SLTT and nongovernmental analytic entities. Finally, this integration and analysis function shall support DHS's ability to maintain and share, as a common Federal service, a near real-time situational awareness capability for critical infrastructure that includes actionable information about imminent threats, significant trends, and awareness of incidents that may affect critical infrastructure.

INNOVATION AND RESEARCH AND DEVELOPMENT

The Secretary of Homeland Security, in coordination with the Office of Science and Technology Policy (OSTP), the SSAs, DOC, and other Federal departments and agencies, shall provide input to align those Federal and Federally-funded research and development (R&D) activities that seek to strengthen the security and resilience of the Nation's critical infrastructure, including:

1. Promoting R&D to enable the secure and resilient design and construction of critical infrastructure and more secure accompanying cyber technology.
2. Enhancing modeling capabilities to determine potential impacts on critical infrastructure of an incident or threat scenario, as well as cascading effects on other sectors.

3. Facilitating initiatives to incentivize cybersecurity investments and the adoption of critical infrastructure design features that strengthen all-hazards security and resilience. and

4. Prioritizing efforts to support the strategic guidance issued by the Secretary of Homeland Security.

IMPLEMENTATION OF THE DIRECTIVE

The Secretary of Homeland Security shall take the following actions as part of the implementation of this directive.

1) Critical Infrastructure Security and Resilience Functional Relationships. Within 120 days of the date of this directive, the Secretary of Homeland Security shall develop a description of the functional relationships within DHS and across the Federal Government related to critical infrastructure security and resilience. It should include the roles and functions of the two national critical infrastructure centers and a discussion of the analysis and integration function. When complete, it should serve as a roadmap for critical infrastructure owners and operators and SLTT entities to navigate the Federal Government's functions and primary points of contact assigned to those functions for critical infrastructure security and resilience against both physical and cyber threats. The Secretary shall coordinate this effort with the SSAs and other relevant Federal departments and agencies. The Secretary shall provide the description to the President through the Assistant to the President for Homeland Security and Counterterrorism.

2) Evaluation of the Existing Public–Private Partnership Model. Within 150 days of the date of this directive, the Secretary of Homeland Security, in coordination with the SSAs, other relevant Federal departments and agencies, SLTT entities, and critical infrastructure owners and operators, shall conduct an analysis of the existing public-private partnership model and recommend options for improving the effectiveness of the partnership in both the physical and cyber space. The evaluation shall consider options to streamline processes for collaboration and exchange of information and to minimize duplication of

effort. Furthermore, the analysis shall consider how the model can be flexible and adaptable to meet the unique needs of individual sectors while providing a focused, disciplined, and effective approach for the Federal Government to coordinate with the critical infrastructure owners and operators and with SLTT governments. The evaluation shall result in recommendations to enhance partnerships to be approved for implementation through the processes established in the Organization of the National Security Council System directive.

3) Identification of Baseline Data and Systems Requirements for the Federal Government to Enable Efficient Information Exchange. Within 180 days of the date of this directive, the Secretary of Homeland Security, in coordination with the SSAs and other Federal departments and agencies, shall convene a team of experts to identify baseline data and systems requirements to enable the efficient exchange of information and intelligence relevant to strengthening the security and resilience of critical infrastructure. The experts should include representatives from those entities that routinely possess information important to critical infrastructure security and resilience; those that determine and manage information technology systems used to exchange information; and those responsible for the security of information being exchanged. Interoperability with critical infrastructure partners; identification of key data and the information requirements of key Federal, SLTT, and private sector entities; availability, accessibility, and formats of data; the ability to exchange various classifications of information; and the security of those systems to be used; and appropriate protections for individual privacy and civil liberties should be included in the analysis. The analysis should result in baseline requirements for sharing of data and interoperability of systems to enable the timely exchange of data and information to secure critical infrastructure and make it more resilient. The Secretary shall provide that analysis to the President through the Assistant to the President for Homeland Security and Counterterrorism.

4) Development of a Situational Awareness Capability for Critical Infrastructure. Within 240 days of the date of this directive, the Secretary of Homeland Security shall demonstrate a near real-time situational awareness capability for critical infrastructure that includes threat streams and all-hazards information as

well as vulnerabilities; provides the status of critical infrastructure and potential cascading effects; supports decision making; and disseminates critical information that may be needed to save or sustain lives, mitigate damage, or reduce further degradation of a critical infrastructure capability throughout an incident. This capability should be available for and cover physical and cyber elements of critical infrastructure, and enable an integration of information as necessitated by the incident.

5) Update to National Infrastructure Protection Plan. Within 240 days of the date of this directive, the Secretary of Homeland Security shall provide to the President, through the Assistant to the President for Homeland Security and Counterterrorism, a successor to the National Infrastructure Protection Plan to address the implementation of this directive, the requirements of Title II of the Homeland Security Act of 2002 as amended, and alignment with the National Preparedness Goal and System required by PPD-8. The plan shall include the identification of a risk management framework to be used to strengthen the security and resilience of critical infrastructure; the methods to be used to prioritize critical infrastructure; the protocols to be used to synchronize communication and actions within the Federal Government; and a metrics and analysis process to be used to measure the Nation's ability to manage and reduce risks to critical infrastructure. The updated plan shall also reflect the identified functional relationships within DHS and across the Federal Government and the updates to the public-private partnership model. Finally, the plan should consider sector dependencies on energy and communications systems, and identify pre-event and mitigation measures or alternate capabilities during disruptions to those systems. The Secretary shall coordinate this effort with the SSAs, other relevant Federal departments and agencies, SLTT entities, and critical infrastructure owners and operators.

6) National Critical Infrastructure Security and Resilience R&D Plan. Within 2 years of the date of this directive, the Secretary of Homeland Security, in coordination with the OSTP, the SSAs, DOC, and other Federal departments and agencies, shall provide to the President, through the Assistant to the President for Homeland Security and Counterterrorism, a National Critical Infrastructure Security and Resilience R&D Plan that takes into account the evolving threat landscape, annual metrics, and other

relevant information to identify priorities and guide R&D requirements and investments. The plan should be issued every 4 years after its initial delivery, with interim updates as needed.

Policy coordination, dispute resolution, and periodic in-progress reviews for the implementation of this directive shall be carried out consistent with PPD-1, including the use of Interagency Policy Committees coordinated by the National Security Staff.

Nothing in this directive alters, supersedes, or impedes the authorities of Federal departments and agencies, including independent regulatory agencies, to carry out their functions and duties consistent with applicable legal authorities and other Presidential guidance and directives, including, but not limited to, the designation of critical infrastructure under such authorities.

This directive revokes Homeland Security Presidential Directive/ HSPD-7, Critical Infrastructure Identification, Prioritization, and Protection, issued December 17, 2003. Plans developed pursuant to HSPD-7 shall remain in effect until specifically revoked or superseded.

DESIGNATED CRITICAL INFRASTRUCTURE SECTORS AND SECTOR-SPECIFIC AGENCIES

This directive identifies 16 critical infrastructure sectors and designates associated Federal SSAs. In some cases co-SSAs are designated where those departments share the roles and responsibilities of the SSA. The Secretary of Homeland Security shall periodically evaluate the need for and approve changes to critical infrastructure sectors and shall consult with the Assistant to the President for Homeland Security and Counterterrorism before changing a critical infrastructure sector or a designated SSA for that sector. The sectors and SAs are as follows:

Chemical: Sector-Specific Agency: Department of Homeland Security

Commercial Facilities: Sector-Specific Agency: Department of Homeland Security

Communications: Sector-Specific Agency: Department of Homeland Security

Critical Manufacturing: Sector-Specific Agency: Department of Homeland Security

Dams: Sector-Specific Agency: Department of Homeland Security

Defense Industrial Base: Sector-Specific Agency: Department of Defense

Emergency Services: Sector-Specific Agency: Department of Homeland Security

Energy: Sector-Specific Agency: Department of Energy

Financial Services: Sector-Specific Agency: Department of the Treasury

Food and Agriculture: Co-Sector-Specific Agencies: U.S. Department of Agriculture and Department of Health and Human Services

Government Facilities: Co-Sector-Specific Agencies: Department of Homeland

Security and General Services Administration

Healthcare and Public Health: Sector-Specific Agency: Department of Health and Human Services

Information Technology: Sector-Specific Agency: Department of Homeland Security

Nuclear Reactors, Materials, and Waste: Sector-Specific Agency: Department of Homeland Security

Transportation Systems: Co-Sector-Specific Agencies: Department of Homeland

Security and Department of Transportation

Water and Wastewater Systems: Sector-Specific Agency: Environmental Protection Agency

DEFINITIONS

For purposes of this directive:

The term "all hazards" means a threat or an incident, natural or man-made, that warrants action to protect life, property, the environment, and public health or safety, and to minimize disruptions of government, social, or economic activities. It includes natural disasters, cyber incidents, industrial accidents, pandemics, acts of terrorism, sabotage, and destructive criminal activity targeting critical infrastructure.

The term "collaboration" means the process of working together to achieve shared goals.

The terms "coordinate" and "in coordination with" mean a consensus decision-making process in which the named coordinating department or agency is responsible for working with the affected departments and agencies to achieve consensus and a consistent course of action.

The term "critical infrastructure" has the meaning provided in section 1016(e) of the USA Patriot Act of 2001 (42 U.S.C. 5195c(e)), namely systems and assets, whether physical or virtual, so vital to the United States that the incapacity or destruction of such systems and assets would have a debilitating impact on security, national economic security, national public health or safety, or any combination of those matters.

The term "Federal departments and agencies" means any authority of the United States that is an "agency" under 44 U.S.C. 3502(1), other than those considered to be independent regulatory agencies, as defined in 44 U.S.C. 3502(5).

The term "national essential functions" means that subset of Government functions that are necessary to lead and sustain the Nation during a catastrophic emergency.

The term "primary mission essential functions" means those Government functions that must be performed in order to support or implement the performance of the national essential functions before, during, and in the aftermath of an emergency.

The term "national security systems" has the meaning given to it in the Federal Information Security Management Act of 2002 (44 U.S.C. 3542(b)).

The term "resilience" means the ability to prepare for and adapt to changing conditions and withstand and recover rapidly from disruptions. Resilience includes the ability to withstand and recover from deliberate attacks, accidents, or naturally occurring threats or incidents.

The term "Sector-Specific Agency" (SSA) means the Federal department or agency designated under this directive to be responsible for providing institutional knowledge and specialized expertise as well as leading, facilitating, or supporting the security and resilience programs and associated activities of its designated critical infrastructure sector in the all-hazards environment.

The terms "secure" and "security" refer to reducing the risk to critical infrastructure by physical means or defense cyber measures to intrusions, attacks, or the effects of natural or manmade disasters.

GLOSSARY

Adaptability: It includes designing risk management actions, strategies, and processes to remain dynamic and responsive to change.

Advisory Councils: They provide advice and recommendations to the government or to private agencies about the best methods to protect critical assets. Councils are also able to develop better methods for information sharing between and among the public and private agencies. Two significant councils are the National Infrastructure Advisory Council (NIAC) and the Critical Infrastructure Partnership Advisory Council (CIPAC).

Capability Target: Capability targets define success for each core capability and describe what the community wants to achieve by combining detailed impacts with basic and measurable desired outcomes based on the threat and hazard context statements developed in Step 2 of the Threat and Hazard Identification and Risk Assessment (THIRA) process.

CARMA: Cyber Assessment Risk Management Approach is used alongside the Cybersecurity Framework to assess risk. CARMA provides a methodology for sector stakeholders to define key business functions that must be protected, and identifies risks posed to their functional viability.

CARVER Plus Shock Method: It is used by the food and agriculture sector to determine the vulnerabilities in its assets, systems, and networks. This is accomplished by encompassing the consequences and threats.

Communications Sector-Specific Plan Risk Framework: It is built on the goals of the CSSP, the plan attempts to increase the resilience of the communications sector. These basic risk assessment goals include a more resilient infrastructure, diversity, redundancy, and recoverability.

Computer Crime and Intellectual Property Section (of Department of Justice): It investigates and prosecutes cyberattacks on critical assets and also participates in policy and legislation issues. The agency coordinates with other federal agencies to work on issues related to critical infrastructure protection.

Consequence: The possible impact or result of an event, incident, or occurrence, such as the number of deaths, injuries, property loss or damage, or interruptions to necessary services. The economic impacts of an event are also critical consequences, as many events have both short and long-term economic consequences to communities or even to the nation.

Context: A community-specific description of an incident, including location, timing, and other important circumstances.

Convergence: The interconnected nature of critical infrastructure such that harm to one asset results in harm to other assets. At the same time, it means that if one sector is unable to provide a service, another asset may be able to provide that service.

Core Capability: It is defined by the National Preparedness Goal, 31 activities that address the greatest risks to the nation. Each of the core capabilities is tied to a capability target.

Critical Infrastructure: The framework of man-made networks and systems that provide needed goods and services to the public. This includes any facility or structure, both physical and organizational that provides essential services to the residents of a community to ensure its continued operation. This term includes things such as buildings, roads and transportation systems, telecommunications systems, water systems, energy systems, emergency services, banking and finance institutions, and power supplies. In addition to physical structures and assets, the term incorporates virtual (cyber) systems and people. Critical infrastructure can be found in the local, state, and federal systems, and can be owned and operated by private and/or public organizations.

Critical Infrastructure Assurance Office: Located in the Commerce Department, this office provided support to the sectors as they developed their protection plans, as well as providing assistance to National Coordinators as they integrated the sector plans into the National Plan.

Critical Infrastructure Information (CII): The data or information that pertains to an asset or critical infrastructure, such as knowledge about the daily operations of an asset, or a description of the asset's vulnerabilities and protection plans. CII can also include information generated by the asset such as patient health records or a person's banking and financial records, or evidence of future development plans related to the asset. It can also be information that describes pertinent geological or meteorological information about the location of an asset that may point out potential vulnerabilities of that facility (e.g., a dam at an earthquake-prone site).

Critical Infrastructure Partnership Advisory Council (CIPAC): It was established by DHS in 2006 to help foster effective communication between federal, state, local, tribal, territorial, and regional infrastructure protection programs. It provides a forum for these groups to discuss activities to support and coordinate resource protection. CIPAC membership plan, coordinate, and implement security programs related to critical infrastructure protection. The Council also includes representatives from federal, state, local, and tribal governmental groups who are members of the Government Coordinating Councils for each sector.

Critical Infrastructure Protection (CIP): Actions that are geared toward protecting critical infrastructures against physical attacks or hazards, or toward deterring attacks (or mitigating the effects of attacks) that are either man-made or natural. Most CIP activity includes preventative measures, but it usually refers to actions that are more reactive. Today, CIP focuses on an all-hazards approach. The primary responsibility for protecting critical infrastructure lies with the owners and operators, but the federal government and owners/operators work together to identify critical infrastructure.

Critical Infrastructure Warning Network: An agency managed by the DHS to provide secure lines of communication between the federal government and other federal, state, and local agencies, the private sector, and international agencies.

Cybersecurity: Any actions taken by government or by private operators to prevent damage to, unauthorized use of, or exploitation of, information that is stored electronically. This includes any activity that is intended to protect or restore information networks and wirelines, wireless satellite, public safety answering points, and 911 communications systems and control systems.

Cybersecurity Framework: On February 12, 2013, President Obama issued Executive Order 13636 in which he described the development of a cybersecurity framework to increase protection to protect the nation's cybersecurity. This framework would establish standards, methodologies, procedures, and processes that the owners of critical infrastructure could use to reduce their cybersecurity risks.

Cybersecurity Framework Components: The three components of the cybersecurity framework are the core, implementation tiers, and profile. The framework is a voluntary risk-based framework focusing on enhanced cybersecurity that can be used by organizations of any size in any of the 16 critical infrastructure sectors that either already have a mature cyber risk management and cybersecurity program, or even by those that do not have such programs.

Cybersecurity Workforce Assessment Act: It required the Secretary of Homeland Security to conduct a yearly assessment of the cybersecurity workforce in DHS.

Cyberspace Policy Review Committee: It was established in May 2009, by President Obama, this Committee was asked to review the nation's cyberspace security policy and make recommendations to the president about ways to improve cyber security. The Committee recommended that the president appoint an Executive Branch Cybersecurity Coordinator and that the Executive Branch work more closely with all key players who are involved in US cybersecurity policy.

Department of Homeland Security (DHS): It was created in November 2002 when the Congress passed the Homeland Security Act (PL 107-296). The DHS is a cabinet-level department that is responsible for developing a comprehensive national plan for securing the country's assets and for recommending policies to protect the Nation's critical infrastructure and key resources.

Desired Outcome: The standard to which incidents must be managed, including the time frames for conducting operations or percentage-based standard for performing security activities.

DHS Risk Lexicon: It was initiated in 2008, the DHS Risk Lexicon provides a common language to improve the capability of the DHS to assess and manage homeland security risk. At first, the document contained 23 terms that served as a tool to improve capabilities of DHS to assess and manage homeland security risk. In 2010, the second edition of the DHS Risk Lexicon was published with an additional 50 new terms and definitions.

DHS Risk Management Process: It encourages comparability and shared understanding of information and analysis in the decision-making process. This is comprised of seven planning and analysis efforts, including defining and framing the context of decisions and related goals and objectives; identifying the risks associated with the goals and objectives; analyzing and assessing the identified risks; developing alternative actions for managing the risks and creating opportunities, and analyzing the costs and benefits of those alternatives; choosing among alternatives and implementing that decision; and monitoring the implemented decision and comparing observed and expected effects to help influence subsequent risk management alternatives and decisions. Risk communications underlies the entire risk management process.

Enhanced Cybersecurity Services Program: It allows classified information on cybersecurity threats and other technical information to be shared with infrastructure network service providers.

Executive Order 13010: It is a document signed by President Clinton in 1996 in which he revealed his plans to establish the President's Commission on Critical Infrastructure Protection (PCCIP) that would investigate the scope and nature of potential vulnerabilities and threats to the country's critical infrastructure, with a focus on cyberthreats. Clinton also identified eight critical infrastructure sectors in the Executive Order, including telecommunications, transportation, electric power, banking and finance, gas and oil storage and delivery, water supply, emergency services, and government operations. The third change that Clinton identified was the expansion of the term "infrastructure."

Executive Order 13228: It was signed by President Bush on October 8, 2001, to create the Office of Homeland Security. The agency was to coordinate efforts to protect the US and its critical infrastructure from another attack, and maintain efforts at recovery.

Executive Order 13231: It was signed by President Bush on October 16, 2001, the document announced the president's intentions to create the President's Critical Infrastructure Protection Board. The board was responsible for recommending policies and programs to protect information systems for critical infrastructure.

Executive Order 13563: It was issued on January 18, 2011, by President Obama, this document was also entitled "Improving Regulation and Regulatory Review." In this document, Obama directed all federal agencies to develop a Preliminary Plan to review their regulations to determine whether any of the existing rules should be updated or altered in any way to make the agency's regulatory program more effective.

Executive Order 13636: It was issued by President Obama on February 12, 2013, this document, also entitled *Improving Critical Infrastructure:*

Cybersecurity, stressed the need to protect the nation's critical infrastructure and cyber environment. Obama stressed the need for better communication and cooperation between the owners and operators of critical infrastructure and the federal government. In another part of the executive order, Obama sought to develop a cybersecurity framework to improve the nation's cybersecurity.

Executive Order 13691: It was issued by President Obama in February 2015, Executive Order 13691, also called Promoting Private Sector Cybersecurity Information Sharing, focused on the importance of sharing information pertaining to cybersecurity. Obama created Information Sharing and Analysis Organizations (ISAOs) to further this goal.

Federal Emergency Management Agency (FEMA): It is the nation's federal agency that oversees the federal response to disasters, both natural and man-made. The agency provides support for citizens so they can protect against, respond to, recover from, and mitigate all hazards.

FEMA Grant Program: It is an annual grant program overseen by the Grant Programs Directorate that provides financial assistance for programs that seek to increase the nation's infrastructure protection and security of its assets. The focus is to promote communication with state, local, and tribal stakeholders and increase the nation's level of preparedness. The grant program helps to fund many activities related to homeland security and emergency preparedness, including planning, organization, equipment purchase, training, exercises, and management.

Financial Services Information Sharing and Analysis Center (FSISAC): It is a program to increase the financial sector's cybersecurity information sharing capabilities.

Fusion Centers: They are one important way for federal, state, local, tribal, and territorial agencies to facilitate information sharing. Fusion centers have been established in many states and large cities to share intelligence within their own jurisdictions as well as with the federal government. The fusion centers ensure that both classified and unclassified information can be shared among the group, with expertise at all levels sharing information.

Hazard: It is a source or cause of harm. There are different types of hazards, including natural hazards (caused by acts of nature such as hurricanes or wildfires); technological hazards (such as a hazardous materials releases, dam or levee failures, an airplane crash, power failure, or radiological release); and human-caused hazards, which include incidents that are the result of intentional actions of an individual or group of individuals. Examples of this include acts of terrorism, an active shooter, biological attacks, chemical attack, cyber incident; a bomb attack, or a radiological attack.

Hazard Effect: The overall impacts to the community, were an incident to occur.

Homeland Infrastructure Threat and Risk Analysis Center (HITRAC): HITRAC, found within DHS, HITRAC is the Department's Intelligence—Infrastructure Protection Fusion Center. The Center's membership includes analysts from both the Office of Infrastructure Protection and the Office of Intelligence and Analysis who have the expertise to carry out infrastructure risk assessment responsibilities. HITRAC carries out Sector-Specific Threat Assessments, Sector-Specific Risk Assessments, Individual State Threat Assessments, and other assessments as needed. To assist in this process, they have a Critical Infrastructure Red Team that examines threats, vulnerabilities, and plans for mitigating risk to critical infrastructure.

Homeland Security Act of 2001: The legislation was passed by Congress after the terrorist attacks of 2001 that created the Department of Homeland Security.

Homeland Security Information Network (HSIN): HSIN is a secure web-based system established by DHS to increase information sharing and collaboration efforts between government agencies and the private sector groups that have a concern with protecting critical infrastructure. HSIN is comprised of communities of interest (COI) that allows users in all 50 states to share information with others in their communities through a safe environment in real time.

Homeland Security Presidential Directive 7: A document released on December 17, 2003, by President Bush that defined the responsibilities of various agencies that played a role in protecting critical infrastructure. The roles of sector-specific agencies were more clearly defined. The Directive also reiterated the importance of establishing effective relationships between the federal government and agencies in other areas. Bush also asked for a comprehensive National Plan for Critical Infrastructure and Key Resources Protection.

Human-Caused Hazard: It is a potential incident resulting from the intentional actions of an adversary.

IT Sector Baseline Risk Assessment (ITSRA): It serves as a foundation for the IT sector's national-level risk management activities.

Impacts: The impact of an event on an asset, such as the property damage caused or the disruption in services; how a threat or hazard might affect a core capability.

Information Sharing: It is communication between agencies. This is essential between the private and public sectors to protect assets.

Information Sharing and Analysis Centers (ISAC): These agencies comprise representatives from both government and the private sector that would facilitate greater information. Information could also be shared after an incident to analyze why that event happened and how to make changes so prevent a similar event in the future.

InfraGard: It is a cooperative, outreach effort between the federal government and private sector businesses, academic institutions, and state and local law enforcement agencies, who work cooperatively to increase the security of the nation's assets. The goal is to increase information exchange between these groups so that assets are better protected.

Infrastructure Protection Executive Notification Service: It is located within DHS, the agency serves as a way for DHS to communicate more effectively with the chief executive officers of major industrial firms to inform them of any incidents or threats that pertain to them.

Institutional Risks: Risk associated with an organization's ability to develop and maintain effective management practices, control systems, and flexibility and adaptability to meet organizational requirements. These risks are less obvious and typically come from within an organization. Institutional risks include factors that can threaten an organization's ability to organize, recruit, train, support, and integrate the organization to meet all specified operational and administrative requirements.

Integrated Risk Management (IRM): It was established in May 2010, by then Secretary of Homeland Security, Janet Napolitano, and the plan formalized many of the organizational aspects of the DHS risk effort. The policy supports the idea that security partners can most effectively manage risk by working together, and that management capabilities must be built, sustained, and integrated with federal, state, local, tribal, territorial, nongovernmental, and private sector homeland security partners.

Interdependencies: Many sectors are interconnected so that damage to one leads to damage in others. For example, a disruption in water service caused by a natural hazard or terrorist act may threaten other sectors such as emergency services, healthcare, and transportation.

Likelihood: It is the chance of something happening, whether defined, measured, or estimated in terms of general descriptors, frequencies, or probabilities, or in terms of general descriptors (e.g., rare unlikely, likely, almost certain), frequencies, or probabilities.

Management Directorate: It is a part of the DHS, this organization is responsible for the budgets and dispersing funds earmarked for protecting critical infrastructure. Many grant programs that help fund protection plans originate or are managed by this office.

Maritime Transportation Security Act of 2002: Maritime Transportation Security Act of 2002 is a law that requires ports and facilities to carry out vulnerability assessments of infrastructure and then develop plans to keep them safe.

Mitigation: Any activities geared toward lessening the possible impact of an event. This can include increasing physical security measures, hiring additional security guards, or installing barriers around a building.

National Advisory Council (FEMA): It was established in June 2007 by the Post-Katrina Emergency Management Reform Act (PKEMRA) to develop more effective coordination of federal policies for preparedness, protection, response, recovery, and mitigation for all events. The Council was given the responsibility to develop the National Preparedness Goal, the National Preparedness System, the National Incident Management System (NIMS), the National Response Framework (NRF), and other national plans.

National Coordinator for Security: A position created in the PDD-63 who would serve as the chair of the Critical Infrastructure Coordination Group.

National Counter Intelligence Executive: It was established under Executive Order 14231 and PPD-75, the NCIX works with the President's Critical Infrastructure Protection Board to address potential threats from hostile foreign intelligence services. The agency helps to identify critical assets located throughout the nation, implement counterintelligence analyses, develop a national threat assessment, formulate a national counterintelligence strategy, create an integrated counterintelligence budget, and develop an agenda of program reviews and evaluations.

National Infrastructure Advisory Council: It was created by Executive Order 13231, the Council was an advisory agency to the president regarding the security of information systems for critical infrastructure. The Council was also to increase partnerships between public and private agencies.

National Infrastructure Assurance Council: A position created in PDD-63 as an advisory group to the president that included private owners, representatives from state and local government, and representatives from relevant federal agencies.

National Infrastructure Protection Center: It was created as part of PDD-63 and housed within the Department of Justice and the FBI, this agency was responsible for defending the nation's public and private computer systems from possible cyberattacks and responding to illegal acts carried out by the use of computers and information technologies.

National Infrastructure Simulation and Analysis Center (NISAC): DHS's modeling, simulation, and analysis program that seeks to analyze critical infrastructure and key resources, along with their interdependencies, consequences, and other complexities. NISAC provides three types of products: preplanned long-term analyses, preplanned short-term analyses, and unplanned priority analytical projects. The reports provide information for mitigation design and policy planning and address the cascading consequences of infrastructure disruptions that could occur across all 18 CIKR sectors at national, regional, and local levels.

National Plan for Critical Infrastructure and Key Resources: It was outlined by President Bush in HSPD-7, the document was to include (a) a strategy to identify, prioritize, and coordinate the protection of critical infrastructure and key resources, including how the department will work with other stakeholders; (b) a summary of activities to be undertaken in order to carry out the strategy; (c) a summary of initiatives for sharing critical infrastructure information and threat warnings with other stakeholders; and (d) coordination with other federal emergency management activities.

National Plan for Information Systems Protection: It is issued by the Clinton Administration in January 2000, the plan focused on protecting the nation's cyber-infrastructure.

National Protection and Programs Directorate (NPPD): Under PPD-21, the NPPD develops ways to identify the nation's critical infrastructure and prioritize them so that funds can be distributed accordingly. Officials in the agency also seek to reduce possible risks to critical infrastructure, including both physical and virtual threats. One way this directorate achieves their goal is by training others (owners and operators) about identifying risks and mitigating them.

National Security Staff: It was created when President Obama merged the Homeland Security Council and the National Security Council into one agency.

National Strategy for Homeland Security: A document that sets out government efforts to protect the nation against terrorist threats of all kinds. It also added public health, the chemical industry, and hazardous materials, postal and shipping, the defense industrial base, and agriculture and food to the list of sectors that have critical infrastructure in them. It also combined emergency fire service, emergency law enforcement, and emergency medicine as emergency services and eliminated those functions that belong primarily to the federal governments. The report also introduced key assets.

National Strategy for the Physical Protection of Critical Infrastructures and Key Assets: It is a document published in February 2003, by the Office of Homeland Security that defined "key assets." It also identified the roles and responsibilities of agencies and people, actions that needed to be taken, and guiding principles for protecting the nation's key assets.

National Strategy to Secure Cyberspace: A 2003 document that stressed methods to protect critical information and data stored electronically or available on the Internet.

Natural Hazard: It is a potential incident resulting from acts of nature.

NIMS-Typed Resource: It is a resource categorized, by capability, the resources requested, deployed, and used in incidents.

The National Infrastructure Protection Plan (NIPP): It was first published in 2006. This document outlined a national plan for managing risk for the country's critical infrastructure. The updated plan, published in 2013, emphasized goals of critical infrastructure security and resilience, including the identification, deterrence, detection, and disruption of threats, along with reducing vulnerabilities.

Office of Cybersecurity and Communications (CS&C): It is the sector-specific agency for both the communications and information technology (IT) sectors. The CS&C coordinates national-level reporting that is consistent with the National Response Framework and works to prevent or minimize disruptions to critical information infrastructure in order to protect the public, the economy, and government services.

Office of Homeland Security: An agency created after the terrorist attacks of 2001 that would develop and coordinate a comprehensive strategy to keep the US safe from terrorist threats and attacks.

Office of Intelligence and Analysis (I&A): This office seeks to improve information sources to assist other agencies in protecting critical infrastructure. The Information Analysis and Infrastructure Protection Directorate (IAIPD) carries out many tasks such as gathering and disseminating information from other sources that will assist them in identifying and assessing the risk of a possible terrorist threat, and assessing the vulnerabilities of critical infrastructure to determine the possible risks posed by attacks.

Operational Risks: Risk that has the potential to impede the successful execution of operations with existing resources, capabilities, and strategies. Operational risks include those that impact personnel, time, materials, equipment, tactics, techniques, information, technology, and procedures that enable an organization to achieve its mission objectives.

Partnership Engagement: Collaborating with sector partners and encouraging continuous growth and improvement of these partnerships.

Partnership for Critical Infrastructure Security: It is an agency established in December 1999 as a way to share information and strategies for infrastructure protection and to identify potential interdependencies across sectors.

Physical Security: Both cyber and physical security measures are needed to protect critical infrastructures against potential threats. Physical security measures prevent the unauthorized access to servers, and other technologies which carry sensitive information.

Post-Katrina Emergency Management Reform Act (PKEMRA) of 2006: The law passed by Congress after Hurricane Katrina that reformed the Federal Emergency Management Agency (FEMA) to make it more effective in responding to national emergencies. Congress opted to keep FEMA as part of DHS but clarified FEMA's mission, which included: to lead the nation's efforts to prepare for, respond to, recover from, and mitigate the risks of, any natural and man-made disaster, including catastrophic incidents; implement a risk-based, all-hazards strategy for preparedness; and promote and plan for the protection, security, resiliency, and post-disaster restoration of critical infrastructure and key resources, including cyber and communications assets.

Preparedness: Activities that are planned to prepare for an event. This can include establishing guidelines, protocols, and standards for training responders, or purchasing needed equipment.

President's Commission on Critical Infrastructure Protection: Established by President Clinton, the Commission was to assess the vulnerabilities of the country's critical infrastructures, and then create a new plan to protect them. The final report indicated the need for greater exchange of information by all participants in critical infrastructure protection as a way to predict or prevent an attack.

President's Critical Infrastructure Protection Board: Established by President Bush, the Board was responsible for recommending policies and coordinating programs geared to protecting information systems for critical infrastructure.

Presidential Decision Directive 63 (PDD-63): PDD-63 stressed the importance of partnerships between the government and private ownership to protect critical infrastructure. The document described critical infrastructure as composed of five essential domains: banking and finance, energy, transportation, telecommunications, and government services. Specific critical infrastructure assets that required protection were referred to as "sectors" and included information and communications; banking and finance; water supply; aviation, highways, mass transit, pipelines, rail, and waterborne commerce; emergency and law enforcement services; emergency, fire, and continuity of government services; public health services; electric power, oil and gas production, and storage.

Presidential Policy Directive-8: Signed by President Obama on March 30, 2011, this document, also called National Preparedness, was a way to increase the nation's security and resilience by focusing on preparation. Obama concentrated on an all-hazards approach to security that included planning for possible terrorist acts, including cyberattacks, technological events, and also natural disasters. Additionally, the president recognized that national preparedness and security must involve the government, private sector, and individual citizens.

Presidential Policy Directive-21: Announced in February 2013, by President Obama, this document, entitled *Critical Infrastructure Security and Resilience*, established a policy to strengthen critical infrastructure that is also resilient to attacks. Both physical and cyber infrastructure was included. Throughout the document, the need for cooperation between private sectors and the government was stressed. The number of sectors and how they were changed as well.

Private Sector: Any unit that is not operated by the state or federal government, such as companies, corporations, private banks, television or radio stations, or nongovernmental organizations. Since the goal of these entities is to make a profit, their actions are geared toward minimizing any financial risk.

Private Sector-Preparedness Program: It was initiated by FEMA in 2009, the program initiated ways to improve the preparedness of the private sector and nonprofit organizations for an event. The program involves establishing guidelines, best practices, regulations, and codes of practice.

Private Sector Resources Catalog: A list of DHS publications aimed specifically toward the needs of private sector owners. This includes resources on training, guidance, alerts, newsletters, programs, and other services. They have also created the *Critical Infrastructure Protection and Resilience Toolkit* as a way to assist the owners and operators of critical infrastructure assets at both the local and regional levels to help them prepare for, protect against, respond to, mitigate against, and recover from any possible threats or hazards.

Protective Security Advisors (PSA) Program: It was originally developed in 2004, the PSA program is part of the National Protection and Programs Directorate (NPPD) of the DHS. The PSAs are experts who have been trained in critical infrastructure protection and in mitigation procedures for infrastructure protection. These analysts ensure that the owners and operators of critical infrastructure in the private sector are also given essential information. The PSA program focuses on three areas: enhancing infrastructure protection, assisting with incident management, and facilitating information sharing.

Public Sector: It is an agency that is owned or operated by the government, such as federal, state, or local departments and agencies, water treatment plants, and power plants. These groups often get financial support from the government through taxes.

Public–Private Partnerships: An agreement between a public agency and a private sector agency. The goal is to draw on the skills and resources of each separate group so that a task can be accomplished efficiently.

RAM-W: A risk assessment tool that is widely used across the water and wastewater sector.

Recovery: The ability to adapt and withstand any disruption that may occur after an emergency or event. It refers to the ability of a community to recover rapidly and bounce back, or regroup, after a disruption.

Resiliency: See Recovery.

Resilient Infrastructure: Critical infrastructure and their communications capabilities should be able to withstand natural or manmade hazards with minimal interruption or failure.

Resource Requirement: An estimate of the number of resources needed to achieve a community's capability target. A list of resource requirements for each core capability is an output of the THIRA process.

Resourcefulness: The capacity to mobilize needed resources and services in emergencies.

Risk: The probability that an asset will be the object of an attack or another adverse outcome. Risk is the likelihood that an adverse event will occur, and is related to consequences (C), vulnerabilities (V), and threats (T), in the following relationship:

$$Risk = (function\ of)\ (CVT)$$

Risk Analysis: An attempt to identify the probability, and possible consequences, of an attack. A risk assessment asks, "What can go wrong? What is the likelihood that it will go wrong? What are the possible consequences if it does go wrong?" This way, the probability of an incident occurring and the impact of that incident will be better understood. The analysis can also be used to determine what assets are more critical and how should money be spent to protect them.

Risk-Based Decision Making: Determination of a course of action predicated primarily on the assessment of risk and the expected impact of that course of action on that risk.

Risk Communications: A key element of the risk management process is effective communications with stakeholders, partners, and customers. According to DHS, a consistent, two-way communication will ensure that decision makers, analysts, and officials are able to implement any decision and share a common understanding of what the risk is and what factors may contribute to managing it.

Risk Fundamentals: Risk fundamentals are a doctrine to support homeland security practitioners. This doctrine includes promoting a common understanding of, and approach to, risk management; establishing organizational practices that should be followed by DHS components; providing a foundation for conducting risk assessments and evaluating risk management options; setting the doctrinal underpinnings for institutionalizing a risk management culture through consistent application and training on risk management principles and practices; and educating and informing homeland security stakeholders in risk management applications, including the assessment of capability, program, and operational performance, and the use of such assessments for resource and policy decisions.

Risk Management: It is an effort to decide which protective measures should be implemented to reduce the risk of an event occurring.

Risk Transfer Products: They occur when insurance companies offer customers the ability to transfer financial risks under a multitude of circumstances.

Science and Technology Directorate: A part of DHS, and this agency supports research and development regarding critical infrastructure protection. The agency carries out research in explosive detection, blast protection, and safe cargo containers. They monitor threats and develop ways to prevent those threats. There are three directors within the Science and Technology Directorate, including the Director of Support to the Homeland Security Enterprise and First Responders, the Director of Homeland Security Advance Research Projects Agency, and the Director of Research and Development Partnership.

Sector Coordinator: A person appointed by the private sector organizations in each sector who cooperated with others to develop plans for protecting assets.

Sector Liaison Official: A sector official who communicates with others in private sector organizations to build methods to protect assets.

Sectors: Categories of assets which help to organize the country's critical infrastructure and protection plans.

Sector-Specific Plan (SSP): A way for each sector to tailor their response plan depending upon the unique operating conditions and risk landscape of its particular sector.

SEMS: Security and Environmental Management Systems.

State, Local, Tribal, and Territorial Government Coordinating Council (SLTTGCC): The SLTTGCC, under the NIPP, helps to ensure that state, local, tribal, and territorial homeland security officials or their designated representatives are integrated fully as active participants in national CIKR protection efforts. The SLTTGCC provides the organizational structure to coordinate across jurisdictions on state- and local-level CIKR protection guidance, strategies, and programs.

Strategic Homeland Security Infrastructure Risk Analysis (SHIRA): It provides a common framework that sectors can use to assess the economic, loss of life, and psychological consequences resulting from terrorist incidents as well as natural hazards and domestic threats. It is a threat-based approach and is the result of an integrated "fusion" effort between the infrastructure protection and intelligence communities. Typically, intelligence initiates the planning and all functional areas participate in the entire process.

Strategic Risks: Risk that affects an organization's vital interests or execution of a chosen strategy, whether imposed by external threats or arising from flawed or poorly implemented strategy. These risks threaten an organization's ability to achieve its strategy, as well as position itself to recognize, anticipate, and respond to future trends, conditions, and challenges. Strategic risks include those factors that may impact the organization's overall objectives and long-term goals.

Technical Resource for Incident Prevention (TRIPwire): An online information sharing network for groups including bomb squads, law enforcement personnel, and other emergency services personnel that informs them about current terrorist tactics, techniques, and procedures. The agency was developed by the DHS Office for Bombing Prevention (OBP), which continues to maintain it. The group relies on expert analyses and reports alongside relevant documents, images, and videos that were gathered directly from terrorist sources to assist law enforcement to anticipate, identify, and prevent incidents.

Technological Hazard: It is a potential incident resulting from accidents or failures of systems or structures.

Threat: A natural or man-made event, person, entity, or action that has the potential to harm life, information, operations, the environment, and/or property. Threats can stem from humans, natural hazards, or technology.

Training and Exercise Support: It is initiated by DHS, there are many programs to help local communities train their first responders and others for an event. Three levels of training are provided: awareness level training, performance level training, and management level training.

Transportation Security Administration (TSA): TSA became a part of DHS when it was formed in 2002. The TSA oversees the security of the nation's transportation sectors. Officials screen airline passengers and their baggage to ensure that no dangerous material is brought onboard an aircraft. TSA also regulates the installation and maintenance of equipment to detect for explosives. Agents provide security for airport perimeters. They also oversee the air marshals.

Unity of Effort: It reiterates that homeland security risk management is an enterprise-wide process and should promote integration and synchronization with entities that share responsibility for managing risks.

US Computer Emergency Readiness Team (US-CERT): US-CERT makes information related to computer-related vulnerabilities and threats available to others, and provides information about responses to incidents. US-CERT collects incident reports from others around the country and analyzes that information to look for patterns and trends in computer-based crime. Officials here manage the National Cyber Alert System, that provides general information to any organization or individual who subscribes.

USA PATRIOT Act: Legislation signed by President Bush after the terrorist attacks of September 11, 2001. The law defined critical infrastructure and added new terms to the homeland security lexicon.

VSAT: Vulnerability Self-Assessment Tool.

Vulnerability: A physical feature or attribute of critical infrastructure that leaves it vulnerable to an attack or natural event. This could be a weakness or flaw in an asset that may cause it to be a target for an attack. In most cases, an attacker will identify a vulnerability in an asset and plan their attack on that use that liability to strike the asset.

Whole Community: An approach to emergency management that reinforces the fact that Federal Emergency Management Agency (FEMA) is only one part of our nation's emergency management team. We must leverage all of the resources of our collective team in preparing for, protecting against, responding to, recovering from, and mitigating against all hazards; and that collectively we must meet the needs of the entire community in each of these areas.

TIMELINE

1947: National Security Act of 1947 passed by Congress

1950: Civil Defense and Disaster Compact

1982: FIRESCOPE

July 15, 1996: President Clinton signed Executive Order 13010: Established the President's Commission on Critical Infrastructure Protection (PCCIP)

May 1998: Presidential Decision Directive 63 (PDD-63): To establish a national capability within 5 years that would provide for protection of our critical infrastructure

September 11, 2001: Terrorist Attack on New York and Washington, DC

October 8, 2001: Executive Order 13228: Established the Office of Homeland Security and the Homeland Security Council within the Executive Office of the President

October 29, 2001: President Bush issued the Homeland Security Presidential Directives: The first HSPD: Concerned the organization and operation of the Homeland Security Council

2001: Critical Infrastructure Protection Act

October 29, 2001: HSPD-1: Organization and Operation of the Homeland Security Council

October 29, 2001: HSPD-2: Combating Terrorism through Immigration Policies

2001: USA PATRIOT ACT passed by Congress

2001: Homeland Security Act passed by Congress that established the Department of Homeland Security

March 11, 2002: HSPD-3: Homeland Security Advisory System (Color System)

December 2002: HSPD-4: National Strategy to Combat Weapons of Mass Destruction

February 28, 2003: HSPD-5: Management of Domestic Incidents: Created National Incident Management System (NIMS)

September 16, 2003: HSPD-6: Integration of Use of Screening Information

December 17, 2003: HSPD-7: Critical Infrastructure Identification, Prioritization, and Protection

2003: National Strategy for the Physical Protection of Critical Infrastructure and Key Assets

2003: HSPD-8: National Preparedness

January 30, 2004: HSPD-9: Defense of US Agriculture and Food (by President George W. Bush)

HSPD-10: Build Defense for the 21st Century

2004: Intelligence Reform and Terrorism Prevention Act of 2004 (Amended by PATRIOT Act Reauthorization Act of 2005)

August 27, 2004: HSPD-11: Comprehensive Terrorist-Related Screening Procedures (by President George W. Bush)

August 27, 2004: HSPD-12: Policy for a Common Identification Standard for Federal Employees and Contractors (by President George W. Bush)

December 21, 2004: HSPD-13: Maritime Security Policy (Also NSPD-41)

April 15, 2005: HSPD-14: Domestic Nuclear Detection (Also NSPD-43)

2005: USA PATRIOT Act Improvement and Reauthorization Act of 2005

August 2005: Hurricane Katrina hits the Southern US

HSPD-15: US Strategy and Policy in the War on Terror

HSPD-16: Aviation Strategy

HSPD-17: Nuclear Materials Information Program

2006: Pandemic and All-Hazards Preparedness Act of 2006

2006: Secure Fence Act of 2006

2006: First NIPP

2006: Post-Katrina Emergency Management Reform Act of 2006

January 31, 2007: HSPD-18: Medical Countermeasures Against WMD (by President George W. Bush)

February 12, 2007: HSPD-19: Combating Terrorist Use of Explosives in the US

June 2007: National Advisory Council established

HSPD-20 Annex A: Continuity Planning

May 4, 2007: National Continuity Policy in the National Security Presidential Directive (HSPD-20) by President George H. W. Bush

October 18, 2007: HSPD-21: Public Health and Medical Preparedness

January 8, 2008: Homeland Security Presidential Directive 23 (HSPD-23): National Cyber Security Initiative (by President George W. Bush) (NSPD-54)

June 5, 2008: HSPD-24: Biometrics for Identification and Screening to Enhance National Security (by President George W. Bush)

National Strategy for the Physical Protection of Critical Infrastructures and Key Assets.

PPD-21: Critical Infrastructure Security and Resilience

2008: A Guide to Critical Infrastructure and Key Resources Protection at the State, Local, Regional, Tribal, and Territorial Level

September 2008: Hurricane Ike

2009: National Infrastructure Protection Plan: Partnering to Enhance Protection and Resiliency (16 sectors)

2010: Quadrennial Homeland Security Review Report: A Strategic Framework for a Secure Homeland

2010: Critical Infrastructure Protection: Key Private and Public Cyber Expectations Need to be Consistently Addressed

2010: DHS Risk Lexicon

March 30, 2011: Presidential Policy Directive-8 (PPD-8): National Preparedness (by President Obama): With goals and 31 core capabilities

2011: Empowering local partners to prevent violent extremism in the US

March 30, 2011: PPD-8: Presidential Policy Directive: National Preparedness (by President Obama)

2011: National Preparedness Goal

2011: National Preparedness System

October 2011: National Preparedness Goal

December 2011: Strategic National Risk Assessment (SNRA): Secretary of Homeland Security identified the types of incidents that pose the greatest threat to the Nation's homeland

2011: A Whole Community Approach to Emergency Management: Principles, Themes, and Pathways for Action

2011: Community Resilience Task Force Recommendations

2012: Threat and Hazard Identification and Risk Assessment Guide: Comprehensive Preparedness Guide (CPG) 21

October 2012: Federal Continuity Directive

October 2012: Hurricane Sandy

July 2013: Federal Continuity Directive 2

2013: National Cybersecurity and Critical Infrastructure Protection Act of 2013

2013: National Infrastructure Protection Plan re-do: NIPP: 2013: Redone every 4 years

February 12, 2013: Presidential Policy Directive/PPD-21L Critical Infrastructure Security and Resilience

February 12, 2013: Executive Order 13636: Improving Critical Infrastructure Cybersecurity (by President Obama)

February 25, 2013: Establishment of the Cyber Threat Intelligence Integration Center (by President Obama)

February 12, 2014: Framework for Improving Critical Infrastructure Cybersecurity released by National Institute of Standards and Technology (Obama Administration)

February 13, 2015: Executive Order 13691: Promoting Private Sector Cybersecurity Information Sharing (by President Obama)

INDEX

Printed in the United States
by Baker & Taylor Publisher Services

Printed in the United States
by Baker & Taylor Publisher Services